THE
BREAST
CANCER
BOOK

A personal guide to help you through it and beyond

Val Sampson and
Debbie Fenlon

VERMILION
LONDON

To Mary, Jackie and Liz

3 5 7 9 10 8 6 4 2

Text © Val Sampson and Debbie Fenlon 2000

Val Sampson and Debbie Fenlon have asserted their right to be identified as the authors of this work under the Copyright, Designs and Patent Act 1988.

First published in 2000 by Vermilion
an imprint of Ebury Press
Random House, 20 Vauxhall Bridge Road, London SW1V 2SA

Random House Australia (Pty) Limited
20 Alfred Street, Milsons Point, Sydney, New South Wales 2061, Australia

Random House New Zealand Limited
18 Poland Road, Glenfield, Auckland 10, New Zealand

Random House South Africa (Pty) Limited
Endulini, 5A Jubilee Road, Parktown 2193, South Africa

The Random House Group Limited Reg. No. 954009

A CIP catalogue record for this book is available from the British Library.

ISBN 0 09 185613 2

Printed and bound in Great Britain by Mackays of Chatham plc, Kent

Papers used by Vermilion are natural, recyclable products made from wood grown in sustainable forests.

Contents

Acknowledgements

We would like to thank the following individuals who have contributed to this book: Penny Wark; Mark McCallum; Christine Fogg; Mary Pole; Audrey Jones; Ruth Marriott; Paul McCloskey; Linda Payne; Melanie Payne; Amanda Payne; John Jennings; Clare Southard; Lynda McGilvray; Tony Yates; Dave Morgan; Mavis Morgan; David Morgan; Alison Peacham; Sally Reygate; Margaret Phelps; Sue McEvoy; Elly Pearce; Gweneth Roberts; Dominic Fielder; Fran Davies; Ali Kennett; Judy Allen; Garner Thomson; Richard Curtis.

We would also like to thank our families, especially Colin and Oliver Jones-Evans, for their encouragement and support throughout.

Foreword

Breast cancer touches the lives of most people in this country sooner or later, whether personally or through the experience of family or friends. The scale of the problem is enormous and these days media interest is intense. Yet for those trying to come to terms with breast cancer it can be difficult to find information that is appropriate, accurate and easy to read.

Val Sampson understands the issues as well as any expert and better than most: she has had breast cancer twice herself. Her account of the experience makes compelling reading. Her insight into ways of dealing with the illness is invaluable, because she has been there herself. She discusses the most difficult questions, 'What do I tell the children? How do I handle my friends?', with sympathy and sound common sense. Debbie Fenlon gives practical advice and information. Her approach comes from her wide experience as a breast cancer nurse and her knowledge of the kind of questions that people ask when they come into contact with hospitals.

The Breast Cancer Book has a unique combination of practical advice, information and personal experience that will be of enormous benefit to women and their families. This book should be essential reading for anyone wanting to know more about breast cancer.

Ian E. Smith,
Professor of Cancer Medicine, Medical Director,
Royal Marsden Hospital and the
Institute of Cancer Research

Introduction

If you have just found out you have breast cancer, you can feel that everything you know is under threat. Your trust in your health and your future has been torn apart. It can seem as if everything is stained with the knowledge that you have cancer and your world will never be the same again.

But you are not alone. The purpose of this book is to offer you hope. It will guide you through what lies ahead, helping you to feel stronger on all levels: physical, emotional and spiritual. It is a practical guide which provides essential information about breast cancer treatments in hospital and offers a round-up of complementary medicines which can help you feel better.

It explains the sometimes confusing choices you need to make, and sheds light on how to manage your life and your relationships with people inside and outside hospital. It answers questions about talking to your children, whether they are toddlers, teenagers or parents themselves; and it offers suggestions to help you deal with the men in your life and their reactions to breast cancer.

I hope it will prove to be a companion you can turn to through your experience of breast cancer and beyond. I hope too that it will destroy the feeling that fate has singled you out for an unpleasant battle you have to fight on your own. These are big claims for a small book, but one of the things the experience of having breast cancer has taught me is that small goals are good, but big goals are better.

My first diagnosis

When I was first diagnosed with breast cancer in August 1994, I was working as a freelance journalist. Two months earlier, I had interviewed Mary, a doctor whose response to the discovery of a small, malignant lump in one breast was to have both breasts and her ovaries removed. It seemed an extreme and frightening course of action, and the article, which appeared in the *Daily Mail*, focused on the fact that in those days, the levels of care nationally for women with breast cancer were patchy.

There was so little information generally available that even Mary, a high-flying hospital consultant, needed to agonise over the treatment she should have.

When I found a lump in my right breast one Monday morning, I phoned Mary that night. Because she had been through the same experience 18 months earlier, she talked me through the steps I needed to take. She didn't dismiss my panic by saying, 'Don't worry, you'll be fine', but she didn't terrify me either. She gave me the information I needed to talk to my doctors and she phoned to see how I was when I got back from those first hospital appointments. She urged me to think for myself, and I chose a different medical route from her, but her friendship was unwavering.

When I started my first course of chemotherapy, I felt an urge to do something outrageous that I had never done before, and I blasted my Barclaycard by treating us both to lunch at The Ritz. We drank champagne and toasted the next 20 years of our lives. We talked about our fears of dying; of leaving our children before they grew up; about our husbands and our friends. And we still managed to laugh together. It was a meeting I shall always remember. Mary offered me the kind of informed support I hope this book will give you.

Why was this book written?

Although I have spoken to other women who have contacted me when they have been diagnosed with breast cancer, I have often felt that I couldn't give them the right kind of support. Partly because I can't summarise enough of my own experience in normal conversation to be certain that I meet another woman's needs at that time. And partly because there isn't enough of me to go round. So my thoughts and feelings about breast cancer, plus as much useful information and guidance as I can come up with, are in this book.

I have never wanted cancer to take up more of my life than absolutely necessary. Which is why, if I hadn't had a second malignant lump diagnosed in my left breast in 1998, I probably wouldn't have written this book. But I was trudging down the cancer treatment path again and it seemed right to do it. The vague thoughts about this that were going through my head at the time were crystallised one night when the phone rang. A friend of my mother's apologised for troubling me, but her 38-year-old daughter had just been diagnosed with breast cancer. The whole family had been hit by a hurricane of conflicting emotions and panic. What should they do?

I talked her through the initial steps to take, but what I wanted to do was point her in the direction of a book that would offer her family accurate medical information, emotional and psychological support and which, with a bit of luck, would raise their spirits and give them a sense of hope. I couldn't do it because no such book existed. It was at this point that I realised it was down to me to write it.

I hadn't intended ever to write about my cancer. Although I earn my living as a national newspaper and magazine journalist, it's an aspect of my life which I had preferred to keep private. Not because I felt a stigma or shame attached to it, although initially I did have a weird feeling that by getting cancer I had somehow let everyone down, but because I have always dreaded being the victim of people's sympathy. If anyone touches my arm, puts on a caring face and whispers 'How *are* you, dear?' I feel an impulse to invent a crazy Latin lover and tell them I am about to rush into his arms for hours of wonderful sex. I've not succumbed yet, but that thought has sprinted through my mind more than once.

When I was first diagnosed with breast cancer, I was treated with a lumpectomy, four months of chemotherapy and six weeks of radiotherapy. After the diagnosis of another primary tumour in my left breast in September 1998, I had a bilateral mastectomy and immediate recon-struction (the tissue from both breasts was removed and replaced with implants), followed by more chemotherapy. Although I have experienced the sharp end of a lot of the current breast cancer treatments, I felt it would be better if the chapters devoted to orthodox medicine – the clinical treatments you can expect to receive from physicians and surgeons in hospitals – were written by someone with medical training and expertise.

About my co-author

Debbie Fenlon, my co-author, was my breast care nurse at the Royal Marsden Hospital. She was introduced to me by Dr Ian Smith, the cancer specialist who has looked after me, and who also wrote the fore-word for this book. She was the person I phoned in the early days if I was worried about my health, but didn't feel the worry was significant enough to make an appointment to see my consultant.

After 12 years working with women with breast cancer, Debbie is now a lecturer with the Institute of Cancer Research in association with the Royal Marsden Hospital. Three years ago, she asked me to become involved in a seminar on Language and the Concept of Cancer for nurses studying for a diploma or degree in cancer nursing. It was intended that I would talk to the students about the way the media portray cancer, and de-mystify the workings of newspapers, magazines and television in relation to cancer and the public perception of the disease. These sessions included a more general discussion of the way the medical profession and patients use language around cancer and the extraordinary power of the language that we all use, which helps or hinders patients' progress.

Debbie seemed exactly the right person to contribute to this book. Not just because she knows hospitals inside out and has helped hundreds of women with breast cancer over the years, but because our different personalities should help bring a balance to the way our book is written. To be frivolous, Debbie finds the idea of wearing makeup a chore; I wore lipstick and mascara to have radiotherapy. Debbie admits that losing her hair wouldn't bother her too much ('because it always looks such a mess, anyway'). I spent £400 on a wig because I was devastated by losing my hair after chemotherapy. She is a reminder to me that not all women (in fact very few) would bother, like me, to apply fake tan before an operation. And perhaps I am a reminder to her that girly trivia, like changing your foundation because chemotherapy alters the balance of your skin, matters to some of us because it keeps us feeling feminine and in touch with who we are beyond our lives as cancer patients.

The structure of this book

Debbie's chapters will offer a step-by-step guide to all aspects of hospital treatment and tips to help you to get the best treatment for you. They can be used for reference if a doctor uses technical terms you are unsure of, and they will clearly explain the processes of treating breast cancer in a hospital setting.

We have deliberately put the chapter on living with secondary cancer in the middle of our book, rather than tacking it on as an afterthought at the end. Some women live for more than 20 years with so-called 'advanced' disease, when the cancer has spread beyond its first, localised site. A decade ago, these women were often disregarded by embarrassed and awkward doctors who couldn't offer them a 'cure'. But palliative care – treatment which does not offer a cure but can manage symptoms – has progressed enormously in the last ten years. Diabetes is not 'curable' but its symptoms can be managed over a lifetime. Similarly, increasing numbers of women are living with secondary breast disease for far longer than could once have been expected.

The medical sections of the book will be clearly sign-posted. You don't have to read anything with which you are not comfortable. If you think you'll be up all night worrying if you read about symptoms associated with secondary tumours – then don't. Or if, like me, you feel a horrible compulsion to read everything about cancer, even if you suspect it will trouble you, make sure you look at the chapter on how to handle fear and anxiety straight afterwards.

Why this book is different from medical textbooks

Most books on breast cancer are written by doctors and begin by asking 'What is cancer?' and then, 'What is breast cancer?' While these are, of course, important questions, as a patient I had more pressing queries, like 'How do I handle the knowledge that I have a life-threatening disease?' 'How do I talk to my family and friends about this?' 'How can I stop feeling scared?', even 'Should I abandon traditional medicine and take complementary therapies only?'

So our first chapter is 'Hoping and coping'. It is my story. As every leaflet you pick up is at pains to stress, everyone's experience is unique and I don't expect my experience will reflect yours. But it might give you new insights into the way *you* are coping with *your* breast cancer.

Fear and the medical profession

Fear is a word that is hardly ever mentioned in hospitals. Nurses and doctors talk about managing physical pain and sickness with drugs, but hardly anyone discusses emotional pain. Some people feel a lot more afraid of breast cancer than others. This is partly to do with your personality type and your background. If you have a close relative who has died of the disease, say a mother or an aunt, you may feel a lot more concerned about dying soon than someone like me, who didn't know anyone who had died from breast cancer, but has a mother-in-law who survived it more than 20 years ago. Some women take one step at a time, confident they are having the right treatment, and give little thought to what will happen if it is not successful. Others plan their funeral and choose the hymns within days of a diagnosis. I discuss personality types and the different ways people react to the crisis of illness in the chapter 'How to get support from the people around you'.

Reducing your anxiety levels may be easier than you think. 'Fear and how to handle it' suggests techniques you can use; try different ones until you find one that works for you. Remember that feeling afraid is a perfectly normal reaction to the stress you are facing; handling it is hard at first, but it does get easier as time goes on.

Language and cancer

Have you ever picked up a newspaper or magazine and felt your heart sink as you read about someone 'losing their brave battle against cancer?' The print and screen media constantly describe cancer as a battleground. In 'Cancer and the power of language' I look at why the print media are so keen to describe cancer as a nasty personal war and why that approach is so unhelpful to a lot of women.

Who hears your news and how?

One of the first decisions a woman with cancer needs to make is who she will tell about her illness. In 'Who to tell?' I describe the decisions I have made – to tell only a handful of family and friends the first time around and lots of people the second – and the different impact that had on me and my life each time. Also included is information on how to talk to children about cancer. Every woman who is a mother worries about what she should tell her children. A child psychologist will give guidance on what children can cope with at various ages and what their reactions are likely to be. I've also spoken to children whose mothers have had breast cancer and they have definite ideas about what they would find helpful too.

This book is not just for women and about women

Around 30,000 women and 200 men are diagnosed with breast cancer each year. This book is aimed primarily at women and their partners, although I hope there are plenty of elements in it that would be useful to men who are diagnosed with breast cancer.

Cancer does not just affect the person who has the disease. Couples, families and friends discover that it has an impact that is often unwelcome and unexpected. Relationships can be stretched under the strain of ill health or operations that a woman may feel undermine her femininity or sexual confidence.

It may be a cliché to suggest that men don't talk about their feelings or that they repress their emotions, but it is probably true to say that most men handle their feelings differently from women. In 'How to get support from people around you', I have tried to de-mystify the way men react to cancer, first by talking to men whose partners have had breast cancer, and secondly by explaining the different way men tend to react to a crisis. I have also looked at personality and the impact it has on our reaction to breast cancer. In doing this I have introduced the thinking behind the Myers-Briggs Type Indicator®, which might explain why your partner prefers to do something practical and look up breast cancer on the Internet, rather than talk through your innermost fears.

Complementary treatments

I had been practising a form of mantra meditation for two half-hours a day (when I could manage it) for several years before I was diagnosed with cancer at the age of 34. The fact that I had a regular, built-in 'switch-off' time, helped me immeasurably in those early days, although I have lost count of the number of times I used to meditate with tears running down my cheeks; it was a strange kind of calm crying. Knowing that the meditation was helping me, I decided to explore other things I could do that would lessen the shock that the surgery and chemotherapy were bound to give my system. So I tried using a hypnotherapy tape before I went to the Marsden for chemo and around the same time I became interested in reflexology.

Although I admire *The Times*' journalist, John Diamond, for his lacerating humour and his deeply honest account of his experience of cancer, chronicled in a weekly column in *The Times Magazine* and in his book, *C*, we have very different ideas about the value of complementary medicine. He dismisses it as 'pixie dust for the middle classes'. I feel it's saved my sanity at times and boosted my morale, and my immune system, on numerous occasions. As a result, two chapters of this book are devoted to complementary therapies, all of which can be used in conjunction with orthodox hospital treatment.

I have read accounts of people who have walked away from surgery and chemotherapy and saved their lives by switching to different diets or consuming vast quantities of vitamins, but I didn't have the courage or determination to do that myself. I wanted the best of both worlds; hospital medicine helped by complementary treatments.

There is talk among New Age philosophers and some complementary practitioners that we 'create' our own illnesses and all that we have to do to get rid of them is change our thinking. This encourages people who have illness to feel that perhaps in some way they are to blame for their own predicament, and that if they don't get better they are not 'trying'. To point your finger at someone with cancer and tell them it is all their fault is unhelpful, to say the least.

If changing your attitude helps you to cope with your illness, by all means change your attitude. But don't waste valuable time agonising over how you may have brought your illness on yourself. How you handle it now and in the future is what counts. Remember the saying: 'The past is history; tomorrow is a mystery, but today is a gift. That's why it is called the present.'

Looking good

The chapter 'Looking good and feeling better' suggests ways in which you can boost your spirits and self-esteem. You know you genuinely look good when someone who knows about the cancer says 'you look well' and sounds surprised. But even if you manage to astound your friends and family by continuing to look great throughout your treatment, there will be days when you feel fed up. That's when it's worth flicking to 'Twenty things . . .' (on page 188) and trying a couple of those; or the whole lot if you have the time and the inclination.

Looking forward

The final chapter, 'The way ahead', is my philosophy on the cancer experience. I have learnt over the last six years that there is a lot more to me than my physical body. And that my spirit is just as important as my body, if not more so. Cancer can be an opportunity as well as a burden, but I say that as someone who has lived with it for a while now. I am not ready to assume sainthood yet. There are plenty of times when I feel less in touch with my soul and more in touch with my credit cards. I had no idea that the urge to spend could be so life-affirming.

Although newspapers and magazines dwell on breast cancer as though it is a modern epidemic, it has been around for a long time. The Roman writer Celsius recorded an operation for breast cancer in Provence, and there are references to it on Egyptian papyrus, thought to be written by the physician Imhotep in 3000 BC. In 1811, the writer Fanny Burney had a mastectomy for breast cancer without anaesthetic, carried out by one of Napoleon's surgeons. Although her graphic description of the operation is terrifying, it saved her life and she lived without a recurrence of cancer for another 29 years.

And there is good news for this century. Mortality from breast cancer has been falling steadily since 1989, and it has one of the highest survival rates of all cancers in adult women.

Journey metaphors are understandably popular with cancer writers. It is a venture into the unknown for all of us, and none can be sure of its outcome. For me, cancer is like climbing a hill (sometimes a mountain), that ultimately offers a sweeping view of your life. Gradually, I've learnt to choose my path and my companions with care and to give up the panic about the destination. If nothing else, cancer has taught me the value of living in the present, and given me a fuller picture of what that means.

1
Hoping and coping: my story

I had planned on having a quick shower one Monday morning in late August 1994 before starting work on an interview I had done with the comedienne Victoria Wood a couple of weeks earlier. As a journalist, I specialised in writing about celebrities, and I was planning to turn the tape recording of our conversation into a piece for the *Daily Mail*.

My husband, Colin, a management trainer, was away working. Downstairs, someone was helping me to look after our two-and-a-half year old son, Oliver, while I wrote for newspapers and magazines. We had recently moved into a new house and we felt confident about our future. In the shower, I ran my hand over my right breast and felt a hard lump. I swore and panicked at the same time. Minutes later I was on the phone to my GP, making an appointment for that morning. As I sat alone in the doctor's waiting room, I rehearsed a conversation in my head about having a second child and a home birth, trying to convince myself that the lump would turn out to be nothing. But deep down I suspected I had cancer. I don't know why I had feared it for so long. Had I sensed that cancer was to be part of my life's pattern? Or had I somehow created it by thinking about it and fearing it too much? Who knows? I didn't consciously set out to make it happen. My only option then, as now, was how to handle it.

My GP said the lump felt like 'knotty breast tissue' and she would refer me straightaway to a specialist. I felt very scared when she seemed to take it so seriously. Of course, I was hoping to leave the surgery with the knowledge that I had nothing to worry about, but I owe her a debt and, possibly, my life. Although the odds were heavily stacked against a 34-year-old having a malignant lump in her breast, she didn't dismiss me, but sent me to a breast surgeon and for a mammogram that afternoon. As I left her consulting room, this usually brisk, reserved woman said 'Good luck'. I knew then that I needed it.

The mammogram revealed nothing abnormal, but in a young,

pre-menopausal woman that is not unusual; the breast tissue is too dense to show up tumours. I didn't know that at the time, and I took some comfort in the normal result as I sat on a bench outside the hospital, having torn open the envelope with shaking hands.

Because we were both self-employed, Colin and I had paid for BUPA cover as we wanted to be able to get treatment quickly if ever we were ill. For us, like so many people nowadays, being freelance means that if you are ill and can't work, you don't earn. The upside of private care was that I saw a surgeon quickly, although measures are now being put in place to make sure that women with breast problems see specialists on the NHS within two weeks.

That Monday night, Colin and I sat opposite a kindly, middle-aged man who did his best to disguise the fact he thought I probably had cancer. When he tried unsuccessfully to take a needle biopsy from the lump, his demeanour became more concerned, and he suggested that I have an operation to remove it in three days' time. 'Let's cross that bridge when we come to it,' was his initial reply when I asked him what would happen if the lump turned out to be cancerous. It's a frustrating phrase I've heard in hospitals many times since. I even thought about titling this book 'Crossing Bridges', as I seem to have ended up always needing information doctors initially want to withhold. But I decided against it – it sounded like a guide to a walking holiday in Venice.

How much information you can handle in the early stages is down to the individual, but I have always liked to gain an overall picture so that I can put some kind of positive spin on it, rather than have huge worries about the unknown crashing around in my mind. When coaxed by me, the surgeon explained that if the lump was malignant, he would then hand me on to an oncologist (cancer specialist) at the Royal Marsden Hospital. A very nice chap, he said, as if he was recommending a really good painter and decorator.

I have my husband's permission to tell you that he didn't handle that first meeting very well. In fact he had to lie down on the couch in the consulting room, while I talked to the surgeon about the operation later in the week. We giggle about it now, but at that traumatic time, it was an indication of the fact that breast cancer places a huge strain on partners which is very often ignored. The problem is that the women in their lives, who may be their usual source of comfort in terms of emotional support, are going through agonies themselves, which leaves the men alone to come to terms with what is going on. And, let's face it, not that many men are terribly good at getting their emotional needs met. It is quite possible that a man is using up all his resources handling the fact that his partner has a life-threatening illness, which is why he has nothing left to offer you. It is not that he no longer cares, or doesn't care enough. I talk more about this in 'How to get support from the people around you'.

I cried in the car on the way home. Nine out of ten breast lumps in women are benign, the surgeon had said, but I sensed mine wasn't. It was a question of getting through the next two days until the operation.

I phoned my parents that night. I tried to play it down; breast lumps were terribly common, I reassured them, but I was terrified. That night, Mary, the doctor I had interviewed about her breast cancer for the *Daily Mail* three months before, phoned me back to offer consolation and support, and as I spoke to her, my legs felt as if they had steel rods running from my thigh to my ankle. I was rigid with fear.

The next day I got up and sat down at my computer to write the Victoria Wood interview. I was in emotional chaos. Every time I looked at Oliver I wanted to cry. I was working full-time then and employed someone to take care of him. This meant that his routine carried on virtually unchanged while I was in hospital, first for the operation, and then as an out-patient for chemotherapy and radiotherapy. But hearing him laugh and chatter as I sat working in another room made me want to howl like a wounded animal. Would I be there for him when he started school? Would I see his first football match? Would he have a mum to help him with his spellings? I drifted away on a stream of unutterably gloomy thoughts.

My work, however, came to my rescue for those two days before the operation. I was worried that my magazine and newspaper employers would no longer want to use me if they thought I was ill, so I decided that I wouldn't mention it to anyone connected with work. I could be typing with tears running down my face, but as soon as the phone rang, and I picked it up, my voice was strong and normal. I guess it was at this point that I decided I would limit the number of people I would tell about the forthcoming operation. Val Jones-Evans (my married name) was a hospital patient. Val Sampson (my professional name) was going to carry on being a journalist, no matter what the following Thursday held.

Colin was due to be away, and although he offered to cancel his work and take me into the hospital, I persuaded him not to. Initially, I wanted this experience to disrupt our lives as little as possible. So it was my Dad who arrived on the Thursday morning to drive me to that first operation. I breathed in the familiar scent of his old car and cried again. I felt I was taking the first step into a foreign and frightening world of hospitals and sickness. I was an unwilling participant in a marathon I had not trained for and I was terrified I wouldn't complete the course.

We pulled up outside the hospital and I was reminded that immediately opposite was a hospice. I felt about hospices the same way I feel about skiing holidays. I am perfectly prepared to accept that people have a wonderful time skiing, but I have no desire to confront my fear of heights and rock unsteadily in a fragile chairlift high above a ravine. Likewise with hospices. They are, by all accounts, places full of friendship and warmth and love. But I wasn't yet ready for either learning curve.

I looked fit and healthy (and felt it, which was why the thought I might have a serious illness was so bemusing) and the nurses assumed it was my Dad who was the patient. Once the confusion was sorted out, I was shown to a corner room and I was pleased to see trees immediately outside the window. The view from a hospital window has always mattered to me. If you are reading this before you go into hospital, do your best not to get a bed facing a brick wall. This may sound strange, but you are going to be confined to a small space for a few days and the outlook from your bed will affect you. If there's no option, get a friend to bring a picture you like to look at. Sometimes it's hard to concentrate on reading in hospital, and you'll benefit from something uplifting to look at if you just want to sit and gaze for a while.

On one of my hospital sojourns, one of my chief supporters brought in a stunning photograph of the Grand Canyon, a candle and a crystal and immediately a sterile hospital space became personal and comforting. Physically and emotionally you have a tough time in hospital, no matter how caring the staff are around you, so do your best to create an environment where you feel reasonably OK.

After I had unpacked and sent my Dad away I managed to meditate for about ten minutes. A decade before I had begun to do a mantra meditation a couple of times a day, when I could manage it; it was, and continues to be, a lifesaver for me. Stilling your mind gives you back a sense of balance and control. (See Chapter 11 on 'Mind therapies'.) Shortly afterwards my surgeon appeared in those surprisingly workmanlike pale blue operating theatre overalls and explained that he was going to take out the lump and, if necessary, some glands from my armpit. He talked about the *axilla* (armpit), but I got confused and thought that somehow he might take out *auxillary* or extra breast tissue. I should have clarified exactly what he meant, but at that point I was so desperate to get the whole thing over with I just signed the consent form, let him draw on me with a blue marker pen and put on the operating gown.

There's an important lesson here. Most surgeons will happily talk to you about your operation until seconds before you fall unconscious from the anaesthetic. This is fine for them – the operating theatre is their work-place – and they are relaxed and happy to chat informally. Some even listen to music while they are operating (apparently Radio Two and Vivaldi are favourites), but even the toughest patient is likely to feel a few qualms before an operation for suspected cancer, so for you it isn't an ideal time to discuss your operation. The place for final decisions, from the patient's point of view, should be the consulting room. Take as long as you want then, and be completely confident that you and your surgeon are in full agreement about what will happen.

When that first lumpectomy was over, I woke in the recovery room and noticed that the clock said 12.15pm. My surgeon had said he expected me to be back on the ward by midday, so I knew that the operation had taken longer than he had anticipated. The word 'cancer' came into my head again, and I sensed the medical staff were treading around me tentatively. A young woman with cancer brings everyone's spirits down. The anaesthetist, who had seemed chatty and relaxed when we met before the operation, told me in a businesslike way she had given me plenty of pain relief and vanished before I had a chance to ask any questions.

I was pushed back to the ward and shortly afterwards the surgeon appeared, dressed in a dark suit and tie. It couldn't have been more obvious that bad news was in store if he had carried a placard with 'It's over, bye bye' on it.

He stood at the end of the bed and said 'I am afraid you have an invasive carcinoma with disease in situ.' I guessed he meant I had cancer. My first question was 'How long have I got?' And this is where it gets better. He could have hedged and said stuff like 'No-one knows how long they have', or 'Cancer is an unpredictable illness'. Instead he said 'Forty or fifty years, we hope'. He added he was going to refer me to the Marsden for chemotherapy and radiotherapy and told me that the anaes-thetist's sister had had breast cancer at my age. That was seven years ago and she had just completed a backpacking tour of Africa. Those two hopeful remarks were to sustain me for years to come.

The ward sister, a motherly woman with six children, stood beside him. When he left the room she said to me 'You'll see your son's gradua-tion'. Oliver was two-and-a-half at the time. Now there are plenty of medical people who will suck in their breath and strongly disapprove of such optimism in the face of a cancer diagnosis. All I can say is that those words got me through those first life-changing months. When I replayed that awful scene in my head, I heard hopeful words too. Of course, they may not turn out to be prophetic; cancer patients aren't gullible idiots. I've had cancer twice by the age of 38 and I realise that I could die soon. But even if I were to get grim news tomorrow, I certainly wouldn't be knocking on their doors and attacking them for the sense of hope they instilled in me in those early days.

My surgeon was frank about what lay ahead – chemotherapy and radiotherapy – but he was optimistic about the outcome. The ward sister encouraged me to believe that I could get well. For a long while, every night when I used to kiss my son's forehead as he slept, I used to murmur to myself 'I'll be at your graduation.' Who knows whether that will turn out to be true. It made me stronger *at the time*, and that helped.

The afternoon of that first operation, I phoned Colin who was working in Stoke that day. He drove down to London and arrived at my bedside around 10pm. We were both in a state of shock and I don't think either of us quite knew what to say. I had been watching a French and Saunders comedy show that was spoofing the *Alien* movie. I should have switched off; the analogy with cancer was too uncomfortable.

My parents had brought in my son during the afternoon, and I had expected to be engulfed by a flood of emotion when I saw him. I was very concerned about hiding the drain that came out from under my arm. I had a terrible vision of him seeing it, screaming and running away from me. Again the ward sister was a gem. She found a way of tucking it behind pillows, so Oliver couldn't see it. Initially he was a little uncertain. The hospital surroundings were unfamiliar to him. So I didn't push it immediately. But within a few minutes he climbed onto the bed beside me, and we read a book together before my parents took him home.

Because Oliver was there we all acted normally, and although I don't believe in denying your feelings, there are occasions when if you simply behave as normal, instead of sinking under the weight of overpowering emotions, it can help you through a tight spot. Handle the emotions at a time that seems right. Breaking down and sobbing with my mum and dad in front of Oliver that first afternoon didn't feel right. I wanted to establish that I was still me, to cling to the me that I knew was still capable of behaving normally.

When Colin turned up that night I think I apologised for getting cancer. His mother had died from ovarian cancer when he was 17 and I felt guilty I was putting him through the cancer business again. For a couple who talk a lot, neither of us really knew what to say. He told me later that he had driven down the motorway literally bracing himself against the steering wheel, and gritting his teeth in preparation for something terrible that he felt lay ahead. When he arrived at the hospital he didn't want to burden me (as he saw it) with his fears, and he felt guilty that he hadn't been there when I was given the news. Small wonder that it was hard for us to talk.

Fairly quickly, we decided to limit the number of people he would tell. In those early days, one of Colin's employers had been awkward when he asked if another trainer could take over one day of a management course he was due to run, as he needed to go to the hospital with me. This man had been uncompromising and difficult. From then on we told no one connected with work. We made the decision that it was going to be tricky enough getting through the next few months without having to handle any extra burden that telling people would create in our working lives. This approach was right for us and because we are both self-employed we could juggle our work commitments around hospital visits. Clearly, it isn't right for everyone. If you are an employee, your company will need to be told as you will require time off work and, to be fair to a lot of companies, they can also be an excellent source of support.

The surgeon recommended that I stay in hospital overnight and the next morning the phone rang with a well-meaning relative telling me how desperate she was to hear my news. I tried to calm her down, and soon realised that people want to know you are OK for their own peace of mind. That was the first in a long line of phone calls where I reassured everyone that I was going to be fine and that I felt extremely positive about the whole episode. This wasn't strictly true, but after a couple of days of agonising uncertainty, at least I knew what I had to handle. The implications of it all still had to sink in.

Probably the main reason I did feel fairly positive in those early days, was because of the support I had from the surgeon and nurse in hospital. But taking care of other people's feelings is tiring, especially when you can't be entirely sure of your own. Be prepared to delegate someone else to talk to other people about your news. Talking to others can be a valuable source of support, but you won't be able to share your innermost thoughts and fears with *everyone*. (And you shouldn't feel obliged to.) Neither will it be immediately apparent among your friends who will be best to turn to.

Give yourself a few days at least to find out who you think you will be most comfortable talking to. It may not be the friends you would have assumed would be there for you before your illness. Some people just can't deal with the idea of cancer because of their own fears or past experiences, and such people won't do you any good. There are those who play it down so much it seems less important than a common cold, (just plain thoughtless) or who get so weepy and dramatic you suddenly feel you're centre stage in the final act of a particularly tragic opera (equally thoughtless on their part). What both sets of people are doing in those instances is putting their feelings above yours. You don't need them. And, by the way, some friends simply don't call at all.

So many people have said that it is only after something really bad happens, like a bereavement or a divorce, that they learn who their 'real' friends are. So it is with breast cancer. There are a handful of friends who have held me when I have cried, either physically or metaphorically, and with whom I feel I can be competely honest. For everyone else, I feel obliged to put up a sort of front. Cancer isn't common currency in our conversation, and that's what I'm happy with. Everyone has to find their own way through their friendships, but don't feel too let down if the people you first thought would be there for you aren't. They probably have other qualities that matter to you. And stay open to the idea of making new friends. It happens less often when you grow older, but it's my belief that friends – old and new – are good for your health.

Colin and I waited for further results from the surgery over the August Bank Holiday weekend. Black humour helped us both. We talked about what might happen if the news was very bad. I didn't feel like booking a round-the-world cruise or a fabulous holiday if I didn't have long to live. I just had a very strong desire to make the most of what I had. I didn't know quite how to do it then, but I've been learning ever since.

When we turned up at the Marsden for the first meeting with the oncologist I wore my sexiest bright red suit, (the one I turned to for tricky meetings with the bank manager), jewellery and lipstick. I wanted to look positive. I thought if I looked well, the people who treated me at the hospital would feel morally obliged to keep me looking good. Dubious rationalisation, I know, but I was convinced it would work at the time.

We walked into Dr Ian Smith's consulting room and his opening words were 'This must have come as a shock for you'. I was taken aback; I hadn't expected such a human response. I liked him straight away. He talked us through the prospect of chemotherapy and he agreed that as we had a one-week holiday booked in Norfolk, I could start the chemo two weeks later. At the end of our discussion, he introduced me to Debbie with the words 'This is Val Jones-Evans, she is a journalist and she has a two-year-old son'.

I have since described that moment as feeling as if someone had lifted a blind and let sunshine in. I suddenly remembered that there was more to me than breast cancer. My life had more to offer than chemotherapy and possible hair loss. Naturally, that was going to feature prominently for a while, but somehow I was bigger than the cancer. Please God, let it stay that way.

Debbie had a serious but friendly approach. She explained that she would be my link with the hospital and I could call her with any worries or concerns. She recommended that I think about getting a wig for when the chemotherapy started. Strangely enough, we came home from the Marsden on a high. At this point, it didn't look as if the cancer had spread to my lymph nodes, and although it was aggressive, Ian Smith had played it down by remarking that this was normal for younger women.

It was my Dad who I asked to take me for chemotherapy at the Marsden when Colin was away, and the hours that we spent together then sustained me through a very difficult time. I speak to my mother on the telephone nearly every day, so the visits to the Marsden with my father gave us time with each other that we would otherwise never have had. An unlooked-for bonus from breast cancer.

Although usually I have chosen to go for check-ups on my own, and I drove myself to radiotherapy every day, having someone with you while you hang around for chemotherapy is always a good idea. Even if your anti-sickness drugs do a wonderful job (I swore that ondansetron made me invincible. Climb Everest? Sure, if I have ondansetron first), you may not feel like tackling public transport alone or driving on your own afterwards.

For some reason, chemotherapy nearly always involves hours of waiting. Having someone to talk to passes the time. During my second lot of chemo four years later, I used to disappear off to the nearby town for a coffee and spot of shopping while waiting a couple of hours for the drugs to be made up, and that was much more fun to do with a friend than alone. The shopping was a bigger boost for both of us than sitting in the corridor outside the chemotherapy suite reading tatty back copies of *Woman's Own*. My hair fell out after my first lot of chemotherapy. It had a profoundly negative effect on me which I discuss in Chapter 13, 'Looking good and feeling better'.

Radiotherapy was different. I got myself booked into a 9.15am slot and I'd be home by 10am ready to start the day. Some people get very tired while having radiotherapy. I found that going relatively early in the morning, before delays in appointments set in, meant my life wasn't disrupted too much, and I didn't get tired. Because you lie under a radio-therapy machine for only a couple of minutes the whole process is much speedier than chemo. One thing to beware of though – when they plan the radiotherapy they usually take a photograph of you. I was given this photograph, clipped to the outside of my file which I then proceeded to carry the length of the hospital. I had no idea why people were giving me sneaky glances as I strode along the corridors with a topless picture of myself pinned to the front of the file I carried in my arms . . .

When my treatment ended, roughly six months after the first opera-tion, I was surprised not to feel more euphoric. It is probably because as far as other people are concerned, when the treatment is over, the cancer is over, and that is not the case. You still have fears of recurrence to handle, and the knowledge that you are not immortal changes you in ways you might not expect.

For me, finishing the treatment was like phase one of the experience coming to an end. My hair grew back, a sign to the outside world that I was back to 'normal', but the person beneath it had started to change.

The beauty therapist I used to visit to have my legs waxed began to offer reflexology treatment and I had decided shortly after starting chemotherapy that I would like to try it. I had no idea whether a type of foot massage could have any benefit to the rest of your body, but I have always loved having my feet stroked, so I decided to give it a try. I still have regular reflexology. I find it soothing and enjoyable, and if it helps me physically, which I feel it probably does, then that's a wonderful bonus.

I had practised a form of self-hypnosis when I gave birth to my son, which had been so effective that the doctor monitoring my labour had declared that she had rarely seen anyone so relaxed before giving birth. That gave me the belief that what goes on in our subconscious is enormously powerful, if we can tap into it.

I contacted the hypnotherapist before starting chemotherapy, and she recorded a tape which began with a relaxation exercise. She then gave me lots of positive messages about feeling calm while I was at the hospital, and believing that the drugs would help me get well quickly. I used to listen to the tape the night before I went to the hospital and it did help me to calm down. The reflexology that I used to have on the Saturday after my Wednesday chemotherapy also helped me feel as if I was doing some-thing positive for my own well-being. But I knew that if I was going to take time to heal, I had to change the pattern of the life I was leading.

I cut down my work from five days a week to three, and decided that I would no longer think that I would one day get around to doing something when I wasn't so busy. I would start it there and then. So I began to learn tap dancing, joined a local amateur drama society, signed up at a gym, took up yoga and developed an interest in spiritual healing. I am, as my husband puts it, a woman with many hobbies. I prefer to say that I've got off a treadmill and got a life.

I returned to the Marsden for three-monthly and then six-monthly check-ups. It was during such a routine check-up in September 1998, four years after my first diagnosis, that Dr Ian Smith found a lump in my left breast. I stared at the ceiling as I heard the disappointment in his voice. I couldn't believe it was happening to me again. In his measured, professional way he said he thought he'd better take a needle biopsy to check it. I had a sleepless night, but the result the next day was clear. I felt like I had been let out of prison and we went out to lunch to celebrate. Nevertheless, we agreed that I should have the lump removed 'to be on the safe side'.

I returned to the surgeon I had seen four years before, but opted to have the operation done in another hospital which didn't have such traumatic memories. The lump was taken out a couple of weeks later, and he reassured me that it had all looked perfectly normal, 'very different from last time'. So far so good. Then, five days later I turned up alone to get the final results. Colin had left for America that morning, and I felt confident that all was well. I walked into his consulting room and he said 'I'm very sorry, but it's another tumour. You'll have to talk to Ian Smith about this.' I felt numb.

Outside the hospital, I sat in the car as an irritating red security light blinked up at me. I called my mother on my mobile phone. 'Bugger', she said. She only swears about once every 25 years, so I knew she was distraught. I phoned Steve, a family friend, who was preparing to go out to celebrate his mother's birthday. 'You're joking,' he said. 'Believe me, this isn't something I want to chuckle about,' I replied.

I got home and talked to Colin in America. My Dad insisted on coming to stay and when he arrived that night we sat and talked about what I might do. I knew that I needed to phone Ian Smith the next morning and Steve rang during his dinner party to say he would be with me the next day.

I usually helped out at my son's infants school on Wednesday mornings and I decided to go into school as usual. Again, it was all to do with reminding myself that I was bigger than the cancer. Ian Smith phoned later that day. He was pretty stunned by the news. He explained that the chance of getting another primary in the opposite breast rises each year by one per cent. It was four years on, so I had a four per cent chance of it happening. And a 96 per cent chance that it wouldn't. Val Jones-Evans beats the odds again. I felt that somehow my breasts had become unreliable. I had lost confidence in their ability to stay clear of cancer. I said I wanted a mastectomy and reconstruction. He agreed we should talk it over and we fixed an appointment.

Steve offered to take me shopping (a perennial distraction from bad news for me) and I wandered around John Lewis, choosing curtain material. Occasionally I clung to his hand like a little girl. Life felt ordinary and yet strangely out of kilter. But I felt very loved. I had cried on my Dad's shoulder the night before, but I sensed that if anything, I was better equipped to handle cancer the second time around. I had become a broader and stronger person, not simply because I had acquired a range of hobbies and interests, but because the experience of cancer had already pushed me to explore beyond my immediate surroundings, mentally, physically and emotionally. Within days, it didn't feel so much like 'here we go again', but 'here is the next step on my journey'. And I'd bought some great curtains.

The following week Colin and I went to see Ian Smith at the Marsden. I said I wanted both breasts replaced by implants (a bilateral mastectomy with immediate reconstruction). He explained that it wasn't strictly necessary and that I could have a lumpectomy, chemotherapy and radiotherapy as before. But I had a fixed idea in my mind that mastectomy was the right thing to do. I couldn't be sure that no other lumps would appear. And – this is where the vain part of me steps out in kitten-heels and a swimsuit – I wanted breasts that matched. Neither could I face losing my hair again. There are no guarantees with chemotherapy the second time around, so when Ian Smith suggested I try vinorelbine, a new chemotherapy drug with remarkably few side-effects that didn't cause hair loss, I leapt at the chance.

First I had to meet Nigel Sacks, a breast surgeon at the Marsden, to make sure he could reconstruct my right breast as I had already had radiotherapy on it. He decided that the skin was still sufficiently soft and flexible, and he didn't think there would be a problem. I arranged to have the operation at the end of November, six weeks later. I was acting in a play locally and I didn't want to give up my part in it. Breast cancer is rarely an emergency. Although it is important to be seen quickly when you have found a lump, and not be kept waiting for ages for the results of tests, *you don't have to rush into treatment within days*. Naturally, some people prefer things to swing into action quickly, but if you are someone who likes to take a while to think about your options, you are pefectly entitled to say this to your doctor and to take a week or ten days to mull things over.

Giving up my part in the play would have made me feel I was missing out on life because of cancer, and that is something I have been loath to accept. I don't see my actions as a 'fight' against cancer, but I do see myself as someone who turns down cancer's invitation to a cosy dinner for two with no other guests present. This is a flip way of saying I don't want to get involved with cancer more than is strictly necessary, so if I have to create lots of other things in my life to take my attention away from it, that's what I'll do.

Learning lines, attending rehearsals and moaning about the director are all part of the amateur actor's lot, and were a brilliant distraction from the forthcoming operation. The play finished on the Saturday night, and it would be a more dramatic story if I could say I took the final curtain call with a heavy heart, knowing that I was facing a major operation in a few days' time. Actually, I didn't even think about it. I went to the party, dissected the play with the other actors and went home feeling pretty happy that I had remembered my lines (mostly), my friends had enjoyed it, and it had all gone well.

For me, distraction plays a major part in coping with difficult situations. I was later to learn that psycholgists call this cognitive therapy (see Chapter 2, 'Fear and how to handle it'). I could have sat at home on that Saturday with a feeling of dread in the pit of my stomach and dwelt miserably on what lay ahead. Instead I had other things on my mind, and that helped. When I arrived at the Fulham Road branch of the Marsden the following Friday, it felt as if life was carrying on as usual. Yes, I had a sinking feeling on a par with the *Titanic* as I climbed the steps to the entrance hall, but I had limited it to the actual day of the operation, I hadn't had to live with it for the week before too.

It took a while for the bed manager to sort out my bed and I began to get twitchy. I hadn't eaten or drunk anything since the night before and the smell of other people's coffee in the waiting room made me feel unfairly singled out. Losing both breasts was one thing, having to give up my early morning cup of tea felt like adding insult to injury. Eventually, after blood tests and a chest X-ray everything sprang into action. I saw a young doctor from Nigel Sacks' team who examined me, chatted aimably about nothing much, and I began to unpack. No lunch of course. I wondered if they planned to economise on the anaesthetic; shortly I'd pass out through hunger.

The friend who had taken me into hospital disappeared to buy me some flowers. I put on the operating gown, pulled on those hideous white stockings they make you wear and picked up my book. No sooner had I settled down to read around 3pm, comfortable at last, than the doors swung open and a nurse appeared with a porter and a trolley. For a moment I was shocked by the reality of it. The trolley looked alarmingly medical. I was actually going to have this operation.

Surgeons carry out a mastectomy in various ways. (See Chapter 8, 'Surgery and reconstruction'.) My breast tissue was replaced by two inflatable saline implants, but the outer skin was left intact. The operation took around three hours and I woke up in the recovery room with two drains in either side of me and a huge dressing that covered my chest and stomach like a surgical suit of armour. I felt like Joan of Arc minus the French army.

To my horror, I wasn't wheeled back to the nice bed I had left before the operation. 'I don't want to go to the High Dependency Unit,' I declared, 'take me back to my bed.' The nurses looked bemused, then they checked. Someone had got their information mixed up, so I was returned safely to my familiar pre-op surroundings where my friend was waiting. Don't ever be afraid to query what hospital staff do, if you think they've got it wrong. They are busy with lots of other patients, not just you, and it's not surprising that they do make errors occasionally. But if you are aware of what should be happening to you, the chances are that it won't be *you* who suffers as a result of someone else's blunder.

Some people feel ghastly after an anaesthetic. I felt drugged but surprisingly perky. Perky enough to request a cup of tea and toast. A big mistake. I'd recommend that no matter how well you may feel after a major operation, don't eat or drink anything more than water, at least for several hours. The milk in the tea suddenly tasted like solid cream and I felt incredibly sick. The sickness made me feel weak and I slumped back on the pillows. Water was my sole comfort for the rest of that night.

I stayed in hospital until the following Tuesday. I requested visits only from Colin, Oliver, now aged seven, two close friends and my Mum and Dad. I wanted to spend the time I had, between swallowing antibiotics and having my blood pressure and temperature taken, feeling calm and working on my mental state. Visitors are draining. Unless you are absolutely certain that the person sitting beside you is doing you good, postpone seeing them until you are at home and feeling stronger.

For me, a hospital visitor needs to be someone who will make me laugh and raise my spirits. Anyone who looks concerned or worried, no matter how well-meaning, or who feels obliged to tell me about the problems they are having in their life – in a skewed attempt to level the playing field of bad luck between us – is to be avoided.

When I returned to have the dressing taken off several days later, I wasn't sure what to expect. So when I saw a bruised and battered bosom I felt a mild euphoria. They weren't *my* breasts, but they would do.

It would be tempting to close this chapter here, but there is a postscript. Six months on, the day before we were due to fly to America on holiday, I felt a small lump under my arm. I had chosen to preserve the lymph nodes under my left arm when I had my bilateral mastectomy, but as it turned out, the cancer had spread to three of the twelve I was to have taken out. It was time to return to the surgeon Nigel Sacks – this time on a floor with an interestingly mixed bunch of fellow patients (facelift and penis extensions were housed along my corridor) at the Lister Hospital in Chelsea.

The operation in July 1999 seemed minor in comparison with the mastectomy, and I felt fine and wanted to leave hospital the next day. But the drain under my arm was still filling with fluid and couldn't be taken away, so the staff nurse came up with an ingenious way of allowing me outside the hospital. It was summer and I have a penchant for loose, floaty frocks. We put the drain inside one of those drawstring makeup bags you can buy in Boots and pinned it to the lining of my dress. No one could see it. I went out for dinner to a nearby restaurant on Saturday night, two days after the operation, and apart from a slight panic when a waiter hovered frighteningly close to my chair, almost clunking into the hidden drain as he poured me a glass of wine, it worked a treat.

The following day was a family tea party for my birthday. I hadn't told my in-laws about the most recent operation – we're back to not wanting cancer to take over life events here – so I went to the party with the drain safety-pinned to the inside of my dress. I didn't join in with my son's football game, but I don't think anyone was any the wiser, and that suited me at the time. The drain came out two days later and it was like losing a ball and chain. I had an urge to cartwheel across the garden, but I've never managed a cartwheel in my life. And the acrobatic lessons are on hold . . . for now.

2

Fear and how to handle it

Fear takes many forms and is different for everyone. For me it's a stomach-churning feeling of dread. At its peak, the tension is unbearable. I discovered the expression 'rigid with fear' was entirely accurate when I was first diagnosed with cancer. I remember lying in bed and feeling my legs stiffen with a horrible combination of anticipation and panic. There have been some ghastly moments since when I have felt my entire body tense in exactly the same way.

Fear forces your mind into a gallop, scattering worries like black confetti across your daily life. It would be tempting to stay in bed and sleep, if only that felt like an escape, but it doesn't. In fact, the longer you lie in bed feeling afraid, the worse it gets. Fear is the opposite of peace and it is one of the hardest things in life to handle.

There are different sorts of fear too. There's the re-kindling of old fears; when you have to return to hospital for a check-up, for instance, and waves of unpleasant memories sweep across your mind. There is the panic when you experience an unexpected symptom which could be linked to the cancer, and there is, of course, the biggest one of all: the fear of dying.

I came across the following quote, attributed to the writer Dorothy Thompson:

'Only when one is no longer afraid to die is one no longer afraid at all. And only when we are no longer afraid do we begin to live in every experience, painful or joyous, to live in gratitude for every moment, to live abundantly.'

I have to say that getting to that place is a long, hard road. Many of us won't face death for a very long time, but that is the point Dorothy Thompson is making. It is fear which paralyses us and stops us from living fully in our daily lives. Whether they have experienced cancer or not, too many people's lives are hemmed in by their fears.

So how do you shake off the fear and get back some of the peace and joy you have lost on the way? Or, for some of us, how do you find that sense of living fully and joyously in the first place?

How to handle fears when you are first diagnosed

A diagnosis of breast cancer is a crisis point in your life. I have found that getting through it is easier if you follow a few simple steps which, incidentally, apply to most crises, whether they are connected with health, getting the sack or your partner leaving.

Step One: Don't make it worse

Your initial reaction is: 'This should not be happening to me'. You feel indignant, angry and in a state of panic. What we then tend to do is to break the first rule of crisis management, which is 'do nothing that will make your situation worse'. Yet this is precisely what a lot of people do. They use unhelpful coping strategies, like drinking heavily, over-eating, or hitting out at people close to them. Even if you have done none of these things, the shock of what has happened tends to make it difficult to think clearly. What you need to do now is to accept that your brain is still reeling, and take time until you feel calmer before you move on to the next stage.

Step Two: Gather information

Before you rush headlong into surgery or a course of treatment, take time to discuss your choices with your surgeon and breast care nurse. If you are not automatically allocated a breast care nurse (and you should be) *ask* to see one. If you have doubts about the people who will be treating you at a certain hospital, return to your GP and ask to be referred for a second opinion. It does take courage to do this at a time when you are feeling especially vulnerable, but it is *your* body and *your* health that is at stake. It is worth repeating that breast cancer is very rarely an emergency, so if you have worries about what is happening to you, make sure they are resolved before you go ahead with treatment.

Step Three: Take practical steps

When you have gained a clearer picture of what your diagnosis means and the recommended course of action, the third rule of coping beckons – take practical steps to make your situation better. Positive activity, no matter how small or seemingly trivial, will improve your situation. It will not only calm you down, but also it will reduce your fears. Part of this third rule involves asking other people for help. That might mean calling an organisation like Breast Cancer Care (see Useful Addresses), where volunteers staff a telephone helpline and specialist nurses can answer your questions, or talking to friends or acquaintances who have also had breast cancer. Bouncing your thoughts off others can be a useful coping strategy because it can help you to think more clearly. Brooding alone usually builds up fear and depression, so if at all possible, try to avoid it.

Step Four: Don't worry needlessly

Easier said than done, of course. Some women are more prone to worry than others. I'm the Queen of the Needless Worry and all I can say is that when I try and limit my worries, life is much better. Oh, chorus my fellow worriers, what if your worries are not without foundation? Suppose you have good reason to worry? I can only answer by offering a personal example.

In June 1999 I fulfilled a lifetime's ambition and went on holiday with Colin and Oliver to America and visited New Orleans. I had found a tiny lump under my arm the day before we left and I was worried that it was a cancerous lymph node. I managed to put the worry out of my mind for most of the holiday and we had a wonderful time. When we returned I saw my surgeon and had it removed. But there's another part of the story. One night, while Colin and Oliver went swimming, I sat in the hotel room and started to worry. I became obsessed with fears about my health. We had thought about going out to a nearby jazz concert that night, but I had worked myself into such a state that I didn't want to go. So we stayed in the hotel room while Oliver slept and Colin and I talked about my health.

Looking back, I regret not abandoning my worries for an evening of jazz in New Orleans. Of course, my worries were proved to have some foundation. But I could have dealt with them another time and I did – when we returned to England. Worry stopped me from having a wonderful night out in New Orleans and now I could kick myself for that.

I wouldn't advocate going to a film or a concert instead of visiting a doctor if you have a concern about your health. You should always pay proper attention to your health and do the best you can to make sure you are taking good care of yourself physically. But I would most certainly suggest that you do something to help your mood after you have been to hospital.

Some people try to distract themselves first and end up burying their heads in the sand, hoping the problem will go away – not a wise move. But if you have done everything you can to help your problem, there is no point dwelling on it.

Symptoms of anxiety

Most of us who have been diagnosed with breast cancer know only too well what the symptoms of anxiety feel like; we have lived with them for days, weeks, months or years. Below is an officially recognised list which may help you realise that forgetting to make your child's packed lunch or shouting at your partner is not a sign that you are going crazy, but a medically accepted pattern of behaviour for people who are under stress.

- **Poor concentration and memory:** when you are under stress, thoughts may become fuzzy and hard to organise. You can become easily distracted and can't take in or remember information as effectively as normal.
- **Sleep disturbance:** worry can make it particularly difficult to 'switch off' and sleep is often affected. This has a build up effect which gets worse over an extended period of time.
- **Short temper, irritability:** because of excessive worry and tiredness, you may find you become more easily frustrated and have little energy for problems outside your most immediate concerns. This can make you feel snappy and short-tempered.
- **Tiredness and lethargy:** worry and tension use up a lot of energy so that you find it difficult to make the effort to cope.
- **Depression:** the feeling that worries are taking over your life, or disrupting normal activities, can understandably lead to feelings of depression and despair. This in turn makes it hard to believe that change is possible or that life can be better. Your motivation goes and you no longer feel like doing things you once enjoyed. Around one in three women will develop an anxiety disorder or depressive illness at some stage in their disease or treatment. You are not unusual if you become depressed. If you are finding it incredibly hard to cope, make sure you talk to your doctor. Some women find that a short course of anti-depressants helps to get them through.
- **Hopelessness:** you may feel it is no longer worth trying and that the future looks black. This makes you feel helpless and unable to cope.

Security is not just about having good health; it is about handling illness well

How do you help yourself when you are frightened and exhibiting some or all of the above feelings? How do you get back a sense of security and control in your life? One of the things I have learnt is that feeling secure is not just about having good health, it is about handling illness as well as you can.

The first lesson I learnt about fear, actually before I had cancer, is that all unpleasant thoughts and emotions aren't stuck in your brain forever. They go. It is quite possible to be in the depths of despair and to be laughing a couple of hours later. What you need to hang on to when you are feeling desperate, is the thought that *this feeling will go*. How quickly it leaves and is replaced by something better is up to you.

Feeling helpless feeds fear and many people who are told they have cancer feel 'helpless and hopeless'. But no one takes away your power over yourself when they give you a diagnosis of cancer. Doctors are there to advise you, and it is entirely up to you whether or not you take their advice. Because we often feel childlike when we are ill, it is tempting to hand over our welfare to a parental figure, like a doctor, and expect them to 'put it right'. If that idea is fine with you, that is of course your choice. Some people compare putting a doctor wholly in charge of their health with handing their car over to a garage or getting a lawyer to sort out a legal problem. They prefer to leave some things to an expert.

I feel uncomfortable relinquishing *all* control over my treatment because that makes me feel less in charge of my life, and feeling at least slightly in control of my life reduces my level of fear. So, if I am going to see my consultant, I picture him as a helpful friend. He knows a lot more about the technicalities of cancer than I do and I am grateful for his knowledge, but I know more about my state of mind than he does. He does not have the power to make life or death pronouncements over me. He can give me information, but it is down to me to decide what to do with it.

Knowing this doesn't stop my heart from thumping as I sit in the waiting room, but whatever news a doctor gives you, you will be able to handle it. It is just a question of finding the best way for you. The aim of this chapter is to make a few suggestions about how to do that.

In her book, *Feel the Fear and Do It Anyway*, Susan Jeffers, a former breast cancer patient, explains that one of the ways of diminishing fear is to develop more trust in your ability to handle whatever comes you way.

As she points out: 'If you knew that you could handle anything that came your way, what would you possibly have to fear? Nothing!'

I once heard about a woman who reacted to her diagnosis of breast cancer with such fear and panic that she was virtually hysterical. She needed psychiatric support to cope in those early days; her biggest fear was that she would suffer a recurrence of the cancer. Four years later her cancer did come back. The nurses who had looked after her braced themselves for a woman who would be terrified. In fact, she was transformed. She explained to them that as far as she was concerned, getting cancer was the worst thing that could happen to her, and she had learned to handle it. It hadn't been as bad as she had feared; she knew she could handle anything after that. Eventually, she died, but that degree of overwhelming fear never returned.

Susan Jeffers' book is about personal development, rather than facing illness, but her arguments ring true for people with cancer. She believes that when you handle fear, you move from a position of pain to one of power.

You do this by accepting that fear will never go away, as long as you continue to grow as a person, and that the only way to get rid of a fear of doing something is to go out and do it. She recommends that you don't blame an external force for your bad feelings about life. In other words, there is little point in blaming cancer for making you feel bad about life, no matter how justified you may be in doing so. You are entirely in charge of your feelings and actions and you need to stay aware of the many choices you have in any situation that comes your way. She suggests you choose the path that makes you grow as an individual and makes you feel at peace with yourself and others.

Of course, this is easy to say, but hard to put into action. Changing ourselves so we cope with cancer better is tough, but I believe we have a more difficult journey in front of us if we bury our heads under the duvet and hope it will all go away.

There are three ways to tackle fear:

- Thinking skills (changing the way you think)
- Problem solving skills
- Relaxation skills

Changing the way you think

Identifying your negative thoughts is the first step in learning to change your thinking. Genuine negative events can be exaggerated and distorted until they seem enormous problems which you cannot hope to solve. If you control these thinking errors you can cut your problems down to size, and devote your energy to solving them rather than worrying pointlessly about them.

Most of us think 'I can't cope' or 'I feel terrible' from time to time. These thoughts, in themselves, can make your situation worse. Cancer patients, like everyone else to a greater or lesser degree, are prone to what psychologists call 'negative automatic thoughts'. Here are some examples:

'No-one will find me attractive if my hair falls out.'
'I know I am going to die from the cancer.'
'There's no point in doing anything because I have no power to change things.'

These thoughts are unrealistically pessimistic, spring from nowhere and automatically enter your mind. They also have the following characteristics in common. Negative thoughts:

- come to mind without any effort from you
- are easy to believe
- are often not true
- can be difficult to stop
- are unhelpful because they keep you anxious and make it difficult to change.

The key to handling these thoughts is to recognise them. Here are four questions to ask if you start having thoughts you suspect are negative:

1. Does the thought make me more anxious or depressed?
2. Does it stop me from doing what I want to do?
3. Is is true?
4. Is there another way I can look at this situation?

If the answer to any of the above is 'yes', try to think of another thought which would help you to get through the situation and feel better about it. For example: 'I can't cope' could be replaced by 'It's thinking this way that stops me from coping. If I slow down and take my mind off these negative thoughts, I'll be fine.'

When people are fearful and under stress they often feel overwhelmed and demoralised. This can lead them to exaggerate the real problems they are facing and to underestimate their ability to cope. Their thinking becomes distorted. The examples below are common.

Overgeneralisation

A single negative event is seen as a never-ending pattern of defeat. For instance, if you have a row with your partner the day after you get back from hospital you think, 'It's the cancer. We'll always be arguing, things will never be the same again. We might as well split up now and get it over with.'

Magnification and minimisation

You exaggerate the importance of things (such as other patients' strengths and coping abilities) while at the same time shrinking other things until they appear insignificant (such as your own efforts at coping). You say 'Everyone is coping better than me. I'm just a wimp.' In fact you are doing the best you can. You have no idea how other people are coping inside; you see only their 'public' face.

All or nothing thinking

You see the world in absolutely black-and-white terms. If a treatment is not 100 per cent likely to be successful you see it as useless. If you are told your cancer cannot be cured, you think 'If I can't be cured, there's no point in doing anything. I might as well die now.' Whereas, with appropriate treatment, you could have months or decades of full, active and enjoyable life ahead.

Selective attention

If you feel depressed, you are only able to think about the negative parts of your life. You selectively attend to these, while ignoring all the positive things that are happening to you. For example, if you are very worried about chemotherapy, you might not be able to see beyond the potential side-effects of the treatment. You ignore the fact that if the treatment is successful you can enjoy the rest of your life. You also fail to see what you can enjoy on a daily basis even during your treatment. I've had day trips to France, weekends away and some great nights out during my months of chemotherapy. Not on the days of the chemo itself, naturally, but within a week or so of the hospital visit.

Negative predictions

The future for women with breast cancer is uncertain, but you can turn this into a negative uncertainty by assuming the worst:

'I know this treatment won't work.'
'I won't be able to cope if the cancer comes back.'
'Even if the cancer is cured, something else will come along to create problems for me.'

Try these **coping statements** instead:

'I've done this before and come out of it alive/sane/still in one piece.'

'I know that worry about my body makes me feel worse. I know that my feelings can be controlled.'

'I am going to approach this situation by practising coping better.'

'I might not be 100 per cent satisfied with the way I handle it, but the important thing is to practise coping skills and build up my confidence.'

'I'll practise relaxation before I go to a clinic.'

'I am deliberately going to change how I feel.'

'I am proud of myself for having the courage and patience to control my anxious feelings.'

'I haven't achieved so much since I sat my exams, started my first job, etc.'

The key to feeling less afraid is to keep practising. Every time a negative thought goes through your mind, try to stop yourself and think of a positive, realistic answer to it.

Mind-reading

Instead of asking people what they are thinking, you jump to conclusions. I assumed that Colin would be horrified when I lost my hair. I thought he wouldn't want to see me without a headscarf or a wig. I was wrong. In fact, as my hair got thinner, he offered to trim it to get rid of the strange-looking spikes I was left with, and we giggled together as he played the role of camp hairdresser, complete with the inevitable questions about was I going out that night and where was I going on holiday. I remember being about to dash up to the bedroom one evening to put on my cotton turban before we sat down to dinner. He said 'Don't worry about that. Just be yourself.' It is hard to describe how reassuring hearing that sentence felt. So my mind-reading on that score couldn't have proved more inaccurate.

'Shoulds' and 'oughts'

You try and motivate yourself with 'shoulds' and 'oughts', but end up feeling guilty: 'Even though I don't feel well, I should still be looking after my children', or 'I've tried to lead a good life, I shouldn't have got cancer'. 'Shoulds' and 'oughts' rarely make anyone feel better. Don't beat yourself up, it won't get you anywhere. Do the best you can and give yourself a pat on the back.

Labelling

You apply a critical label to yourself instead of accurately describing the situation. Instead of saying, 'I didn't do that job as well as I should have done', you say 'I'm a failure'. Or if you find it difficult to concentrate because of the stress you are under you say 'I'm an idiot'. Change the voice inside your head. Coping with cancer and its treatment is tough. Tell yourself you are doing well. You are reading this book for a start – you are taking steps to help yourself through one of the toughest times of your life.

Personalisation

You see yourself as the cause of some negative event for which you are not directly responsible. If your children behave badly you think, 'It's my fault', or if friends cancel a visit you think, 'It must be because I have cancer'. After the initial shock and upset, you may be surprised at how quickly your friends and family can forget you have cancer. Brutal as this may sound, just because it is on your mind a lot of the time, it doesn't mean that it is on everyone else's. Other people tend to behave in a certain way because of the way you treat them or, more importantly, because of what is going on *for them*. Very rarely is their behaviour directly due to your illness.

Action you can take

The best tip I was given in the early days of my diagnosis for coping with rampaging fears was to set aside up to half an hour a day for worry. I chose between 9.30 and 10am. Every time a fear came into my mind at any other time of the day, I would think 'I'm not going to give that any attention now, I'll worry about that tomorrow at 9.30am'. The chances were that by the following day, I wouldn't remember what the worry had been, and as time went on, I forgot to worry at 9.30am. That's not to say that I still can't get trapped in a spiral of panic if I have an unexplained ache or pain. As one woman breast cancer patient said, 'Once you've had cancer, a spot is never just a spot again'. But I am better at managing the fear, and that is down to practice.

Recently I came across a book by the American author, Richard Carlson, *You Can Be Happy No Matter What*. I picked it up and read the title as a kind of challenge – try saying 'you can be happy, no matter what' to someone with breast cancer, I thought, cynically. Nevertheless, I bought it and was surprised by what I read.

Carlson's philosophy – that thinking is an ability rather than a reality – means that we don't have to become the victims of our fears. We can take our negative thoughts, accept them for what they are, that is just negative thoughts, and let them pass. He believes that happiness is our natural state and that it is characterised by feelings of gratitude, inner peace, satisfaction and affection for ourselves and others. This isn't a fleeting thing, but it is essentially us. It is the negativity that we have come to accept as 'necessary' or 'just the way that life is' that is a learned process. This is what interferes with our natural state, which is to be happy.

How does this fit in with breast cancer? Well, it is possible to have happy moments in an unexpected enviroment. Just as it's possible to plan a 'perfect' romantic evening and end up with a disaster.

Three days after my last major operation, I can remember sitting on my hospital bed, listening on a borrowed personal stereo to 'Lifted' by the Lighthouse Family (a song which always raises my spirits), looking out of the window at a tree and a church spire and feeling completely peaceful and happy for no particular reason. In fact, I felt so good that I remember thinking 'I'm amazed it's possible to feel this happy when you are in hospital'. It was one of those rare moments when you can virtually taste the happiness and it took me completely by surprise. I can still remember the quality and texture of that moment.

Richard Carlson says once we are in touch with happiness, we can be more lighthearted and easy going, *whether or not our circumstances seem to warrant this positive outlook.*

The other plus is that when we are in a happy state, we have more access to our wisdom and common sense, we are less defensive and critical and we make better decisions. Obviously, the problems that breast cancer brings with it are real, but once you learn how to handle negativity, they won't stop you from enjoying your life.

Your thoughts do not represent your reality

If a person experiences *every* thought as a reality, then most psychologists would agree that they had a mental health problem. A psychotic will hear a voice inside his head telling him to leap off a building because he can fly and he will try it. Regardless of the contents of his thoughts, he believes them to be reality 100 per cent of the time. Someone whose mental health is in a good state, however, can have any thought run through her head and still understand that 'it is only a thought'.

Thinking is something we do because we are human. You need not confuse it with your reality. If you find it hard to replace a negative thought with a positive one, just practise recognising the negativity as 'only a thought'. Sometimes a worry pounces on me unexpectedly and I feel myself starting to spiral downwards. If I can't think of a positive thought to counter it with – and often I can't – I just say to myself, 'That's just a fear, it might be an understandable fear, but fear is all that it is'. I remember that it's up to me to choose whether or not I want to pay it any attention. That gets me onto the next step of thinking about something else.

The other trick I have found very effective is to meet the fear, rather than to try to avoid it. There is a story about the Tibetan saint, Milarepa, which I have found helpful. He was sitting in his cave one day when three huge, terrifying demons burst into the cave, waving swords and howling. With a big smile, he asked them to sit down and join him for tea. The demons were surprised. 'Aren't you frightened by us?' they demanded, their foul breath filling the cave. 'No, no,' replied Milarepa, gently. 'It is at moments like these when the demons of fear and doubt present them-selves that I am most grateful to be on the path of healing. Your ugliness only reminds me to be aware and have mercy. How do you like your tea?' The legend doesn't specify exactly how the demons reacted, but I like to think they made a quick exit.

Greeting your demons like old friends takes away a surprising amount of their power. We can't overcome fear in one leap, but if we meet it, we can get to know it well. And you can feel more lighthearted about it. You can greet a familiar fear – 'Oh, big surprise, it's you again' – and almost at once the fear starts to shuffle its feet, twist its fingers and start to back away.

Be aware of your moods

It is almost impossible to stay in exactly the same mood for hours and hours. When we are feeling low, we lose our ability to listen and our sense of perspective. That's when we might be inclined to think, 'What's the point of all this treatment, I'll probably die anyway.' Try and learn to question your judgement when you are feeling low like this. When we are feeling low, we don't always have access to our common sense. Remember, everything looks different when we are in different moods. The key to getting through the low times is remembering that inevitably they will pass. Just remembering this can help you shift into the next gear more quickly, too.

Don't try to solve your problems if you are feeling very low. For a start, what you are dwelling on may not be as profound a problem as you think – your mood could be exaggerating its importance. One thing you can be sure of, if you are facing a genuine difficulty, is that it will still be there when you are feeling better – it won't go away. The difference, however, is that you will be feeling much better equipped to handle it when you are in a better mood and thinking more clearly.

Of course, you can't dismiss the feelings of sorrow and anger that having breast cancer arouses. It is perfectly natural to feel profoundly sad from time to time. But there is a difference between experiencing and acknowledging the sadness and having a good cleansing cry, and dwelling for hours on endless fears about your future. It is *completely normal* to feel very frightened at times. But if the fear starts to prevent you from leading the life you want, it's probably time to take steps to handle it better for your own peace of mind.

If you have had a bad day, and felt beset by fears and worries, take some time to look at the structure of your day and how it might have contributed to making your problems seem worse. Are you trying to do too much? Has your day been too empty and given you too much time to dwell on your fears? Compare it with a day when you have felt more in charge. What are the differences?

Relaxation

Practising relaxation is different from flopping in front of the TV although, as a *Coronation Street* addict, I have to say that mentally moving to Weatherfield for half an hour, four times a week, has proved a dependable source of light relief for me. Physical relaxation is something else, however. You can learn how to do it and it will allow you to slow down your breathing and reduce your overall level of tension. There are different sorts of relaxation techniques; try them and stick with the one you like best. Some people don't like progressive muscular relaxation (Debbie says it makes her feel tense); the secret is to find a process that you 'click' with.

To prepare for a relaxation session

If you don't live alone, tell your partner and your family that you need at least 20 minutes every day to practise relaxation undisturbed. It's ideal if you can do it every day, as the best results are noticed over a period of weeks.

- Try to ensure there are no distractions from animals or telephones.
- Wear loose, comfortable clothes and make sure your room is warm.
- Allow sufficient time to finish slowly and gently.

Progressive muscular relaxation

Find a comfortable position, either sitting or lying. Concentrate on your feet. Curl your toes hard and point your feet away from your body. Feel the tension in your feet. Hold the tension as you breathe in. As you breathe out, relax the muscles and let the tension go.

Now press your heels hard into the bed or floor and point your feet towards your body. Feel the tension in your ankles. Hold the tension as you breathe in. Then breathe out, relax and let the muscles go.

Slowly work your way up the rest of your body; tensing and relaxing the muscles in your calves, knees, stomach, hands, shoulders, neck, jaw and face.

When you have finished, begin to move slowly by stretching your toes and fingers, and moving your head slightly. Blink a few times, or have a full stretch or a yawn before you get up.

Breathing

Calm, controlled breathing can be very quick and effective in reducing anxiety.

Sit comfortably in a chair. You may shut your eyes, but it's not essential. Wait a few moments until you feel settled. Then breathe in through your nose to a slow count of four and, as you breathe out through your mouth, slowly count one, two, three, four. Do it at a pace you feel comfortable with. Don't strain for breath. Just concentrate on repeating the numbers in your mind.

When you start to feel relaxed, try saying a word you find relaxing, like 'calm' or 'peace' every time you breathe out.

Imagination

Some people can relax their bodies but not their minds. If you find it hard to switch off frightening thoughts, try this mental exercise:

Close your eyes and try to create a place where you feel happy, relaxed and at peace. Conjure up in your mind as vivid a picture of it as you can. You may be imagining you are in a garden on a warm summer's day, perhaps you can smell newly cut grass or the scent of roses nearby. Or perhaps you are lying on a beach with the sand warm and yielding beneath you, feeling the sun warm your skin and hearing the gentle rush of the waves a few feet away. Whatever your personal picture is, try to create every detail of the scene in your head. If other thoughts try to clamber across your mind, gently let them go, unanswered, and return to your happy scene. Say the word 'calm' to yourself. Tell yourself that you feel good. Stay with the feeling for as long as you wish, then slowly turn your attention to your immediate environment, tune into the sounds around you and open your eyes.

You don't always have to picture the same scene each time you do this exercise. You may want to conjure up another time or adapt it to remember an occasion when you felt confident and good about yourself. Choose what suits you best. Some experts recommend that you invent an ideal scene, rather than choose to recall a real-life occasion. This is because genuine memories are more likely to stir other thoughts which will make it harder to concentrate on the relaxation.

Distraction

Distraction is another way of coping with a stream of negative thoughts that keep you feeling anxious. It teaches you to focus your concentration on things outside yourself.

First, you need to be in a quiet room or somewhere you know you will not be disturbed for several minutes while you are trying to learn this technique. To start with, practise at least two or three times a day.

1. Close your eyes and focus on your worries. This will probably make you feel more uncomfortable, but is to be expected. The point of doing it is to demonstrate how your anxiety changes when you focus your whole attention on it. Do this for only a few minutes.
2. When the thoughts are clear in your mind, say or shout 'stop' either mentally or out loud and open your eyes.
3. Immediately you open your eyes, quickly begin to name and describe all the objects you see in the room. Imagine you are describing the layout of the room to someone who is blind. You can do it inside your head or out loud. Describe the *colours*; *size*; *numbers* of objects or parts of them; *shapes*; *ages*. Imagine that the blind person is firing a lot of questions at you which you have to answer as accurately and *quickly* as possible.

When you have learnt to do this, you can apply it at any time you feel your levels of anxiety begin to build. If you are in a hospital, you can focus on the colour of the corridors, read notices that you pass, and describe the flooring to yourself. If you are with another person, practise listening to them intently, as if you were going to have to describe the conversation in detail to someone else later. This way, you train your attention away from your internal thoughts, which contribute to your anxiety, and turn it outwards, which can make it easier to feel relaxed.

Having breast cancer might present you with problems, but it doesn't mean that you have to stop enjoying your life. My ways of getting through it have actually increased my happiness levels over the past five years. My personal top five tips for banishing fears (taking into account everything I've talked about so far) are:

1. Laugh. As long as you are alive, things can still be funny. It is not physically possible to laugh and feel afraid at the same time. The relaxation response after a good laugh has been measured as lasting as long as 45 minutes. Watch *The Full Monty* or any comedy that makes you smile, or phone the friend you always giggle with. Don't speak to someone who will drag you down if you are feeling low already; you have enough to cope with.

2. Act 'as if' you are feeling fine. Don't deny your feelings all the time, but if you have talked or thought about your fears and worries and now you are getting nowhere, start acting as if you are feeling fine. You'd be surprised at how when you are pretending something, it's easy to start to feel it genuinely; think of the way all those Hollywood stars play love scenes and end up in bed together.

3. Do some physical exercise. You may not be strong enough to go for a run or get out the vacuum cleaner, but a walk to the corner shop to buy a magazine can help you into a different frame of mind.

4. Meditate. Learn to do a mantra meditation (see Chapter 11) or just light a candle and sit peacefully for a while, focusing your mind away from the hamster wheel of worry. This will bring instant relief.

5. Remember the story of the king who asked the wise men in his kingdom to pool their collective wisdom and come up with something that would remind him of happiness when he was feeling sorrow and of peace when he was feeling angry. He was taken aback when instead of arriving with vast quantities of books to consult, the wisest man in the kingdom presented him with a tiny box. The king opened the box and found a ring engraved with the words: *This too will pass.*

3
Cancer and the power of language

Imagine sucking a lemon. Think of biting into its moist flesh and feeling the juice cascade over your teeth and run down your chin. Chew the lemon into little pieces; taste the bitter pips on your tongue . . .

If you concentrate your thoughts on sucking a lemon, you'll soon feel a rush of saliva in your mouth. Your body will respond physically to something that is going on only in your mind. You may be a million miles from the nearest lemon, but your unconscious will be convinced by your thoughts and it will send messages to your body to react accordingly. Such is the power of words on our physical state.

This chapter is not about to tell you that your thoughts – the words going round in your head – can cure cancer, although that's what a few people might claim. But not enough of us recognise the power of language to affect the way we feel and the way we perceive our world – and the role that language plays in cancer.

Fighting spirit

Think for a moment about the phrases people use in connection with cancer. The chances are that words like 'fight', 'battle', 'struggle' and 'victory' come to mind. Much of the language we all use about cancer is the terminology of the battlefield. Cancer is the enemy or an alien inside our bodies which we have to defeat. And if that's not bad enough, if we don't have a 'fighting spirit' we are not helping ourselves. This is something with which I have never felt comfortable. Studies contradict each other as to whether a 'fighting spirit' actually helps people live longer. The latest one suggests that it may not make a great deal of difference to your outcome. So the pressure is off if you feel guilty about not being able turn yourself into Xena, Warrior Princess, when it comes to your cancer.

My own view is that people who told me that I needed to be positive when I was still coming to terms with a devastating diagnosis required a punch on the nose, although I don't think that's what the advocates of 'fighting spirit' intend.

The language of the battlefield

I have never felt easy with the language of the battlefield in relation to my cancer. Although newspapers and magazines are full of phrases like 'brave struggle', 'heroic fight' and people who 'win' or 'lose' against cancer, it has never seemed helpful to me to imagine my body engaged in some kind of war against itself. I would prefer to say that cancer is something I live with; I handle it and try to cope with it as best as I can. Over the past six years, I have accommodated it by accepting it and moving on.

Newspapers and magazines love cancer stories because cancer is perceived as a life or death struggle, and that, it seems, is the kind of drama that some editors believe their readers want to read. Some writers and editors behave extremely responsibly and give useful information about detecting cancer, or handling it, alongside news reports or interviews. But when you read stories about cancer, always remember that editors chose dramatic headlines to grab your attention. For the same reason, they highlight the most frightening statistics available. You will never see a headline: 'I Had Cancer And It Wasn't That Bad, Really.' For the press that is not a story. Information comes at a price; it is likely to be wrapped in emotive and possibly distressing packaging. That's important to bear in mind when you read about breast cancer in the media.

Television is equally to blame. Pictures have to be dramatic and powerful, so a story about childhood cancer will inevitably focus on shots of bald children attached to drips. Nurses have told me how TV crews have turned down the chance to film children with cancer who still have their hair – they are looking for a memorable and instantly recognisable image.

Optimism boosts the immune system

If, like me, you prefer not to turn yourself into a fighting machine in relation to your cancer, you can still exert control over your situation. Widely accepted research has shown that optimism boosts your immune system and depression lowers it. If building up your immune system is one of the best ways to eliminate cancerous cells from your body, then it follows that changing the thoughts inside your head, so that they are optimistic rather than pessimistic, can only be to your advantage.

The virtually unpronounceable study of psycho-neuro-immunology (PNI) has confirmed that positive emotional support boosts the immune system's killer cells which destroy cancerous cells. So how can you give yourself that kind of boost?

Neuro-Linguistic Programming (NLP)

Neuro-Linguistic Programming (NLP) is an increasingly popular tool used to change or predict human behaviour. The principle is that by changing your thoughts you can change your reality and your health. This is *not* the same as not being allowed to express your fears, or forcing yourself to put on a smile when you feel desperate and pretend there is nothing wrong. (This is what some misguided people interpret as 'being positive'.)

It *is* about the messages that you send to your unconscious about your life and your health, and adapting those messages so that they are entirely helpful to your well-being. It is also important to remember that there will be days when you feel completely fed up and you simply can't be bothered to keep an eye on the thoughts that are running through your head. This is completely normal and you should never feel guilty about it, but you may like to try NLP, in a small way, in order to maximise the benefit you can get from your thoughts. I have experimented with it and found some aspects very useful.

The map is not the territory

Garner Thomson is an NLP Meta-Master Practitioner who works with cancer patients. He explains NLP like this: we all respond to the world through our five senses. Everyone is unique and we use these senses in different combinations to create a map of the world outside ourselves. This is where our problems can begin. We start to behave as though the map we have created is real, but it's not. It's just our map, or our ideas about the world. So, in NLP terms, we have to remember that the map is *not* the territory. Garner Thomson says:

> 'It is a lot easier to change the map, or to change a way a person uses their senses as a way of understanding reality than it is to change the outside world. Remember, the unconscious can't tell the difference between what is real and what is vividly imagined.'

For example, if you are highly self-critical it may be that you grew up with a parent or teacher's voice telling you that you were bound to fail, and that's the voice you still hear inside your head. NLP says that it is possible to change that voice inside your head, either to say something different, or just to alter its tone. 'You lying rascal', for example, can be said as an insult, or you can hear it as a jokey term of affection. By changing what we hear inside our head, we change the impact it has on our bodies. Remember sucking the lemon?

NLP also uses presuppositions; in other words, you make positive assumptions about your future. For a person with cancer, that's a scary thing to do. It feels like tempting fate, or risking future unhappiness if your plans don't work out. But if you take away that element of superstition, which roughly equates to 'if I think of something good, something bad is *bound* to happen', what harm can imagining a positive future actually do you? The brain, by the way, doesn't process negation. For example, if someone says 'don't think of a grizzly bear', what is the image that comes to mind? So it is far more effective to think of yourself as someone who is 'well', than someone who is 'not ill'.

A presupposition means saying 'when I get better I shall ...' rather than 'if I get better'. It sends a message to your unconscious mind – the part of you that can't tell the difference between what is real and what is not, in other words, the bit that thinks the lemon is real even though you are only *thinking* about sucking it.

When people feel sick *before* they go for chemotherapy, it is their thinking, or what is going on in their unconscious mind that is creating the sickness, not the actual drugs that they are taking. This is why hypnosis can be helpful in reducing so-called 'anticipatory nausea', because it changes the message that the body receives. Instead of expecting sickness, and creating a reaction to sickness, under hypnosis the brain tells the body to be calm and relaxed instead. I used to listen to a hypnotherapy tape telling me to stay calm and relaxed the night before I had chemotherapy and it certainly quelled a lot of my anxiety as I approached the hospital.

Although I hadn't heard of NLP then, I did know a little about visualisation and as I drove to the Marsden, which like most hospitals is pretty grim from the outside, I used to picture it lit up like a funfair with 'Hello, Val, we are here to cure you' flashing in white lights on the roof. The image is so strong in my mind that when I picture the outside of the Marsden today, I see it still looking like the Blackpool Illuminations. I have no idea whether or not this will help my health long term, but I do know that it helped distract me before chemotherapy and that in itself was a bonus.

During my last operation, I asked my surgeon to say only positive things when I was under anaesthetic. My theory was that my unconscious might pick up the voices around me while I was on the operating table, and I wanted to hear that the operation was helping me to stay well and healthy. (It's the same principle that encourages relatives to play tapes of familiar sounds and voices to coma patients.) I was slightly embarrassed about asking him to do it, but he said he would, and a theatre nurse told me later he kept his word. Did it actually help me? It is hard to be certain, but the operation went smoothly and the knowledge that I had asked him to do something I thought could help, made me feel better at the time. So the answer is yes.

Garner Thomson himself had an early introduction to the individual's power of the mind. His mother was diagnosed with advanced breast cancer when he was three. She was given a mastectomy and then told she had only a few months to live. She had been widowed 18 months earlier, and left with two young children. Garner told me:

'My mother said "I'm sorry, I have two young children to bring up, I haven't got time to die" and she discharged herself from hospital. She simply lived as if she were well and died 58 years later from something entirely unconnected with breast cancer.'

I once read about a woman who had survived all manner of illnesses which would have wiped out most people. Her mother had told her when she was a child, 'You're a skinny little thing, but whatever happens to you, you'll always get over it. You'll live to be 93 and then they'll have to run over you with a steamroller.' The woman went on to survive a major heart attack, a bleeding duodenal ulcer, the death of her husband and breast cancer invading the chest wall. Every time illness strikes, she hears her mother's words.

Plan a future

Most people given a diagnosis of cancer can hardly bring themselves to look beyond the treatment stage. I was taken aback one day while I was being given chemotherapy when the nurse glanced up and said 'Where are you going for your holiday next year?' My initial reaction was 'God, she thinks I'm going to be around next year', fairly rapidly followed by 'I can't begin to think about that, I have to get through this first.' My husband recently reminded me that he had wanted to plan a holiday soon after I was first diagnosed and I had refused. I can't remember this, but I imagine that I was feeling so fearful and uncertain about life that looking ahead wasn't on my agenda at the time. It is an easy and understandable trap to fall into.

In reality, planning a future, even if it's just a weekend in Blackpool rather than a month in Australia, is important. Garner Thomson has researched more than 400 cases of people whose cancer went into spontaneous remission – it disappeared when doctors didn't expect it to – and one of their common characteristics was that they all planned a future and had a higher purpose. In other words, they expected more from life than just basic survival. He explains:

'A lot of people allow their lives to end at the point when they are diagnosed with cancer, but it matters to have a future orientation, a powerful map of health in your mind. You don't have to be positive in a mind-numbingly Pollyanna-ish way. A lot of people who survive cancer against the odds argue with their doctors. They aren't afraid to say "I don't agree, I am going somewhere else".'

There is always a level of wellness somewhere in the mind and body

Garner Thomson agrees with me about battleground metaphors.

'I think if you plan to fight cancer you are setting up another conflict, but it does help to work on and build up health. Most of us have tumour cells and our bodies deal with them constantly. So health isn't just an absence of illness. It isn't a state you reach. I think of health as a process where your body is responding, adjusting and reacting all the time. Nobody is ever completely ill; there is always a level of wellness somewhere in the body and in the mind.

'If you are prepared to spend time on vividly and richly creating plans using all your senses, you can begin to create your own reality: *What will I be doing? How will I be feeling? How will I be looking? What will I be saying to myself? What will other people be saying?* Take a large goal and chunk it into smaller, accomplishable steps. Start thinking about your life beyond cancer.

'Working with cancer patients, I have noticed that one of the advantages of having cancer is that very often it allows people to simplify their lives and find out what is truly valuable to them. If you have a dream – follow it now. If there is something you have always wanted to do – try it now. Not in the belief that one day you might not be able to do it, but because if you are doing something you love, you are maximising your health.'

Everyone has a talent. It may not be the kind that is commonly thought of like singing, dancing or drawing. Your talent may be for friendship, or for looking after an animal. Whatever it is, give it free rein and enjoy it.

Having a sense of direction helps, of course, even if you have no problems with your health. A study of American university students followed up a group of graduates after leaving college. Half of them had made no plans for their future, while the other half had made plans, albeit mostly rudimentary. Thirty years later, the researchers tracked down each graduate and found that each member of the group who had made plans was worth more than the whole of the group who had not. The planners considered themselves happier, more successful and more fulfilled.

This isn't to say that you must impose a rigid future on yourself which you can't adjust and change according to events. As John Lennon said 'Life is what happens when you are making other plans'. But I have found that even my most tentative plans have usually been rewarding.

Over the past five years I have hesitated to book concert tickets, weekends away, even (I'm embarrassed to admit) six-monthly dental appointments, because there's been a subconscious fear: 'What if something awful happens between now and then?' This isn't being paranoid. 'Something awful' – a diagnosis of cancer – has already happened to you once and life may not feel certain for a long time. The alternative is to hide under the duvet and put the rest of your life on hold in anticipation of the next horrible event, which even the most timid might agree would be a sad waste of a life.

Book tickets to see that musical you've always fancied. Go to see the Chippendales. One friend planned her wedding for the middle of her chemotherapy. She and her partner had two young daughters and decided to marry in a castle in Scotland so that in the middle of a lot of upset and turmoil they all had something to look forward to.

Make plans. If your circumstances change and they have to be altered, it's not the end of the world. You may surprise yourself by the number of plans you find you are carrying out.

Make movies in your head

NLP helps people achieve their goals by encouraging them to make films in their heads of the way they want their lives to turn out, and to accompany this with an internal soundtrack. Usually, the bigger, brighter and more colourful they are, the more effective they will be. Think of the difference in the impact of seeing a horror film, for instance, on a massive colour cinema screen compared to a tiny, flickering black-and-white TV.

Try this exercise. You may benefit from having a partner or a friend read the following out slowly, allowing plenty of time to follow instructions and pausing where there is a set of dots. If no one is around to help, read the instructions out loud all the way through, then do the exercise.

Garner Thomson suggests you drink plenty of fresh, clean water during the healing process, a least a litre a day, unless your doctor suggests otherwise.

Do not do this exercise in place of medical treatment. It should be used in conjunction with whatever treatments you have been prescribed.

Before you begin, imagine that you can . . . put your past behind you . . . as a line or a pathway, with all your experiences arranged on it in order: the most recent closest to you, the earliest, furthest away. Do this, and . . . think of how your future opens up in front of you, also as a line or path – broad, bright, and stretching far into the distance . . .

Now, take a moment to think about your immune system. It never sleeps; it carries out millions of protective functions every moment of your life, identifying and eliminating any cells, allergens or pathogens that threaten your well-being.

Sometimes, however, for reasons we don't fully understand, it makes a 'mistake': perhaps a trauma, a powerful virus, some pollutant or other, and begins to behave differently.

But, remember: . . . you are genetically programmed to heal – or, more accurately – to return to a state of ongoing 'healthing' . . . identifying, adjusting and responding appropriately and flexibly to whatever imbalance may come into your body.

So, because your Unconscious is about to be given a new map or template to help 're-set' your inner healing wisdom . . . see, or imagine seeing a 'future you' . . . you're in perfect balance, perfect health . . . notice the way you stand, sit, move, breathe in a relaxed and vibrant way . . . hear the comments and praise of people around you . . . just 'know' this is an image of when . . . you are in perfect health . . .

Now . . . 'mark' this image in some way special as representing perfect health – surround it with a shimmering light, or colour, or flood it with sparkles . . . or . . . use your own imagination to make it a special symbolic image of you when . . . you are in perfect harmony, balance and health.

And . . . when you are in perfect health . . . your Unconscious now . . . has returned to its blueprint or map of ongoing health, because it's . . . your Unconscious . . . that monitors and carries out each and every function of your body . . . working to ensure . . . you're in perfect health . . .

So . . . you can know the Unconscious of the 'you' in front of you contains all the information it needs to help you to . . . return to perfect balance . . . Deep . . . inside, 'you' have the code that triggers all the powerful and appropriate functions of a healthy, responsive immune system. Feel a sense of excitement and anticipation that you are about to have this knowledge passed back to you where it belongs . . .

And, thinking about this, bring the healthy 'you' slowly towards you, drawing her into you so you can . . . allow all that inner knowledge, that complex code, that map or blueprint of healing, to 'download' into your own Unconscious, as if reprogramming a computer. Don't concern yourself with the details . . . just have a sense that . . . your Unconscious knows what to do and how to do it.

(Pause)

Now . . . with a sense of appreciation, and keeping the information you have just been given, thank the 'future you' and allow her to move out of your body and take up a position a little in front of you on the future time-line. Allow some sort of connection to form between you – a line or light or colour that links you to her. It's good, isn't it? To . . . know that, from now on, each step forward you take . . . will be in the footprint of this special being, this . . . 'you' in perfect health.

(Pause)

Now, go inside your body and recall the special characteristics of the 'future you' with the perfectly functioning immune system – that light, colour or sparkles – and allow them to begin to flood your body. See that as your special symbol of 'healthing'. Feel it flow through every muscle, nerve, cell, every atom of your body . . . see, or imagine, it lapping gently up against any tumour or cancer cell

that might be in your body . . . dissolving . . . washing away . . .
clearing and cleansing.

Note: This last part can be done as long as, and as many times a day
as you wish. The more the better – especially at night, as you drift
off to sleep, know that . . . your Unconscious . . . will take over and
continue the good work as you sleep and dream . . .

If you think you cannot yet visualise clearly, just imagine or pretend as
you follow the steps.

It is not just to help your health that NLP can be used. If you want
to take more exercise, lose weight or give up smoking, you can use
an adapted version of the NLP technique outlined above to help.
Alternatively, you can visit a trained NLP practitioner who can work
with you on your goals. (See the list of useful addresses at the back of this
book.)

Conventional Western medicine behaves as though there is a division
between the mind and the body. That's why some doctors treat you as
though you have a screw loose when you ask about the psychological
impact of orthodox medical treatment on your life. It also partly excuses
the few who believe it doesn't matter how they talk to their patients, or
what language they use, as long as their surgery or their chemotherapy
prescriptions are OK.

As you will have gathered by now, I don't agree with this view. One of
the most critical times for a patient is the first diagnosis of cancer. You
may not be able to recall the exact words your doctor used when you
were diagnosed with breast cancer. But many patients remember not only
the phrase he used, but also where they were sitting (or standing) at the
time and the colour and smell of the room they were in.

Alison, a friend who has also had breast cancer, described it like this:

'His actual words were that the cells were being a bit mischievous
and that they would get me into hospital as quickly as possible. My
husband and I were standing in one of those dingy, grey examination rooms and we were told this as we stood, there were no chairs
to sit down. Then the breast care nurse took us into another room.
I felt numb.'

I would describe my memories of being told I had cancer as a kind of
vivid videotape that I can play in my head at will. In the early days after
diagnosis, it played constantly, whether I wanted it to or not. Now I can

summon it up with very little effort, but most of the time it is tucked away at the back of my mind. I was lucky, in NLP terms, because the language my surgeon used was not entirely negative. When I asked how long I had to live, he replied 'Forty or fifty years, we hope'. He didn't lie by assuring me that my cancer could be cured, but he instilled a note of optimism which meant that whenever I play back that encounter in my brain, my unconscious receives a positive message.

If, like Alison, you weren't so lucky, and you were given grim news or depressing statistics by a doctor who omitted any upbeat news at all, you could try and imagine a difference scene. Here's how Garner Thomson suggests Alison could change her recollection:

'Take a few moments to create for yourself an image of the best circumstances under which you could be given the news of your illness.

For example, make the room sunny and comfortable. The specialist is warm and optimistic. He tells you you have a condition that many thousands of women recover from to live completely healthy and happy lives. You will have the best care available and are encouraged to engage the healing powers of your own body and mind by whatever other means are useful and appropriate.

Of course, you realise there will be some adjustments to be made, some work ahead. But, from inside comes a small but firm voice that tells you that you will not only recover, but that you are being presented with an opportunity to rethink many aspects of your life, to decide to make appropriate changes, to do things differently, consciously to create for yourself vibrant, ongoing good health.

Your partner, too, is supportive and optimistic. You both know in a way you can't quite explain that everything will be well.

Now, close your eyes and remember the end of the original experience – ie the nurse is escorting you from the room.

But, suddenly, pretend the whole experience is being rewound. Everything, including yourself, runs backwards to the moment just before you enter the examination room.

Then switch to the second scene and run it from beginning to end, from your point of view, and open your eyes.

Starting again at the end of the original experience, repeat the process at least five times, opening your eyes each time you come to the end of the second scene.

Close your eyes again and begin to let your imagination move into the future. See yourself walking into the future in growing, good health. The further you see yourself move into the future, the stronger, healthier and more positive you become.

We cannot change 'real' history, and your conscious mind will, of course, be able to recall the original incident, but each time you are tempted to run it through, 'rewind' it and run it into the second sequence which runs from beginning to end. The idea is to give your unconscious mind the second option, remembering that your unconscious cannot tell the difference between what is 'real' and what is vividly imagined.

Language, then, isn't just a simple tool for talking to each other. According to NLP, how we communicate with ourselves and with others has a direct effect on our nervous system at the deepest level.

You may feel sceptical or uncomfortable about the exercises described above, in which case they may not be for you. Don't force yourself to try everything, or feel guilty if some approaches to dealing with cancer simply don't appeal. The purpose of this book is to let you know what's on offer. It is up to you to choose what you think might help.

4
Who to tell?

There are no easy ways to tell people that you have cancer. Unfortunately, most of the decisions you need to make about who you will talk to and how have to be made in the early days of your diagnosis when you may be feeling emotionally and physically unsteady. This chapter explores the people you may need to talk to *outside* a medical setting. (See Chapter 6 for the people to talk to who will treat your breast cancer.) Some women choose to tell everyone they know; others prefer to tell only those closest to them. There are advantages and disadvantages to both ways.

Friends and family: telling only a few

I have done it both ways. The first time I was diagnosed, I decided that cancer was a private matter and as a result I told only some friends and family. I chose not to tell anyone connected with my work, partly because as a freelance I was worried that my employers would assume I wouldn't *want* to work and that my income would dry up, and partly because I wanted an area of my life to carry on as normally as possible. I wanted to be able to go out and meet people and not feel as if they were looking at me and shaking their heads with sympathy or pity in their eyes. Pity, I read somewhere, is meeting someone else's pain with fear, and I didn't need that. Cancer, I decided, was going to take up quite enough of my life anyway. I didn't want it invading my workspace too.

Because I work from home, I didn't need to ask for time off for hospital appointments; I simply fitted them in around the rest of my day. And when I turned up to a BBC function for magazine journalists wearing a chestnut, shoulder-length wig after my shortish, highlighted blonde hair had fallen out, everyone there assumed I had grown and dyed my hair. In fact, one woman gazed down at me and asked, 'Your hair's a fantastic colour, how do you manage with the roots?' I think I blushed and muttered 'Oh, I spend a lot of money on it', which was partly true – £400 on a wig is a lot of money, after all. But I have to say that encounter gave my ego a sizeable boost.

Oliver had just started at nursery school during my first round of treatment, and despite the fact that everyone recommends that you tell people who are looking after your child about your situation, I didn't. Because I was fortunate and the chemotherapy and radiotherapy didn't stop me doing most of the things I normally do, I saw no reason to make big announcements about my health. In fact, I treasured the fact that life was going on, pretty much as usual. My husband, Colin, and my Dad took me to have chemotherapy so I didn't need extra help from friends or neighbours. And when I did tell one friend, her response was, 'Poor you, do you know I had a cancer scare a couple of years ago?' She proceeded to talk about herself for the next hour. More than enough to make you keep quiet.

What did happen though, was support from unexpected places. A couple of the handful of friends I told who hadn't been desperately close, rang to say 'Call me at 3am if you feel you want to talk', and, I'm afraid to say, others who I thought were close proved to be a let-down. This, frankly, is tough. When I tackled them about the fact they didn't contact me in the early days, their response was, 'We thought you seemed fine'. Of course I *seemed* fine, every ounce of my energy was going into keeping myself together, but what I needed was those people to show that they cared beyond the standard 'let me know if there's anything I can do'.

What CAN friends do?

Just as it may be hard for you to tell people that you have breast cancer, and handle their reactions, it may also be difficult for those you tell to know what is the right response to offer. The simple answer is that that there is no one right response when someone tells you they have cancer. An extremely organised friend of mine drew up an Action Plan to hand out to her friends and family when she was first diagnosed. It had four useful main points:

1. Remember it may not be helpful to ask the woman concerned questions like 'Have they caught it in time?' No one will know the answer to that for a long time.
2. If your friend has made her decisions and has great faith in the medical team treating her, don't suggest that someone you know has had better treatment or ask for lots of personal, medical details unless your friend indicates she wants to talk about this.
3. Talk about people you know who have responded well to treatment. It's probably not a good idea to tell her about people you know who

are in a worse medical condition than her, even if you are telling her in an attempt to cheer her up.

4. Explain to your children what is happening, and at the same time suggest that the best way they can help your friend's children is to carry on as normal, but be willing to listen and offer support if they are approached for help.

Take a few moments to think about what practical assistance you can give – and then offer that. Whether it's cooking a meal that can go in the freezer, offering to look after children, or taking your friend out for a fun cinema trip, *be specific*. Don't give up if your first offer is turned down; support is always welcome at later stages when the initial flurry of offers of help has subsided. Your friend may grow increasingly tired as her treatment continues. Then she will need you more. One woman told me how wonderful it was when someone just turned up with a cooked meal for her family. She said she would have felt awkward accepting the offer of a meal, because it seemed like a lot of trouble for someone else, but she thoroughly appreciated being presented with a *fait accompli*.

Telling a few

The main advantage of limiting the number of people whom you tell is that it allows some areas of your life to carry on pretty much as before. You don't have to answer questions about how you are from everyone you know – and at times that can be exhausting, no matter how well intentioned the people concerned. The disadvantage is that you are limiting your possible sources of support. As I said earlier, some of my best support the first time round came from people I would not have expected to help. If you limit who you tell, there are fewer people who can turn up trumps.

Telling everyone

When I was diagnosed with another primary tumour in the opposite breast, I was more frank with everyone. I had lived with cancer for four years by then, and I wasn't as frightened of being defined solely by my disease. My sense of self wasn't so shaken, and in the intervening four years, some of my friendships had changed. I had formed a couple of close friendships with people whose lives also had not been plain sailing. You could put it grandly and say that our tricky life journeys are the force that bind us together or you could just say that there are some people with whom you click. You can meet them at any stage of your life and know they will always be friends.

Either way, those people were in place when I was diagnosed the second time and perhaps because they were there, alongside Colin and my parents, I felt emotionally stronger. As a result, I could handle telling other people, including mums from school, that I had cancer and I would be having an operation. Immediately, I had offers of help with Oliver, which I was relaxed enough to take up, and I felt happy to talk about the bilateral mastectomy. I decided to think of it as a form of cosmetic surgery and concentrate only on the bonus it would offer – a slightly larger bust that wouldn't droop – rather than worry about possible negatives. (See Chapter 8 for the medical details of implants.) So I entertained listeners with stories of how I could have my boobs made bigger for Christmas parties, should I fancy it (and not unfeasible if you have a valve left in your implant that can allow your surgeon to add more saline if you want a larger bust).

When everyone knows about your cancer you have more support. But it may mean that people will want to talk about cancer when you are heartily fed up with it and there's no escape. Be guided by the sort of person you are. In times of previous crises, has it helped you to talk to lots of people about it or would you rather rely on just a couple of friends? Think of your family circumstances: will you physically need other people's help to keep life going? Don't be afraid to ask for help, either; most people get a warm glow from helping a deserving friend. But if you need a lot of help, it's probably fairer to spread the assistance out among a group of people, rather than relying on one person.

Talking to children about cancer

Telling adults you have cancer is one thing; talking to children about it is another. As mothers we worry about anything that will make our children's lives harder or will cause them problems in later years. So, once again, we need to be reminded that there is no set text for how to talk to your children about your breast cancer. It is never 'the right time'. If you have done it already, don't worry that you did it wrong. Talking to children about cancer can be an ongoing process, and it is undoubtedly better that they hear your news from you, than that they pick it up from friends or neighbours. If you feel you got the balance wrong at the start, you can put it right later. There are no golden rules, but, along with recognising that what they can handle will roughly depend on their age and level of maturity, there are three things to bear in mind:

1. *What do they know already?* Children are born with an innate instinct to make sense of the world. They notice things. If you find out what has been going on in their minds first, it gives you a chance to correct any misunderstandings they may have, before you venture forth with what you want them to know. Children will know something is wrong, even if they don't have the language to tell you. 'You must be wondering why mummy looks upset' is a possible opening, or 'Have you noticed any changes in our house recently?' Think of a question which allows you to hear their thoughts first.
2. *What do you want them to know?* What do you feel confident enough to manage to say to them? It might be the name of the illness, what the doctors have said and what treatment you are going to have. Or it might be about what is going to happen to them if you have to go into hospital, who will be around to make their tea if you are not there, and information that is very practical.
3. *What would they like to know?* They may not want to ask anything immediately. Or they may ask questions like, 'Is cancer catching?' 'Will you die?' 'Is it my fault?'

Before you sit down with your children it can be a great help to rehearse what you are going to say with an adult first. Your children may not ask any of the things to which you have rehearsed answers, but the chances are that having practised first, you will feel more confident about handling whatever does come up. Also, you can talk to the person you have rehearsed with after you have spoken with your children. Unload your feelings onto someone else afterwards, if it helps. Don't feel you must handle your sad or worried feelings alone.

If you are talking to a group of children, talk in terms that the youngest will understand (see below) and then follow up individually with the older ones. According to Barbara Monroe, Director of Patient and Family Services at St Christopher's Hospice in London:

'It's scary and sad and there is no clever thing you can do that will suddenly make it all right. But if you talk to your kids, even if they get distressed, you will have conveyed an incredibly powerful message that overides anything else. That message is, "You are an important member of this family, and when something important happens I will do my best to include you in it in some way." The value of that message will outshine any of the stumbles and mumbles along the way.'

Sometimes your child will choose the time to talk, and not you. You may have carefully avoided trying to catch them during their favourite TV programme and sat down with them when it seems the right time, only for them to walk away or announce they want to go out to play. That doesn't mean that they don't want to talk about it ever. It just means they don't want to talk about it at that moment.

Although there are no set rules, it is not good to tell your children everything all at once. They need to know what is happening now, what is going to happen next, and they need it updated. It is also fine to answer any of their questions with 'I don't know'. You can then suggest that you try to find the answer by asking a breast care nurse or getting the information from a book or a leaflet. Children learn very early on that their parents don't have the answers to everything.

One friend told her children that it was possible she might die very soon after her diagnosis. Four years later, she was still alive and worrying that her daughters, aged 15 and 12, had lived with a burden that could have been delayed. Although both girls had insisted they wanted to know everything, and she had gone along with that, she was also worried that they had had no one outside the family with whom to share their feelings regularly.

A lot of children whose mothers have breast cancer have told me that it would have helped them hugely to have been able to speak to someone outside the family who would listen and answer their questions every so often. At present, there is no automatic NHS provision for this; and there won't be, until patients begin to request it in large numbers. So talk to your breast care nurse or GP if you feel that your children would benefit from some outside support, and they should be able to help. Health visitors should be available for a family in times of crisis; they are not just there to keep an eye on young babies. However, while older children may prefer to speak to someone outside their immediate family circle, small children are usually more comfortable with someone they know well.

What is frightening for children is to hear information which hasn't been given to them by a concerned adult and which is unexplained. For example, if you haven't used the word 'cancer' and they overhear the parent of a friend use it in connection with you, depending on their age, a child could start to panic. If you are talking to them, even hearing something hurtful in the playground – 'X says you are going to die because you have cancer' – can be tackled along the lines of: 'People say all sorts of things – let's sit down together and talk about what we *know*. I'll answer your questions and let you know what's happening as things change. Anytime anyone at school says anything, you let me know when you come home and we can have a good talk.'

Don't be afraid to show your emotions in front of your children. I wouldn't advise hours of weeping or punching the cushions on the sofa in a public fit of rage, but I think it is OK to shed a few tears when you are sad, if you explain that it is your illness or the treatment that is making you sad and *not them*. If nothing else, your children will learn that as your mood changes and you don't stay sad, their sad feelings won't last forever; and that if you are sad, you don't have to pretend that you are not.

It's best not to share money worries (except as it will affect them) or frightening medical details. Don't make promises that you can't keep, just say 'I think I will be able to . . .' or 'I'll try to . . .'

Below are some general guidelines on how to help children according to their age, but remember no one else understands your child and what they can handle as well as you do.

Under-fives

Young children fear separation, strangers and being left alone. A child's security is built around patterns and stability. Try, if you can, to limit the number of people who help you with childcare, so that your children have familiar people to stay with them if you have to go into hospital. Reassure them that you are coming home from hospital soon and that you think of them when you are apart. If they come to visit you, suggest they bring a favourite toy with them. But be sure they take their own security object back home, and don't leave it with you; they will need it.

Sometimes young children believe they have magical powers and what they wish will come true. They may feel guilty that they felt angry with you and then you got ill, or they may believe they could make you better if they tried really hard. Assure them that nothing they have said or done could have caused your illness and that it is not 'catching'.

One friend of mine wrapped up little presents to take into hospital with her so that when her two under-five daughters visited they had something from Mummy to take home with them. Another sent her children a postcard from the hospital every day to say that she loved them and was thinking of them. You may need to explain that you are lying in bed because you are very tired after taking the strong medicine the doctor has given you to get better.

You may be under a lot of stress, so try and find someone else who could give your children extra attention. It may be a grandparent or a favourite babysitter. Studies have shown that increased time with the non-ill parent can help children adjust to cancer, so if possible let them spend extra time with their Dad.

Ages 6–11

Children between six and eleven may begin behaving like younger children when they feel worried about their Mum. They may worry about the changes in the family's lifestyle and become annoyed at limitations imposed on them as a result of their Mum's illness. It can help to talk to their school so that their teacher can understand the problems at home (if there are any) and do your best to maintain regular routines for them, even when you are not there. They should always know who will be meeting them from school and who will be putting them to bed. For children, news about their mother's health should be given one step at a time. Practical things can help; write the telephone number where they can contact you on the flap of their schoolbag.

When I was first diagnosed, Oliver was two-and-a-half and accepted my explanation that I was going to the bank (a regular trip for a self-employed person) when I went for my chemotherapy and radiotherapy. He was used to me leaving the house regularly in connection with my work. When my hair started to fall out and I thought it was necessary to buy a wig, I decided to introduce it to him gradually.

First, I put it on a wigstand in my bedroom. He wandered in and asked 'what's that?' I replied that my hair was a bit thin and my head was getting cold when I went outside, so I had bought a kind of hat. I called it 'Wilma'. He asked if he could touch 'Wilma', and I said 'OK'. 'Would you like to see me wearing Wilma?' I asked. He said 'Yes'. Then he asked to try on Wilma and he wandered off downstairs to show his Dad. As my hair grew back and I stopped wearing the wig, he occasionally asked to see it. So I explained it was in the top cupboard of my wardrobe, and the fact it was still around seemed to reassure him. He may develop a penchant for girls with long, gleaming red hair in later life, but there are worse crosses to bear . . .

By the time he was six-and-a-half I knew that my second hospital stay would require a proper explanation. I said I had a problem with the cells in my bosom, and I needed a new one. I explained to Oliver that a very clever surgeon could make me a new one, but I would have to stay in hospital for a few days and I'd love him to come and visit me. Then I went out and bought the biggest teddy bear I could find and put it on his bed. When he came home from school, I held the bear close to me and said I was putting lots of love from my heart into the bear. If Oliver got sad or lonely when I was in hospital, all he had to do was to hug the bear and my love would go straight into his heart. I asked him if he wanted to give the bear a special name. 'Yes', said Oliver, and, memorably, we christened him Big Bear. The bear has stayed a special friend. When he has gone to stay with friends and family, Big Bear has gone with him. I don't know how much he helped, but I do know that Big Bear made a difference to Oliver (and me).

Role-playing can help you find out about your child's fears. This will appeal to some kids (and Mums) and not others. If you feel it might help your situation, ask your child to be the mum for the evening while you take turns as the doctor, the child or other people who are important to your child. With younger children it can help to use a doll to explain what is going on. The doll usually takes the place of the child, and you can offer over-the-top love and reassurance to the doll. Your child can then ask questions on behalf of the doll, and might want to play at being Mummy and talking to the doll themselves. This gives you a chance to tune in to their level of understanding of the situation. If your older children are worried about how to talk to their peers, volunteer to play the friend while your son or daughter practises how to tell a friend about their Mum's illness.

Teenagers

According to Ann Couldrick, a counsellor who works with children and young people, teenagers are in transition between childhood and adulthood and don't expect their mother suddenly to need support and attention.

'It is actually quite normal for teenagers to behave in ways that might seem cold and uncaring and closed off from you. They may feel worried sick about what it would be like if you weren't there, and yet you are one of the people they need to challenge in order to grow up.'

It is often helpful for teenagers to have someone outside the family they can talk to in confidence. Sometimes they will say 'No' when help is first offered, because they are frightened that they will be forced to talk about their feelings or, even worse, be told something they don't want to hear. Just because they turn it down at one stage doesn't mean that they won't respond to another offer to talk to someone outside the family on another occasion. If you don't feel comfortable with outsiders knowing about your cancer, help your teenager select which friend(s) they want to tell.

Teenagers, especially daughters, are very image conscious. Aspects of your therapy may embarrass them, especially in front of their friends. They may beg you not to appear without a wig, or a prosthesis if you have had a mastectomy. Try and talk about this openly with your children, and come to an agreement about what you all find acceptable. Don't be hurt by it; their feelings for you are not diminished. One friend suggested that a nurse from a Well Woman Clinic be invited into her daughter's school to talk about women's health issues and cover breast cancer in the talk. She believes it helped her daughter to hear breast cancer discussed openly when her friends were around her.

Occasionally, older children will share in your sadness and may cry with you, but often they don't. They may prefer to act cheerfully when you are around and express their sad feelings when they are with friends. Others won't appear to express any emotion at all; for them the whole ordeal is too overwhelming and it will seem as if they are completely ignoring it.

Remember, all children are different and will have different needs. The actor Pierce Brosnan in a newspaper interview talked about the death of his wife, Cassie, from ovarian cancer and said how he had taken his children to see therapists until his eight-year-old son, Sean, finally said to him: 'I don't need this Dad. If I need someone, I'll talk to my brother or my sister or you.'

'Fair enough,' said Pierce Brosnan. 'We ditched the therapists and we all kind of mucked along.' The lesson here is that although it may be helpful to have outside help, take your cue from your children. If you listen to your children, rather than imposing what you think they need, the chances are that you'll weather the storm together much better.

Most women will not die from breast cancer, but if your prognosis is very poor and you feel you want to talk to your children about death, St Catherine's Hospice in Crawley, West Sussex, has produced an excellent booklet which answers many of the questions children have about death (see Further Reading). These include: Why do people die? Why can't hospitals and doctors stop someone from dying? And what happens to a person's body when they die? I found it a worthwhile read simply because sooner or later children will encounter death, whether it is the death of a beloved grandparent or a family pet, and it is useful to have some answers at your fingertips which will help them.

Good reasons for telling your child you have cancer

Although it is not a task which any parent relishes, there are good reasons for giving your child an appropriate level of information.

1. Children are surprisingly good at adjusting to the truth. They can find even upsetting truths helpful in relieving worry and anxiety over what is really happening.
2. Children can learn they are important and that they are needed by their family in stressful and difficult times.
3. Loving children can be a wonderful support to you. And you won't have the additional stress of trying to keep complicated secrets inside your family.

Tips to make it easier for children to cope

Let your children help. A two-year-old can give mum a hug; an older child can help with adult chores. Make your children feel part of getting the family through a crisis. This gives a child a sense of control and participation. Don't load them down with tasks, they'll need their own space too.

Find a time for humour. Don't be horrified if your kids give a prosthesis a nickname or you find it being thrown around in a ball game. Share stories of amusing incidents that may have happened at the hospital. Humour lightens the emotional load.

Create new rituals to provide stability. Find pleasant activities that you can all do together; whether it's a takeaway and a video on a Friday night or an overnight stay with a friend. It should be something that a child can count on that requires minimal effort from you.

Include older children in your treatment. If they feel happy about it, take an older child to a hospital appointment. Let them talk to the doctors and nurses so that they can see the hospital as a friendly, supportive place rather than somewhere terrifying and remote. When your children visit you, let them explore so they can picture your environment while you are away. Oliver has always enjoyed the nurse call button – he couldn't believe it when he pressed it one day and not one but two nurses appeared. This 'game' needs to be restricted though, if you aren't going to drive the nursing staff mad. When a child visits you in hospital, it may be possible for you to watch a video or TV together.

If you have always been uninhibited about letting your children see you without clothes, show them your scars at an appropriate time. Their reaction may be 'yuck', but they will worry less if they have seen it, rather than letting their imaginations run wild if it is always covered up. If you never undress in front of your children, now is probably not the time to start.

Don't give up on discipline. A breakdown in rules can convince children that things are really wrong and add to their feelings of insecurity. Tell your children that you love them, but you won't accept destructive or bad behaviour. Where possible, use rewards rather than punishments to manage your children's behaviour. Be consistent and help your child to feel secure and that his or her world is under control. And remember, your child wasn't always perfect before.

Issues for adolescent daughters

Relationships between mothers and teenage daughters are often strained and a diagnosis of breast cancer can add to it. Daughters may be uncomfortable talking about issues related to breasts and they may worry that they will be susceptible to breast cancer as well. It may help you to tell your daughter that the vast majority of breast cancers (*90 per cent*) occur in women with no signficant family history. But she should be taught how to examine her breasts once a month, after her period. Doctors are gaining a much better understanding of breast cancer risk with families. (See Chapter 6 for information on genetic counselling.)

Children's feelings

The charity Cancer BACUP has written a very useful booklet 'What Do I Tell the Children?' (see Useful Addresses) which includes the following list of some things that children feel:

- Some children will feel sorry for themselves when a parent is ill, and then feel guilty because they think they should feel sorry for the parent.
- Some children will try to make up for these guilt feelings by being super good and setting impossibly high standards for themselves.
- Some children will cling to you too much, afraid something will happen if they are not there.

- Some children will withdraw from you, unconsciously trying to become more independent in case something else happens to you.
- Some children will resent the fact that they need to help you when the opposite was true before.
- Some children will laugh and behave badly to cover up their real feelings or their lack of understanding (especially in strange situations).
- Some children will pretend to be ill to get attention or because they want to be with a parent. They might make a big fuss about a minor illness.
- Some children will be afraid they will get cancer too.

These things will pass with time, but let your children know that you understand and accept them as they are.

5

How to get support from the people around you

Now you have told people close to you about your breast cancer, you reach the next hurdle: coping with their shock and concern, or sometimes what seems like their lack of it. It can be harder to handle than you might expect. There are two helpful things to remember here. The first is that very often men react differently from women. And the second is that *all* of us are different personality types and will need or be able to offer varying kinds of support. Perhaps the most crucial fact to accept, if you don't feel that you are getting the sort of support that you want immediately, is that everyone around you will be doing their best. It may not be what *you* consider to be their best, but it will very likely be the best they can come up with, bearing in mind their personality and their circumstances.

Initially, I thought about sub-titling this chapter, 'Men and how to handle them', but I didn't want to rebuff or patronise male readers who turn to this for help in talking to their partners. Yet I do want to talk about some of the differences between men and women in the way they react to breast cancer and to give women an understanding of some of the thought processes their partner might be going through. I have used quotes from a number of men who are involved with supporting other men through the charity Breast Cancer Care (see Useful Addresses). I've also included comments from women whose main source of support has *not* been their partners, but whose relationships have survived nevertheless.

I have included a section on the Myers-Briggs Personality Indicator. This is a tool often used by psychologists in business as an aid to personal development and teamwork. It was developed by a mother and daughter team, Katharine Briggs and her daughter, Isabel Myers, over three decades and first published for general use in 1975.

It is useful to talk about personality in relation to breast cancer because it gives an insight into the fact that not only are all of us different, but that we have different preferences from our partners and from the people who treat us.

Finally, I have included 'Ten things a man can say to his partner'. This may seem rather crass, but so many men react to a partner's diagnosis of breast cancer with the phrase 'I don't know what to say' that I've decided to tackle this head on. Naturally, there are far more than ten fairly simplistic things you can say and do, but if you are a man and you feel completely at sea, the list might give you an idea of where to start.

Sometimes men withdraw

In his best-selling book, *Men are from Mars, Women are from Venus*, the American writer John Gray explains that, broadly speaking, men and women function differently in psychological terms. This focuses on two main areas. The first is that, usually, when a woman is worried and frightened, she wants to share and talk about what is on her mind. When a man has worries he tends to pull away and think silently about what is going on, or to seek advice to solve it. Secondly, women talk about their problems to be close, not necessarily to find solutions, whereas men feel like failures if they can't *solve* a problem, whether it's their own, or that of their partner.

Apply these conflicting attitudes to a diagnosis of breast cancer and you can see that immediately there's a strain on your relationship. Quite apart from the initial panic that she may die, a woman diagnosed with breast cancer is likely to feel that her femininity is threatened. She may face the prospect of losing a breast or her hair falling out through chemotherapy. At such a time she will need to feel loved, desired and cherished.

A man may be stunned by the news about his partner. He may feel completely inadequate because he cannot solve her problems; her health is now in the care of the hospital. He won't want to burden her (as he sees it) with his fears about her future, so he withdraws, to think it all over in his head. She senses this and assumes (wrongly) that he wants to abandon her because she is ill. The potential for disaster is obvious.

In her work as a breast cancer nurse, Debbie hardly ever came across men who walked away, simply because their partner was diagnosed with breast cancer, although she did look after one woman who left her husband after 25 years as a direct result of her diagnosis. She decided that she hadn't loved him for more than 20 years, and she couldn't think why she had stuck with him for so long. Cancer gave her the opportunity to walk away from her marriage and do other things with her life; she seized her chance. She only lived for a few years after her treatment, but she told Debbie they were the best years of her life.

Plenty of men turn out to be a wonderful support for their partners, but if your relationship feels strained and as though it is fraying at the edges, don't panic.

Maggie Watson, a consultant clinical psychologist at the Marsden advises:

'If a couple are coping in different ways, it may be that they are both at the limit of their personal resources. They may have to come a point where she says, "What he is doing is not what I would want him to do, but he is coping with the problem of my cancer the best way that he can." If a partner is coping quite well, then he may have resources left over for his spouse, but sometimes he doesn't have anything left over. He needs all his resources for himself, just to keep going.

'Sometimes a woman has to admit that maybe he has to do it his way. And to think "I can't depend on him helping me very much and I have to find other ways." '

So if it feels as though your partner is withdrawing from you, bear in mind that it is his reaction to a period of intense stress, *and not a reflection of his feelings for you*. This is the time to talk to your friends, your family or to ask to be referred to a counsellor at the hospital.

I found the half a dozen counselling sessions I had at the Marsden when I was first diagnosed invaluable. I thought I had plenty of friends and a supportive family, but much to my surprise, I didn't find I could talk about certain things to any of them. I didn't want to upset them, to be honest. I felt they would worry that I was no longer being positive if I aired some of the fears that were buzzing round my mind at the time. Talking to Kate, a counsellor, meant I could say virtually anything, and I didn't have to worry about her response. She was being paid to listen; it was her job. She had chosen to do it. That meant I was free to say exactly what I liked. I can recommend it.

There are rare instances when a woman has to cope when her partner leaves shortly after she is diagnosed. The end of any relationship can be traumatic and this is doubly so. If this happens to you, and you feel completely overwhelmed by troubles, focus on one or two things that you can sort out and which will make you feel better. Take the attitude that you will get around to the other problems eventually, when you feel stronger. And accept every bit of help and support from friends, family and the hospital that you are offered.

Most men, though, don't leave. Neither are they all the beacons of shining support that we might hope for.

Tony

'When the specialist confirmed it was cancer, my wife virtually had to help me out of the room, not vice versa. I wish I could have been a bit more of a help to her at the time.'

Paul

'I was in some sort of denial for quite a long time. I just focused on the practical side of things. I went shopping at the supermarket and reverted to my student days. I bought baked beans and steak and kidney pudding, the kinds of things I was capable of cooking. I didn't know at the time, but later on, my wife told me that she assumed that I didn't think she was going to survive, I was acting as if I was preparing for a siege. Actually, I didn't know what I was feeling.'

Dave

'I never told my wife I was scared stiff of her suffering or dying. I thought, 'I can't burden her with my fears, she's got enough to think about. So I ran around like a blue-arsed fly trying to look after the children and turn up at the hospital in an immaculately ironed shirt, desperate to hide the fact I was worried sick.'

These are men who have gone on to become volunteers for Breast Cancer Care; arguably they are now models of support for their wives, but as you can see, at first they didn't know what to do. In 1994, Breast Cancer Care set up The Partner Volunteer Service, to address the fact that men have so little support themselves when their partner is diagnosed, because everyone's focus is on the woman. But men need help too. Ring Breast Cancer Care if you are a man and would like to speak to another man about your situation. (See list of Useful Addresses at the back of this book.) Your call will be treated in confidence, and it may help to speak to someone who has already been through the experience you are going through.

How can a woman get emotional support from a man?

What can women do to enable their partners to support them as well as they can? The golden rule is to remember that *you will need to ask*. Because a woman will automatically offer emotional support to a man she loves, she assumes that, if he loves her, he will do the same. So most women don't ask and sometimes they are bitterly disappointed. You might think 'I have breast cancer, if he really loved me he would be cherishing me, sharing this experience with me and listening to me'. Your partner, meanwhile, is out plundering the supermarkets or trying to prove he can iron shirts just as well as you can, in the hope it will help. Probably it just makes you feel sidelined and hurt.

Take a step back and look at the situation again. Demanding support from your partner in an angry way won't help. You may feel that it is perfectly legitimate to declare: 'I've been told I have a life-threatening illness, I'm frightened of the treatment and I'm scared I won't live to see my grandchildren, the least you could do is offer to take the kids out for the afternoon.' This probably won't work. In the short term your partner may go along with your demands out of a sense of guilt, but long term your relationship won't be helped. Men don't respond well if they feel blamed or criticised and, in my experience, withdrawing your approval from them leaves a yawning gap between you.

In *Men are from Mars, Women are from Venus*, John Gray suggests that you start to get support from a man by appreciating what he is doing for you already. It may seem superfluous to thank your husband for driving you to the hospital; after all, he isn't the one who is going to hear difficult news about *his* health, but take a moment to think. If it was a friend or neighbour giving up their time to help, you'd probably be openly grateful, you might even buy them a small box of chocolates or flowers as a thank you. Why withhold appreciation from your partner? Few women actively dislike praise or encouragement and men are the same.

If you make demands and act as if you don't trust your partner to be there for you, you come across as clinging and needy. Tough as this sounds, a lot of men are repelled by this kind of behaviour. If, on the other hand, you appreciate what you are already getting and you talk to your partner as though you trust what they will do, the chances are that you won't end up feeling let down. It is down to the critical difference between neediness (which implies behaviour that is demanding and draining for both of you) and needing and trusting that you will get something legitimate, like care and concern (which is an entirely acceptable part of a relationship).

Being assertive

There are four basic guidelines that apply to assertive behaviour, whether it is connected to getting your needs met by your partner or getting the service you require from a shop, and they have nothing to do with getting aggressive or angry.

1. Be brief and be direct. Don't just pose a problem. For example *don't* say 'The children are driving me mad, my mother is due in ten minutes and my arm is sore; I don't know how I am going to manage to take out the rubbish'. *Do* say 'Would you take out the rubbish, please?'
2. Use 'would' and 'will' instead of 'could' and 'can'. A lot of women think that using 'could' and 'can' in requests to men is somehow more polite. Actually, it can sound wishy-washy and not definite. 'Could' and 'can' somehow beg the answer 'Well, of course I could, I am capable of it,' rather than 'Yes, I'll do it now'. With 'would' and 'will' there is no room for doubt.
3. Ask for what you want *and then remain silent*. Ignore the temptation to give lengthy explanations of why you need help or why you can't do the job yourself.
4. Thank him.

This of course applies to physical tasks. If you are seeking emotional reassurance, choose the right time. If your partner isn't dealing well with your diagnosis and seems to have withdrawn from you, he may take time to come up with the words you want to hear, but if your relationship is generally good, there's probably no harm in prompting him gently. Something along the lines of 'I need to hear that you are on my side right now' will probably produce more loving concern than you expect.

John Gray's theory is that men retreat into their 'caves' when they are confronted by a difficult situation. In other words, they withdraw mentally to mull over their response. Asking them a lot of questions about their feelings at this stage is a pretty pointless exercise. In fact, the more you try to get a man to talk, the chances are the more he will resist.

When he no longer feels under pressure to get everything off his chest in relation to your breast cancer, he may start to talk about it. But first he has to feel that you don't think he is inadequate or that in some way it's his fault and he is somehow to blame.

If you feel angry about your diagnosis, which is understandable, resist the temptation to transfer that anger to your partner. It may be easier to shout at your husband for leaving dirty dishes in the sink than to confront your fears about cancer, but it won't help your relationship. And you need his support. If you share your fears and anxieties with him in a calm and non-judgmental way, so that he does not feel *he* is the source of your distress, he will be much more able to support you in return.

Remember it isn't always possible for your partner to be your number one source of support when you are diagnosed with breast cancer.

Linda

'When I was first diagnosed in the early 1980s, I couldn't talk to my husband about it at all. He just went to pieces. After I had my operation he just said, "Right, that's finished now". I don't feel he ever wanted to know about my experiences with cancer. I don't mean that in an unkind way, but it is as if he prefers to be on the periphery, rather than deeply involved. And I've accepted that. Initially, I kept a diary and I would write down the positive things that I had done, and that helped me feel strong. And then I found a support group and that has been wonderful. Talking to other people who had suffered was a great help to me.'

Sally

'Just after my operation, my husband came to visit me on his way to work. I was in pain and I sat up in bed and burst into tears. My husband looked devastated. His face just crumpled. I stopped crying because I knew I couldn't unburden myself to him because he already had enough to handle, having a wife with breast cancer.'

Alison

'My emotional support came through my girlfriends and my sister. I knew I could unload onto them. I felt my partner had enough to cope with, it was very hard for him too.'

All three of the women quoted above are still with their partners in successful relationships. Because they chose to turn to other people to get them through the crisis of breast cancer, it didn't mean that their relationships eventually fell apart. In fact, being able to get support from people outside their marriages removed a potential source of stress and disappointment. So don't despair if you feel your husband or boyfriend in some way is not coming up to scratch. See if you can get support from somewhere else without making a big deal of it, so he isn't made to feel that he is failing you.

Getting support from other women

Even if your partner deserves a gold medal for all the help he gives you, there will probably be occasions when work or other family responsibilities mean he can't be there for you. This is the time to turn to your friends and neighbours. If they offer support, swallow your pride, or whatever it is that means you might turn it down, give a gracious smile and say 'Thanks very much'. Many women try and carry on, even if they are feeling dreadful; everyone assumes they are coping well, and offers of help dry up, or don't materialise in the first place.

If you find yourself wondering why no one has called to offer assistance, cast your mind back to who you told about your breast cancer *and how you told them*. I know that when I was first diagnosed, the handful of friends I decided to tell were given strong 'I'm managing fine' signals from me. I even forbade one good friend from work to tell her partner, because I was determined to minimise the effect my cancer could have on my friendships. (That's how I saw it then.) By taking such an unwavering approach I made it difficult for that friend to give me any extra support. What was she supposed to say to her husband if I needed her to call round unexpectedly? In fact, she obeyed my instructions to the letter, and we carried on talking about work – mine and hers – and gossiped as normal about mutual colleagues. I valued the fact that with Penny my life was going on as normal.

Where my Superwoman theory collapsed was with friends from whom I needed more emotional support. I gave off exactly the same 'I'm fine' messages, but expected that somehow they would see through it and offer me extra help. When they didn't I felt upset and let down. I blamed them for not being true friends. What I didn't realise was that girlfriends, like partners, are not mind-readers. If you say you are fine and all is well, they accept that. So, ask. Tell them what you want from your friendship with them. If you need help and ask for it, they are only too happy to give it. Breast cancer gives you permission to get help. Even a Superwoman has off days, and there is nothing to be gained by anyone if you get stressed out and miserable trying to struggle on as if you weren't coping with a diagnosis of cancer. You may be surprised how much other people enjoy being able to do something practical for their friend. Give them a chance to show that they care.

Alison

'I'd say always take someone with you for chemotherapy. The first time I went on my own it was such a miserable experience. Every time after that, my sister came with me so I had someone to chat to and it felt more normal. We used to have breakfast together in a café across the road from the hospital before my treatment and doing something nice like that first made a difference.'

Mavis

'I had friends who came in to see me after my operation and I'd be talking to them and suddenly I'd burst into tears and I couldn't say why. None of them said 'pull yourself together', they just waited until I had finished crying and we carried on. No one said anything silly; they were just there.'

Some people find it easier than others to release their feelings through a good cry with a friend. I have always found it hard to cry in front of my friends, I've preferred to keep positive in public and have an occasional weep on my own, but last year I burst into tears in the most inappropriate and public place I could have chosen. A girlfriend from university and I decided to visit the Glastonbury music festival, before we both hit 40, and we left our husbands looking after the children one blazing June weekend. We were having a wonderful time listening to the music and watching the multi-coloured, multi-talented world go by, pretending we were 19 again. Then it started to rain and we took cover under a tent where a woman was painting henna tattoos. For some reason, she started to tell me her life story. It was tragic. She had been a drug addict who had nearly killed herself on numerous occasions and generally she had treated her life as though it was worth little more than an old tissue.

I sat and listened politely to all of this, thinking I was sad to hear it but otherwise unaffected. We moved on to a Buddhist café for a drink, I sat down with my peppermint tea and burst into a flood of tears. In comparison with the drug addict, I felt as if I had spent the last five years clinging on to life by my fingertips, and there was someone who was deliberately choosing to wreck hers. And she expected my sympathy. It seemed so unfair. Karen, my friend, just put her arm around me. Alarmed and uncertain, some of the heavily tattooed and body-pierced young music fans near us edged away. Karen said nothing. She just sat and held me gently until my tears dried up. As I began to gain a bit of perspective, I realised that I didn't want to die because my life is so good. The drug addict wasn't bothered about staying alive because, from her point of view, her life was so bad. It's a crucial difference. And she didn't have a friend who was prepared to sit and support her through her tears. She had to talk to me, a stranger.

I suppose the moral of this story is that it can be a relief to cry in front of the right friends. If they are good friends they won't object to a few tears. Holding back for so long did nothing to help me.

What can friends offer?

If you are reading this because you have a friend or relation who has been diagnosed with breast cancer and you don't know what to say or how to help, Cancer BACUP produces an excellent leaflet, *Lost for Words: How To Talk To Someone with Cancer*. (See list of useful addresses at the back of this book.) An important thing to remember is that it isn't what you say, but how you listen to your friend. Equally, thoughtful offers of practical help are virtually guaranteed to be welcome. If you can cook a meal for the freezer, be a chauffeur or pick up shopping, offer those skills. In terms of emotional support, here are five basic tips to start with:

1. Make sure your friend wants to talk about her cancer. Sometimes a patient needs to see friends to catch up on the 'normal' side of life that doesn't include hospital appointments, waiting for test results or scans. She may not want to confide her deepest fears to you. She may want to talk about mutual friends, a book you have both read or a film you have seen. Let her choose the subject of your conversation.
2. Show her that you are prepared to have a proper conversation. If you are visiting, take your coat off and sit down; don't hover in the doorway and look uneasy. If you are visiting someone in hospital, draw your chair up so that you can make eye contact easily, so the person in bed doesn't have to twist round to talk.
3. If your friend wants to talk about her illness, don't change the subject. If you feel uncomfortable, it's OK to say 'I'm not sure what to say'. It's all right to describe your own feelings after you have listened to those

of your friend. But don't expect her to take on the burden of support-ing you.

4. Don't ever say 'if I were you'. If you are desperate to make a sugges-tion to your friend, try 'have you thought about?' Don't undermine her confidence in the treatment she has chosen.

5. Respond to humour. Nothing is harder work for a patient than hav-ing to cheer up her visitors. Don't blast her with jokes if she is feeling low, but be prepared to laugh with her. If your friend's sense of humour stays intact it will help her to cope with breast cancer in the days ahead.

The Myers-Briggs Type Indicator® and how it can help

You may be wondering what a psychologists' tool used by large corpora-tions for the personal development of their staff has to do with breast cancer patients. I've discovered it can help a great deal. In simple terms, the Myers-Briggs Type Indicator (MBTI®) is, as the name suggests, an indicator of the way we are likely to react to any situation. There are four principle categories and we are all a combination of these four. Having some insight into your own preferences, as well as those of your partner, your friends and the hospital staff treating you, can give you a clearer perspective on your thoughts and feelings about breast cancer and the way you and others handle it.

Unless you have completed the MBTI questionnaire, of course, you won't know for sure what your type is, but I will be giving an explana-tion of the categories which you may find illuminating in terms of your relationship with your friends and family, and with the medical staff who treat you. What you *can* do is note from the style of behaviour people are displaying with you what their preference might be. You can adjust your response accordingly.

A clue to noticing when someone else is using a difference preference from you is that you may suddenly feel negative or uncomfortable about what the other person is saying; often it is then that we are dealing with a type difference. Other ways of spotting other people's preferences will become clearer later in this chapter.

Judy Allen, a former nurse who is now a researcher and consultant working with the MBTI in healthcare, has co-written a book, *Healthcare Communication Using Personality Type*, which recognises the importance of MBTI among patients and practitioners. She maintains that the most important thing to remember about the MBTI is that it is a indicator of preference, and all of us use all the preferences all the time. Equally, there is no *good* or *bad* type preference. As we know, there are differences between us, and MBTI simply provides a framework for understanding these differences better. There are four dimensions of the MBTI.

Introvert or Extrovert

This is not, as we usually assume, only to do with who is good at parties and who would rather stay at home and read a book. In the MBTI, this first dimension is concerned with where people get their energy from; whether they prefer internal stimulation or external stimulation. In other words, is their approach to life:

- think things through first,

or

- talk about things first?

If you generally prefer to think things through first, you may not want to talk to lots of people about the decisions you need to make about your breast cancer. You may prefer to mull it over in your head for a while at least. Indeed, you may never share some of your thoughts with anyone else. If you prefer to talk things over, however, you may need to talk to as many people as possible who have had a similar experience. Your energy for dealing with your experience will come from talking to others.

As someone who prefers to talk about things first (extroversion), I find that I often don't know what my thoughts are until I am in the middle of a conversation with someone else, and suddenly find myself saying exactly what I think. It's almost a surprise. Colin, my husband, has a preference for thinking things through first (introversion), and prefers to consider everything in his head before he makes any decisions. As a result, he can plan something and be quite a long way down the road with it before he mentions it to anyone, if he ever does. Neither approach is necessarily 'better', but they are different.

Sensing or intuition

This dimension works on how people gather information. People with a preference for sensing tend to use their five senses to focus on facts and details, on what *is*. People with a preference for intuition, however, tend to use a sixth sense, or a hunch, and look for patterns and concepts and possibilities, rather than the facts in front of them. Colin, who prefers sensing, drew up a brilliant schedule for all the tablets I had to take during my first round of chemotherapy. People with a preference for sensing are at their best with routine and practical tasks. As an intuitive, my interest lies in the overall picture, rather than in detailed facts. Rather than read up on breast cancer in reference books, I met my oncologist, knew he was the right consultant for me and decided that I would trust his judgement in matters medical. And that is what I have done ever since.

Differences in type between couples can add to your strength as a unit, if they are recognised and valued. If you are an intuitive, it is possible that you will imagine all kinds of dramatic scenarios which may never happen. Normally, intuitives can trust their hunches, but they are not always right. If you live with a look-at-the-facts sensing partner, it can be incredibly helpful to have someone around to rein in your spinning thoughts and vivid imagination. Equally, someone with a sensing preference can find it helpful to see the big picture; a partner with a preference for intuition can give valuable support here.

Thinking or feeling

Having received information, either through our sensing or our intuition, we then have to make a decision about what we are going to do with it. People with a preference for thinking tend to look first at cause and effect. Those with a preference for feeling may make decisions based initially on human values, or what makes things better for people. Given a diagnosis of breast cancer, a woman with a preference for thinking may not be comfortable at first with being quizzed by others about her feelings and her fears. She may find it intrusive and prefer to ask direct and objective questions herself. A woman with a preference for feeling, however, will want her feelings to be widely acknowledged and respected by those about her; she will want to know that whoever is treating her has her best interests at heart.

Those with a thinking preference tend to see situations from the outside, so they behave more as onlookers, whereas feeling types tend to see life from the inside out, as full participants. Both can lose their sense of perspective if they don't take account of the other.

Difference in type between partners can create difficulties. One (feeling) woman was upset that her (thinking) husband kept incredibly detailed notes of every consultation and treatment that she had throughout her illness, but he never once told her how much he cared about her. As far as he was concerned, his note-taking *demonstrated* his love for her. Similarly, a (thinking) female friend of mine became irritated when her (feeling) husband abandoned his work in order to stay by her bedside when she was first diagnosed with breast cancer. She wanted him to prove his love by carrying on working and being sure to keep up with the mortgage payments, rather than sit beside her and hold her hand. These are extreme examples and many of our relationships fall some way in between; but it is useful to remember that the differences between us are often partly due to personality type, rather than signs of neglect or unkindness.

Judging or perceiving

The final dimension of the MBTI relates to the way in which you manage your life, whether through the judging or perceiving process. People with a judging preference can be goal-orientated: they like decisions to be made. They tend to used words like 'planned', 'decided', and 'organised'.

People with a perceiving preference like to keep their options open. They tend to use words like 'gathering', 'wondering' and 'considering'. They enjoy the process of gathering information and their energy to complete a task usually comes towards or even after the deadline. So a breast cancer patient with a preference for judging will probably like a clear-cut treatment plan. If they are persuaded not to make immediate decisions, they may need to conclude in their heads that not making a decision is a decision in itself, as in 'I've decided not to decide anything yet'. A perceiving patient, on the other hand, may need to gather as many options as possible and then mull them over before finally coming to a conclusion.

How you can make the MBTI work for you with doctors

You won't know what MBTI type your doctor is, but once you have some idea of what your preferences might be, the most important thing is to be able to communicate to whoever is treating you what *your* needs happen to be. If you have a preference for introversion, you may want to say to the doctor that you take time to absorb a lot of detail and you may need to be able to contact someone later for more information. You could say 'Perhaps it will help you to know that I can only deal with so much at a time', or 'Can I take a moment to write that down?' An extrovert might want to say 'I need a moment to talk this through with you'. (Sometimes you can't alter the dynamics of a medical consultation, but it can help to be aware of how you are all behaving.)

A doctor won't know that you are a sensing type who requires all the facts, if you don't tell them. Alternatively, if your doctor begins to spout a lot of information that you find baffling, it is perfectly possible to say 'I just need a general lie of the land, and if you give me too much information, I may have trouble remembering it'.

Having a list of questions usually helps everyone. Introverts find it useful, especially if a doctor moves on before they have had a chance to think through what has been said, and a list helps to keep extroverts on the right track, so they don't get distracted and find themselves talking about everything in a consultation but the one thing they really wanted to ask.

The other important point is that in times of crisis, you may act out of type. There have been occasions when I have walked into a meeting with a doctor, and said (politely, of course) that I didn't want to exchange pleasantries, I just wanted the results of my tests. I abandoned my usual feeling preference (to be chatty and warm) because my health was at stake and I just needed a no-frills delivery of some critical information.

If you have some understanding of your preferences and of those around you, it can help to explain the differences in the way you react to the same piece of information. If you remember that it is not a question of better or worse, but simply the differences between us, you can save yourself a measure of pain, unhappiness or disappointment.

One last aspect of MBTI that is worth remembering is that a large proportion of nurses have a preference for feeling. In other words, they tend to be people who consider the feelings and values of others first. Doctors, and I base this on my personal experience rather than a scientific survey, are more likely to have a thinking preference. This could account for the general perception of nurses as caring and doctors as factually minded and bordering on arrogant, though, of course, this is a gross distortion of reality. What it does suggest is that your treatment from health professionals is much more due to their type preferences, than their perception of you.

We can all access all of the preferences; it is up to you to tell the people looking after you what your needs are and for you to adjust accordingly. So if you are a thinking type, you may be made to feel uncomfortable or hemmed in by a feeling nurse who appears to be concerned primarily with your emotions. You may even be made to feel there's something wrong with you for not showing *enough* emotion. If this happens, you simply have to explain that you prefer to think things over by yourself for a while, and when you need information or personal support, you will let them know.

Equally, if you have a preference for feeling and are hurt by being addressed in an apparently cold and overly businesslike way by a thinking doctor, it will help if you understand that the doctor is not being cruel or unkind, it is simply the behaviour he or she uses at work. So if you are being asked to respond to a set of logical options and you want time to talk about your reaction, just ask the doctor for time to think, or to talk to a friend who will let you explore your feelings.

If you want to explore more about your personality type you can contact a qualified MBTI practitioner at the British Association of Psychological Type. (See Useful Addresses list at the back of this book.)

Finally, I've included a list for the benefit of men who want to do or say something, but have no idea where to begin. Of course, if your ideas are better, act on them.

Ten things a man can say or do for his partner

1. Don't reel off a team talk: 'You're tough – you'll beat it'. It's not helpful because it's a barrier to communication. Instead let your partner talk and don't end every conversation with a motivational speech. Do maintain a positive attitude; something like 'We'll handle this the best way we can', is fine.

2. Tasks like driving her to appointments are important, but listening to her feelings matters just as much. Don't worry, you don't have to fix her or make her stop feeling frightened yourself – just the act of listening will help her.

3. You may want to show that you are sensitive by telling her that you love her, not her breasts, but a woman can hear this as 'Your breasts are unimportant to me, so they shouldn't matter to you'. You are minimising how she feels about herself. Breasts are a part of body image. How would you feel if she said to you 'Your penis means nothing to me'? Acknowledge her loss. Offer reassurance and explain that you are sad about what has happened to her, but that your relationship can withstand any physical changes that might take place. Remind her gently that a woman's attractiveness is made up of much more than one aspect of her physical appearance. I have consulted some of my more sensitive male friends and these are their suggestions:

'This shouldn't have happened to you. But to me your attractiveness goes beyond just your breasts. What I see before me now is a
very attractive woman – there's no change there.'

Or: 'This must be really hard for you. But what we have had so far
   has been great, and as far as I am concerned, nothing is going to
   change that in the future.'

Or: 'When I first saw you, I saw a beautiful woman, and today I still
   see a beautiful woman.'

Or: 'I am with you because of *all* of you, not just a part of you. If all
   I cared about was breasts, I could go anywhere. I can't get *you* anywhere.'

Or even: 'You are still the person that I want to be with, and I hope
   that one day you can let it not affect you as much as it truly
   doesn't affect me. You are far more important than just a part of
   you. I still adore *you* and want to be with *you*.'

These suggestions are to offer you ideas – they aren't a script.
Think about it, find a form of words that you feel comfortable with
and choose the right time to say them – preferably when it's just the
two of you and you can give her a cuddle at the same time.

4. Note-taking can be a great help during hospital consultations. If your
   partner feels overwhelmed and forgets what has been said, you can
   refer to your notes to clear things up. Don't inundate her with facts;
   just have the answer ready if she asks.

5. If your partner needs a breast reconstruction or mastectomy, she may
   be embarrassed to show you her scar. Ask to see the scar while she is
   still in hospital or soon after she comes home. If you are worried that
   you might be horrified (and the chances are that you won't feel like
   that), privately ask a doctor to see pictures of a mastectomy or reconstruction beforehand. Above all else, a woman doesn't want to feel
   repulsive; she does want to feel loved and wanted. Don't just tell her
   she looks great, no matter what. Try saying something like 'I know
   this is tough on you, but I love you and I think you're great'.

6. Some men want to buy their partners presents to make them feel better. Yes, a thoughtful gift may give her a boost, but don't act as if an
   expensive handbag can compensate for the loss of a breast. That's
   superficial and upsetting for a woman.

7. Immediately after an operation, a woman may be uninterested in sex,
   but she will still want affection. Chemotherapy can trigger the

menopause which in turn can create vaginal dryness. Use a lubricant when you have sex, so that it is never uncomfortable for her. Caress her whole body and treat her as you did before, unless she tells you otherwise. One couple swapped sides of the bed so the husband could still cradle his wife and touch the breast that hadn't been operated on.

8. Don't treat her with kid gloves the whole time. A lot of partners try to steer clear in order to give their women 'space'. This can leave a woman feeling hurt and ignored. Don't avoid normal, day-to-day constructive conflict either. It's not a good time to instigate a huge row, but if you act as if you fully expect her to live, she is getting a positive message about her health.

9. When the treatment is over and her hair has grown back, men tend not to want to think about it any more. But breast cancer is never over for a woman. She will have to handle the experience for the rest of her life. If she wants to talk about it (again), just listen. You may want to forget everything; she can't.

10. Give her a card on the anniversary of her surgery. Tell her that you admire her and are proud of her. Twelve months on and the experience will still be on her mind. A thoughtful gesture from you will be appreciated.

6

What is cancer and who should you talk to?

When women are told that they have breast cancer, the diagnosis is usually not only a shock, but for many it is a complete surprise. I have heard many women say that they had never felt so healthy in their lives and that they find it difficult to believe that they have cancer as they feel so well. Often they show a real sense of anger. They eat a good diet, don't drink, don't smoke and do everything they can to keep fit. They say that there does not seem to be any logic or justice in why some women get breast cancer.

For this reason, it can be helpful, therefore, to try and understand why breast cancer occurs. Many people also want to know what they can do to help their bodies deal with the cancer and prevent it from occurring again. Many women are also anxious that their daughters should have good information about preventing breast cancer.

What is cancer and how is it caused?

There is a lot of research being conducted in this area, and as a consequence a great deal is known about cancer and, in particular, about breast cancer. But it seems that the more that is known, the more it becomes clear that the development of cancer is a very complex issue. Adult cancers, such as breast and prostate cancer, take many years to develop. This is not to say that there is a lump growing that has just not been detected yet. It is rather that cancer cells need to change and evolve so that they can overcome all the normal checks to growth and spread.

The cells in your body are constantly dividing in order to repair damaged cells or replace old ones. This process is governed by messages being passed from DNA (deoxyribonucleic acid) into the rest of the cell. These messages are then acted on to make the relevant proteins for certain tasks. During this process there are many places where errors can occur and they often do. Errors are nearly always picked up at a very early level and corrected. However, occasionally they are not detected and there can be a snowball effect. This occasionally results in a group of cells growing without the normal checking mechanisms so that they get out of hand and grow in an abnormal way. Quite often, even at this stage, the body can pick up these cells and eliminate them. Those cells that are not checked can grow into a lump or start to spread around parts of the body that they were not designed to be in. This is called cancer. As your body gets older, it is not quite so good at correcting mistakes and so they are more likely to result in a problem. As a result, older people are more likely to get cancer. Some people have mistakes in their DNA passed to them from their parents. Other factors can cause damage to the DNA and make cancer more likely, such as radiation, certain chemicals (such as cigarette tar) or constant hormonal stimulation. It is not known for certain exactly how breast cancer is caused, but it is probably a combination of factors.

What causes breast cancer?

Breast cancer is more common in Western countries than it is elsewhere in the world. Many reasons have been suggested for this and much research has taken place to try and track the differences. It is hoped that this will give clues about the causes of breast cancer. Researchers often come up with new theories and the media would have us believe that there is a single cause that we just have not found yet. People often come up to me and ask if I have heard the latest theory about breast cancer being caused by bras, deodorants, milk, etc. Some of these claims may have evidence to support them, but many are based on inaccurate theories about the way that cancers grow and develop. Be suspicious of people who claim that they know the cause or have found the cure for cancer, unless they are prepared to show the evidence and name the people that support their ideas. I believe that other claims are not only unhelpful, but also dangerous. They are misleading, play on people's natural fears about cancer, offer hopes that are based on falsity and raise anxiety as to whether specific products should be avoided.

Some genes have been identified which are definitely linked to an increased risk of breast cancer. These genes may account for 5–10 per cent of breast cancers that occur in the UK. The most common ones are called BRCA1 and BRCA2. These genes are usually involved in regulating cell growth, but in some families the gene has been altered so that it no longer works properly. Even if a woman does have an altered gene, it is not definite that she will get breast cancer and no one can predict when it might occur. This is because each of us has two copies of every gene; so every cell in that woman's body will have one normal and one abnormal gene. It will only be when the normal gene is damaged that the abnormal one will predominate and cancer occurs.

As breast cancer is so common, many people have one or two relatives who have had the disease but this does not necessarily mean that there is an abnormal gene present in the family. Women may be referred for genetic counselling if there are four or more affected close family relatives, or if there are cases where cancer occurs very young (under 40), or if any of the men in the family have had breast cancer. Many of these abnormal genes increase the risk of a variety of cancers. For example, breast and ovarian cancer are linked with the BRCA1 gene.

However, this still leaves the 90 per cent of women who get breast cancer without having inherited an abnormal gene. The causes here are much less clear. The clearest risk factors for breast cancer all point to a hormonal cause. Women who never have babies or who start to have them when they are over 30 are more at risk. This does not mean that those who have lots of children will not get breast cancer, just that the chances are fewer. Those who start their periods early (before 12) or finish them late in life (after 55) are also at a higher risk. The common link in these factors is not all the female hormones, but specifically oestrogen. It seems that the more oestrogen a woman is exposed to over many years, the higher her chances of getting breast cancer.

This raises the concern as to whether the contraceptive pill and hormone replacement therapy (HRT) could cause breast cancer, but it is still not clear. It seems that if the contraceptive pill contains high amounts of oestrogen it might increase the risk of breast cancer. However, modern contraceptives contain a balance of oestrogen and progesterone and some only contain progesterone, so they do not appear to be a cause. Hormone replacement therapy is usually given to older women when the breasts are less vulnerable to risk factors as the rate of cell growth is slower. The amounts of oestrogen given are very small in relation to what the body would normally produce and often progesterone is given as well, but there is a possibility that if HRT is given over a very long period of time (more than ten years) it might increase the risk of breast cancer.

Our diet may also be a contributory factor to breast cancer. In the West we consume much higher levels of animal fats and lower levels of plant and fish proteins and also low levels of dietary fibre, than they do in Eastern and developing countries. In these places breast cancer is much less common. It may be that a higher intake of soy protein and fatty fish, such as tuna or mackerel, could be protective. There are also many vitamins, found in fruit and vegetables, which probably protect against cancer. It seems sensible to try to reduce the amount of animal fats that we consume in terms of meat and dairy products and to increase the amount of fish, fruit and vegetables.

Smoking certainly contributes to many cancers, but almost certainly not to breast cancer. However, alcohol does. An average of one drink a day is enough to increase your risk, and the more you drink, the higher the risk.

Women who have had breast cancer once are more likely to develop a second cancer than women who have never had it. This is presumably because if you have a tendency to develop breast cancer then you continue to have this tendency. While it is believed that this increases by about 1 per cent a year, ultimately what this means is that it only affects up to 4 per cent of women over 50 and 14 per cent of women under 50.

Unfortunately, we all know people who follow every recommendation and still get breast cancer. There is as yet no formula for avoiding it, so it seems pointless to follow guidelines slavishly when no-one can guarantee any benefits. Some people make huge efforts and spend large amounts of money to alter their diet and lifestyle radically. I feel that this can sometimes do harm because of the stress that it causes, and that it is impossible to be sure of any benefits. Many women, however, find it helpful to think seriously about their lifestyle and can make changes that are positive and improve their enjoyment of life. For some people this restores a feeling of control when the cancer seems to take control away. Other women feel that this is something positive that they can do to help themselves. It may also prevent a new cancer from arising in the other breast.

Can breast cancer be prevented?

There are indications that in the future we will know more about how to prevent breast cancer. There may be clearer guidelines about our diet (see above) and it certainly makes sense to minimise alcohol consumption. There is some evidence to suggest that exercise might be protective. I certainly think that it is worth encouraging adolescent girls to get into the habit of regular exercise. This also strengthens their hearts and lungs and makes osteoporosis less likely in old age.

Some major studies in the USA have shown that the anti-hormone, tamoxifen, can reduce the incidence of breast cancer. It does not prevent it altogether and does have some side-effects, so the way in which tamoxifen should be used is still being investigated. Because of these concerns, tamoxifen should only be used for prevention if it is part of a study. I also generally feel that it is better for us to find out the causes of disease and prevent these, rather than give drugs.

Some women who are at very high risk of breast cancer consider having both their breasts removed surgically (bilateral mastectomy). Unfortunately it is not possible to remove all the breast tissue in the body. Because it extends a long way under the arm and up under the collarbone, there will always be some breast tissue left behind. It does look as though it will reduce the chance of breast cancer from occurring, but it does not eliminate this chance.

Detecting a change in your breast

Most of you reading this book will already know that you have breast cancer and will know what to look for in your breast. However, you may have been surprised that the changes in your breast turned out to be cancer. Many people describe that they find a thickening, or a puckering, rather than a real lump. Often cancer is found by a screening mammogram and there is nothing to feel in the breast at all. The vast majority of women who find lumps in their breast discover that these are not due to cancer at all. So how can you tell if you have cancer? The answer is that you can't unless you are experienced in telling the difference between normal lumps and abnormal ones. The best advice is to get to know what your breasts feel like normally. You will find that normal breast tissue does feel generally lumpy. You will also find that your breasts feel different at different times of the month. What you are looking for is anything unusual, or anything that is not normal for you. If you find anything unusual, see your GP.

Is a lump always cancer?

Lumps that appear anywhere in the body are called tumours. A tumour is just a name for a swelling of tissue and can be benign or malignant. If it is benign it only grows in one place, does not spread to other tissues and often goes away without any treatment. A malignant tumour is one that can spread into surrounding tissues or to other parts of the body. They are usually called cancers.

Fibroadenoma

The most common sort of lump that appears in the breast is known as a fibroadenoma. This is where the cells have grown abnormally in one area, but there is no tendency for these cells to invade other tissues or any chance of them spreading anywhere else in the body. This is a benign tumour. It is not cancer, nor does it turn into cancer. These tend to occur in younger women.

Cysts

A cyst is a sac filled with fluid and so is very round and distinct. These can often be drained and they just disappear. Sometimes women get many cysts in the breast. These can be clearly seen by ultrasound, which is particularly good at showing images of fluid-filled spaces.

Pain

Pain is a common problem in breasts and is rarely due to cancer. Most breast pain is caused by the changes that occur in the breast during the monthly menstrual cycle. An ill-fitting bra can cause pain, as supporting ligaments may be stretched, so it is worth getting this checked. A high intake of caffeine may be associated with breast pain and cutting down on tea, coffee and cola drinks often helps.

When it is cancer

For every ten women who see their doctor with a lump there will be one that turns out to have cancer. This is where the cells in the breast grow in an abnormal way and are not subject to the normal control mechanisms. There is also the possibility that these cells can break away from the original cluster and spread to other parts of the body through the blood or lymphatic system.

Some of the terms that doctors use to describe cancer can be alarming. One of these is 'invasive ductal carcinoma'. Carcinoma is the name for cancers that occur in lining tissues, such as the gut, the skin and the breast. Invasive means that the cells have been seen to spread into surrounding tissue, which is how it is known to be cancer. Ductal describes the part of the breast where the cancer has been found (the glands that produce milk). These are made up of lobes, where the milk is made, and ducts that carry the milk to the nipple. The majority of breast cancers occur in the ducts. About 10 per cent of breast cancers occur in the lobes and this is known as lobular cancer.

Ductal carcinoma in situ (DCIS)

This is another phrase used by doctors which doesn't mean much to most people. What it does mean is that there are cancer cells in the ducts of the breast. However, the *in situ* part means that it is not yet invasive. When the pathologist looks at the cells under the microscope he can see them growing along the duct but they have not spread through the duct walls. If the cells have not grown through the walls of the ducts then they cannot possibly have spread into the blood or lymph systems and so cannot have spread anywhere else in the body. Sometimes this is known as pre-invasive cancer, or can even be described as a pre-cancerous condition. It has a virtually 100 per cent cure rate when cut out by surgery. This is the kind of cancer that is being looked for when women are called for breast screening by mammography. In a minority of women DCIS tends to occur repeatedly and so sometimes other treatments will be suggested as well as surgery.

Who to talk to if you think you have cancer

The first person to talk to is your General Practitioner (GP). Your GP will make the appropriate referrals for you. If you have cancer you will spend a lot of time seeing specialists at the hospital but your GP is the person who will still be around when the treatment is over. It is a good idea to keep your GP up to date with how things are going for you and how you are coping with it. Sometimes it helps to have someone outside the system with whom to chat things through. If your GP is also the doctor for the rest of your family, remember that they may need support too. It can be helpful for them to be able to talk to someone who understands what is happening but is not emotionally involved. If you or your family would find it helpful your GP can also make referrals to other health professionals, such as counsellors.

If you have cancer, then once you have been referred to a hospital your GP will assume that hospital staff are taking care of all your active treatment and that his role is peripheral to your needs. He will get a record of everything that is happening at the hospital and will be aware of your treatment and progress. Some GPs will ask to see you from time to time, just to monitor how you are getting on. Many others will not. If you feel that he could offer you more positive help and support you may need to ask for it. Sometimes your GP is a good person for other members of the family to talk to as they may feel that the hospital is more geared to answering your needs than theirs.

If you do not have a good relationship with your GP this may mean that you do not get the support that ideally you would want. If you want to change your GP, you can. However, you may feel that you have enough else going on without having to worry about this. Make sure you let the hospital know if you make any changes like this, so that the records can be changed, and be aware that there is a possibility that this could lead to confusion. The records will be changed, but if there are any places where your old GP has been recorded then there is a chance of letters being sent to the wrong address. On the whole, I think it is worth working closely with GPs to get to know them better and to let them know what you want out of your relationship.

Referrals

In the UK, cancer services have now been set up according to strict criteria so that treatment is only carried out by doctors who are up to date and working in centres that are properly set up to deal with cancer. If you have any concerns about where you are being referred to, you can ask how many women with breast cancer the surgeon treats in a year. The recommended minimum is 50 a year. For most hospitals this figure is over 100. Private health care is independent of these regulations, so you might like to check with your consultant where he carries out his NHS work and how many women he treats with breast cancer.

Cancer services have also been organised so that all cancer treatment is carried out either at a designated Cancer Centre or a Cancer Unit. Cancer Centres are specialist centres throughout the UK, where all types of cancer are treated and specialist knowledge and skills, as well as equipment, are all brought together in one place. In order to build up this kind of expertise, there has to be a limit to these Centres as otherwise they would not be able to treat enough patients to develop the knowledge. Cancer Units are satellites of the Cancer Centres, where the more common cancers are treated. They either have resident experts or visiting experts from the Cancer Centres. Women with breast cancer may have surgery and chemotherapy locally at a Cancer Unit, but may often need to attend a Cancer Centre for radiotherapy.

This is a step forward for cancer treatment and care in this country as all Cancer Centres and Units need to be able to demonstrate a certain level of expertise before they can be awarded this status.

Macmillan standards of care

A panel of experts brought together by the charity Macmillan Cancer Relief (see Useful Addresses) has drawn up some guidelines for care. Their ten minimum standards of care for breast cancer are that women should have:

- a prompt referral by a GP to a team specialising in the diagnosis and treatment of breast cancer, including a consultant from within the team
- a firm diagnosis within four weeks of being referred to a hospital by a GP
- the opportunity of a confirmed diagnosis before consenting to treatments, including surgery
- access to a specialist breast care nurse trained to give information and psychological support
- full information about types of surgery (including breast reconstruction, where appropriate) and the role of medical treatments
- a full explanation about the aims of the treatments proposed and their benefits and possible side-effects
- as much time as is needed to consider treatment options
- a sensitive and complete breast prosthesis fitting service, where appropriate
- the opportunity to meet a former breast cancer patient who has been trained to offer support
- information on all support services available to patients with breast cancer and their families.

(From: *Breast Cancer: How to Help Yourself*, Macmillan Cancer Relief, 1998)

In each of the next few chapters I have suggestions for questions you might like to ask your doctor.

Six questions to ask:

What are the changes that have occurred in my breast?

Should I carry on taking hormone replacement therapy?

Is anyone else in my family at risk of breast cancer?

Are there any changes I could make to my lifestyle to help maximise my health?

Is this hospital a specialist centre for cancer?

How many people do you treat with breast cancer every year?

7
Getting into the hospital system

In this chapter I give you an outline of the UK hospital system and how to make the most of it. Getting to know a new system is fraught with anxiety even when you do not have the worry about whether or not you have cancer. The systems are often unwieldy and when you do not know what is going on this can be frustrating. Many people say that they hate hospitals and there are many reasons for this. I believe that one of the most powerful reasons is that while you are the one who is ill and needing help, everyone else knows what is going on and is in charge of what happens to you. I hope this chapter will give you some of the information that you need to get the most out of the system and feel a little more in charge of what is happening.

Once you have been to see your GP, you should be able to get an appointment to see a specialist very quickly. The hospital aims to give you an appointment within seven days of receiving the GPs referral letter. If you can get your GP to fax it over then so much the better. Even specialist centres may not have a clinic for new referrals more than once a week. The current government guidelines say that a specialist should see every woman with a suspicious breast lump within two weeks.

When you get there

Unless you have been to this hospital before, they will need to register you in order to draw up a new set of notes and you will be given a hospital number. I suggest that you get to know your hospital number as this is the way staff trace all the information they hold about you, especially now that most hospitals are computerised. The registration process usually consists of a short interview where you give your basic contact details and information such as next of kin. Once you are registered, you will need to go to a check-in desk for your clinic. This is a good time to check where the loos are, where you can get a drink, how long you might have to wait and how you will know when it is your turn to be seen. It is very common to have to wait a long time in hospital departments. Sometimes this is after you have had a test and the medical staff are waiting for results. It might help to have something to do, otherwise time goes slowly. Many people like easy reading, such as a magazine, as it does not require much concentration. It is a good idea to have someone with you, especially for the first appointment and for results. First, because getting used to the system is always nerve-racking. Secondly, because when people are nervous it is very common for them to miss or forget large chunks of information that they are given.

What will happen

A nurse or health care assistant will usually take you into an examination room and ask you to undress. They should provide you with a gown for while you are waiting. You can take someone with you if you wish. If you are alone, then you can ask for this nurse to stay with you when you are being examined. In some places this will happen automatically, but it is not routine everywhere.

Examination

The doctor, or in some places a specialist nurse, will examine both of your breasts very carefully with the flat of their fingers. Unless you are tender anyway, normally this should not hurt. They will also feel under your armpits and behind your nipples. You will need to be lying down for this examination, but you may also be examined sitting up.

Needle test

If there is a lump in your breast it is usual for the doctor to put a small needle into it to take microscopic cells from the lump and put them onto a glass slide for further examination. This is called a fine needle aspirate (FNA). Sometimes it is possible to tell by looking at these cells under a microscope whether they are cancer cells. I say sometimes because it is not always clear, and depends on how good a sample is obtained and how abnormal the cells are. Also, if the cells are normal cells, this may mean that the doctor has just missed the right area. The needle test is not as painful as it sounds and, in my experience, many women do not find it painful at all. A local anaesthetic would be equally as painful, so most doctors do not give one. After the needle has been withdrawn it is important to apply some pressure onto the area so that no bruising occurs. Bruising does not imply anything serious about your lump, it just means that pressure has not been applied in the right place, or for long enough. If you do get bruising then this can make mammograms or ultrasounds difficult to interpret. It is preferable to have these other tests done before the needle test, just in case bruising does occur.

Biopsy

Sometimes using the fine needle means that not enough cells are obtained so that a larger needle needs to be used. This is called a biopsy, or sometimes a trucut or core biopsy. A local anaesthetic is used and it is common to get some bruising afterwards.

Mammogram

A mammogram is an X-ray taken of the breast. The breast is placed between two X-ray plates and squeezed to try and get it flat. This way a much more accurate picture can be obtained. The reason for this is that the breast is three-dimensional and the picture to be obtained is two-dimensional. If the breast is flattened when the picture is taken, then the image is much more focused. It is also the norm to have two views taken, one top to bottom and one at a slant. This is because your chest wall is curved and one flat image will not get in all the breast tissue. Many women I have spoken to say that the compression of the breast is very uncomfortable, but that it is over quickly. When they understand why it has to be squeezed so tight it helps, so that they realise the radiographer is not just in a bad mood that day! If you can relax your muscles, this helps it to be less uncomfortable. Some women say that for them it is actually painful, so if you are anxious about this or have had previous mammograms that were painful, then I recommend that you take some painkillers beforehand.

Ultrasound

Mammograms are not normally as useful in younger women because the breasts contain more active tissue than older breasts, and this makes a mammogram difficult to read. In this case an ultrasound is more useful. There is no radiation used here, and using high frequency sound waves has no known side-effects. Some gel is put on the breast, and a blunt-ended probe is slid across the breast. An image is seen on a screen, which is interpreted by the doctor, or radiographer, doing the scan. They may need the room to be darkened in order to be able to see the image clearly. Ultrasound is particularly useful at detecting breast cysts. These can be drained and then they usually disappear. Most women that I have come across find ultrasound a fairly straightforward test and quite tolerable. If someone has particularly tender breasts then the pressure of the ultrasound probe over the skin can make them sore but this is not common.

Students

It is very common for consultants at specialist centres to be accompanied by students or visitors. You should be asked if you mind the students being present. Sometimes you may not be asked until they are actually in the room. If you do mind then it is all right to say so; it will not affect your care at all and no one will be offended. I know that often women find this difficult as they do not want to be awkward, but most health professionals realise that women feel particularly vulnerable at this time and consider it perfectly reasonable if you do not want students around.

Results

In some places the results of all these tests can be given on the same day. If this is the case, then you are likely to be at the hospital for a long time. In other places you will need to come back on another day for the results. The waiting can be the worst time – not knowing what to expect can be very difficult to deal with (see Chapter 1 on coping). If given the option to have the results on the same day, most people will say that of course they want them as soon as possible. My view is that it is exhausting, both physically and emotionally, to get the results on the same day as the tests. If the results are given on a different day people have more time to reflect on what their options might be and how they will cope. I have known women who have been perfectly well one day and who have been told the next day that they have cancer and need a mastectomy. Later they say that it was all too quick and that they did not have time to think about what they really wanted. Nevertheless, you should not have to wait more than a few days or a week at the outside. Never go away without knowing whom you can contact in case you have any worries before your next appointment.

Understanding what this means for you

Sometimes the interpretation of the tests is very straightforward and doctors are able to be quite specific about what they recommend. This is helpful as then you can get on with trying to work out what choices you have, what impact this will have on you and how you will cope with it.

Sometimes the tests are not so easy to interpret and you may need to undergo further tests or even surgery to take out the lump before it can be identified for certain. The doctors need to weigh up the evidence from the different tests and decide what is the best treatment for you. If you are a young woman and tend to have lumpy breasts, then it is unlikely to be cancer. In this case it would be unwise to take out every lump that you find. First of all it would create unnecessary scars on your breast and could change the shape of it. It would also cause internal scarring. This can be a problem because it makes it difficult to feel the breast and tell if a cancerous lump has grown. It also makes mammograms difficult to read.

Uncertainty can be one of the hardest things to deal with. Some women say 'Prepare for the worst and hope for the best'. If you work out strategies to deal with 'the worst' then it is much easier to cope if your fears are confirmed.

What does this mean for the future?

When people are given a diagnosis of cancer, they often believe that this means that they will die very soon. One woman asked me if there was any point in watering her flowers any longer as she thought that she would be dead before them! This is very far from the truth. Most women treated for breast cancer will be well with no sign of disease in ten years from diagnosis, and for many it never comes back. This is clearly not the case for everyone and so each individual wants to know what her own chances are. No one can tell a woman for certain what will happen to her in the future but there are signs that suggest that cancer is more likely to come back in some women than in others. Doctors tend to give these chances in percentages. The number of people living at ten years after diagnosis is known as the survival rate.

The information that the doctors have about your chance of a cure is mostly gained after the cancer has actually been removed, although they can give you some information before the operation.

The indicators that are used to work out these figures are:

- size of the original tumour
- grade of tumour
- whether there is any spread to the lymph nodes in the armpit
- how many lymph nodes are involved
- whether the tumour contains oestrogen receptors.

Size of the original tumour

This is fairly straightforward as the smaller the tumour the better. If the lump cannot be felt it is referred to as a T0 tumour, where the T refers to the tumour and the 0 to the size. When it is smaller than 2cm in diameter it is T1 and so forth. A 2.5cm lump is T2 and over 5cm is T3. Some tumours have actually caused an ulcer on the skin and this is a T4 tumour irrespective of how big it is. Survival rates of those with T3 or T4 tumours are much lower than for those who have small tumours at diagnosis.

Grade of tumour

This is much more complex than size, but also very important. Some women with very large tumours when they are first diagnosed can live for many years after the appropriate treatment. This is when the tumour is much more slow growing. An attempt is made to estimate how quickly the cells in a tumour will grow by describing them carefully after surgery, when the pathologist looks at the cancer tissue under the microscope. Some cancers contain cells that still look and behave rather like the breast cells from which they have arisen, even though they are abnormal and growing without the proper controls. Others are extremely abnormal and it is difficult to tell that they originally came from breast tissue. The grade given to the cancer is an indication of how abnormal the cells appear to be. When the cells are very abnormal it is more common for them to grow and spread more quickly and they are more often associated with a worse outlook. Grade I is the least aggressive type; Grade III is the most aggressive type, but it is difficult to be precise about these grades and pathologists can disagree.

Any spread to the lymph nodes in the armpit

If there is any sign of cancer having spread to the lymph nodes, this indicates that there is a possibility that other microscopic cells may have spread elsewhere in the body, but cannot be detected. In this case it is usual to offer an additional (or adjuvant) treatment that is able to treat cancer wherever it may be in the body. This treatment can take the form of chemotherapy or hormone therapy (see Chapter 9).

How many lymph nodes are involved

The fewer nodes that are involved the better, as the more that are affected, the higher the chance that some cells have spread elsewhere in the body.

Whether the tumour contains oestrogen receptors

Cells in normal breast tissue have areas on the surface of the cell which can recognise the oestrogen hormone, and so the cell is able to respond to stimulus by oestrogen. Cancer cells that are still similar to the original cells from which they have arisen still have oestrogen receptor sites. This means that they are more likely to be affected by hormone treatments, such as tamoxifen. In general, oestrogen receptor-positive tumours have a better outlook than oestrogen receptor-negative ones.

Trials

You may be concerned about the necessity of trials. One clinical trial co-ordinator I know asks the women's groups that she speaks to: 'Are you satisfied with the level of cure that we can offer to women with breast cancer?' Most people would reply 'No' to this. There is a need, therefore, to carry out clinical trials to improve treatment and decrease the side-effects of the treatments that are offered. This does not mean that doctors do not know what they are doing, but rather that they are always trying to find something better than what is already available. Val asked me why they always seem to be changing their mind: 'First they said two years of tamoxifen and now they are saying five!' The answer is simple – people always want the latest and the best. If the latest and best drugs are used, then there will still be lots to learn about them, and the more they are used, the more will be known. Questions such as 'How long is the best time to give a drug?' can only be answered if large studies are done with people taking that drug.

Now that most breast cancer treatment is carried out in specialist centres, it is usual to find that doctors in these centres will be involved in trials for new treatments and new ways of carrying out old treatments. There are some figures to show that women who are treated in centres where trials are routinely carried out have a better chance of cure than women who are treated elsewhere. It is also common to have more extensive tests and more careful follow-up if you are in a trial. And being in a trial brings hope: the extra hope that comes out of a new treatment, even though it has not yet been proved. Sometimes this can buoy you up during your treatment. Some women also feel that they are contributing in a positive way for the future, and giving something back to the system that has helped them.

Consequently, it is very likely that you will be asked if you mind taking part in a trial, and maybe more than one. Current medical ethics mean that the treatment you are being offered is either known to be as good as the best available treatment or that it is expected that it will be better. Most modern trials involve one group having the new treatment regimen and another group having the current best standard treatment as a comparison. This comparison group is known as the control group. If you are entered into a trial of this kind you will not be able to choose which of the two treatment regimens you will receive, and nor will your doctors. All clinical trials in this country have to go through strict medical ethics committees before they are approved for people to enter. These committees are made up of scientists (to ensure that the trial is valid and not just wasting your time and effort), doctors and nurses, and also people who are not involved in medicine at all. The hospital chaplain is often asked to be on the ethics committee as he can represent a very different view.

It should be explained very clearly to you exactly what is involved in the trial. This should include information about any new drugs, and whether any new techniques are being used. If extra tests will be required to monitor your progress during the trial this should also be explained to you. You should always receive written information. If you are uncertain about the trial there is no pressure for you to take part. Your treatment will be just as good, whether you choose to take part or not. You may be asked to sign a consent form. This is only to ensure that you have had a proper explanation and does not take away any of your rights. If you want to withdraw from the trial at any time this is perfectly all right. Your treatment and follow-up will be exactly the same even if you do withdraw from the trial. It will affect the trial as every person who is entered into the study in the first place is followed up as though they are still in the study. If you drop out, then it may weaken the results. This is why you should think through carefully whether you want to enter in the first place. However, if you are in the trial and you become unhappy about it, then ultimately you have to think about what is right for you.

One of the biggest problems about trials is that you are probably still trying to cope with the idea that you have cancer and making up your mind about what is the best sort of treatment for you. It took me over ten years to learn what I know about breast cancer. Yet women who get the disease have to find out what they need to know and make decisions about treatments that affect the rest of their life, and they only have a few days to do this. I used to feel that I would like to run a week-long course for women who had just been diagnosed with cancer, teaching them everything they needed to know before they had to make any decisions about treatment. If you feel that you would like a week-long course, how do you go about getting this information? There are lots of sources of help and information that will be discussed in the next section. My advice is to ask everyone everything you can think of. If they think someone else can answer your questions better, they will find that person for you. If you don't ask, they may think that you do not want to know.

Who to ask what

Some people cope with gathering as much information as they can about their illness and treatment. Others rely on the doctors to let them know what is necessary. After all, they are the specialists and they should know best. It can also be very difficult to take in everything that you need to know, especially if it is still near the time of your diagnosis and you are trying to adjust to that, but one of the most frequent complaints about medical care is that people feel they do not get enough information. It can be very hard for doctors to judge just exactly what to say and how much information to give. They have to take their cue from you. The more that you ask, the more they will tell you. For example, Val often says that she likes to know everything that she can, but she did choose not to see any photos before she had her reconstruction. Everyone has a limit. Only you know what yours is and you probably don't know that until you start testing it. It is worth considering this before you see your doctor. Exactly what do you want to know from him and how much do you want to leave in his hands?

The other thing to remember is that some people are better at communicating than others. And you may find that you click with one person more than another. Make sure that you identify and know how to contact someone at the hospital whom you know you can talk to if you have any concerns.

Breast care nurse

Every specialist centre should have a specialist nurse you can call on. She is often called the breast care nurse. This is someone you can ask for advice, information or where to get additional help for specific problems. Very often the breast care nurse carries a bleep or pager so that you can just ring the hospital switchboard and ask for her. Some even have a direct line. If you don't get through, most also have answer phones, so it is worth asking the switchboard if you can leave a message. Not every switchboard will have all this information so if your breast care nurse gives you a card with her details, keep it handy.

When I worked in this role I (or one of the nurses who worked with me) used to try to see every person as they were told that they had cancer, so that they would know who we were and how we could help. Sometimes this was not possible and we would try and contact them later. Some people found we could provide lots of useful information and support. Others just liked to have our number in case they needed us, but never actually called. We did find that the hospital experience could be very confusing for women, as there are different doctors for every part of their treatment: surgery, radiotherapy and chemotherapy. We were the only people who could be a constant point of reference throughout all the treatments. One woman told me that I was the only person of whom she felt she could ask anything. Other women did not use me very much, preferring to rely on their doctors for information. Others find that they get all the support that they need from their friends and family, and that the breast care nurse is an unnecessary extra. But even those who have very close families sometimes find it helpful to talk to someone outside the family. In fact, sometimes it is when families are very close that women don't want to moan for fear of letting the side down. Or they don't want to say something hurtful when they know that everyone is really trying hard to help. Having an outsider to bat some of these ideas about with can help to ease the tension.

Breast care nurses do have a reputation for being a bit sentimental. We have an in-joke that all breast care nurses have to develop a 'head-on-one-side' posture before they get the job. I remember one woman who said that I was scaring her, because I looked so concerned. However, I was concerned because she was so anxious, rather than because there was anything bad about her condition. In the end, the nurse is there to help you, so make use of her. If you find her a bit overwhelming, you could say that you find it really helpful to have the information but you can't cope with her concern.

Most breast care nurses are not trained counsellors (although a few are). They generally have some basic counselling skills to help you through key times, such as at diagnosis or before surgery. If you feel that you need more help, then ask her to help you to find a therapeutic counsellor or clinical psychologist. How do you know when to ask? If you find that it is getting harder, instead of easier, to cope as you go along, or if you find that you are unable to do the things you normally do, due to anxiety or feeling dispirited, then this is the time to ask. This is not a matter of being weak. Cancer is not easy to deal with and different people find that they need help in different ways.

Although you are introduced to the breast care nurse at diagnosis and she will often keep in touch with you around the time of surgery, her role is not limited to these times. If you are having chemotherapy or radio-therapy and are not sure to whom to turn for information, advice or to talk through some worries, she is available for you then too. She is also a good person to get in touch with in between long-term follow up appoint-ments, if you are worried about anything. Women often feel that their concerns are too trivial to bother the doctor with, but if you are worried, then you need to check it out and your breast care nurse could be a good person with whom to do this. I have spoken to many people who are desperately worried about something that is nothing to do with their cancer and I have been able to put their minds at rest. If I can't do this, then I can get them an early appointment to see the doctor.

If you have not been given the contact details of any individual, but want to know what is happening to your referral or any other informa-tion, a good point of contact is the secretary of the consultant to whom you have been referred. If you are still not getting anywhere, then get back to your GP.

Doctors

You will meet a lot of different doctors in your breast cancer journey. They all have a slightly different job and it can feel as though no one really has a clear idea of what is going on for you. One woman recounted that she had been coming to the hospital for four years and in that time had met 19 doctors! This is partly because all the junior doctors are training to be consultants and they do not stay in a job for more than one year at a time. The consultants usually see women at diagnosis and at key times during treatment, but do not necessarily see you on every visit and this becomes more and more infrequent as time goes by. In fact, in specialist centres it can be quite rare to see the consultant. In this case the person that you see most often is a Senior (or Specialist) Registrar. These doctors have many years' experience and are working towards their consultancy post. Initially, some women are concerned that they do not see the consultant, but the registrars are very able to deal with your care and once a relation-ship builds up you may find that you prefer to see them.

The doctors' role is to make a diagnosis and decide on the most appro-priate treatment. They will only give advice about the treatment in which they specialise. In cancer care, as you have a variety of different treat-ments, this means you need a team of specialists. The team should liaise about the best programme of treatment for you, but you will need to ask each specialist about the details of care that they recommend.

Surgeon

The first specialist that you see will normally be a surgeon. Doctors who have completed their training to be a surgeon are referred to as 'Mister', rather than 'Doctor'.

Many surgeons perform a wide variety of surgery, but anyone doing breast cancer surgery should be specialised in this area. They may still do other kinds of surgery as well, but they should see at least 100 women a year with breast cancer. Not every breast cancer surgeon does reconstructive surgery and so may work in partnership with a plastic surgeon. If you need a reconstruction, you may want to think about whether you want two different surgeons – one for the cancer and one for the reconstruction – or whether you would like to be referred to someone who can do both.

Oncologist or radiotherapist

An oncologist is a doctor who specialises in the medical (or drug) treatment of cancer. A radiotherapist is a doctor who specialises in the use of radiation to treat cancer. Sometimes they are the same person. The radiotherapist is the doctor who prescribes your radiation treatment, how much you should have and how it should be given, but he does not actually give the radiation. A radiographer will do this.

A radiologist is also a doctor, but one whom you are unlikely to meet. This person also uses radiation, but uses it for diagnostic purposes, ie X-rays and scans. The radiographer is the technical person who takes the X-rays and the scans, and the radiologist is the doctor who reads them. There are, therefore, two types of radiographer as well: the diagnostic radiographer who uses radiation for diagnosis and a therapeutic radiographer who actually gives the radiation used to treat cancer.

Other doctors

Doctors can specialise in any area of medicine and so you may find yourself being referred to a variety of specialists, depending on your problem. For example, when you have surgery, you will see an anaesthetist. This person is a doctor who specialises in anaesthetics and pain control, and who will look after you during surgery. If after surgery you are suffering pain that the surgical doctors do not seem to be able to help, then you may be referred to a pain specialist.

Levels of doctor

Every area of speciality within medicine has a consultant, who is the most senior doctor on the team. Each consultant has junior doctors working with him or her. These doctors have all qualified to practise medicine, but are in training in the speciality. After doctors pass their initial exams, they become a house doctor, then a senior house doctor, then a registrar and then a senior or specialist registrar. The more junior the doctor, the more areas they need to work in, in order to train. This means that they will not stay long in any one place. The only permanent doctors are the consultants.

Clinical psychologist

A clinical psychologist is a person who has specialised in psychology: a study of why people react and behave in the way that they do. As they understand about behaviour, they are often able to help people to work out ways of coping with what is happening to them. Often in times of shock or crisis, our minds are in such a whirl that it is hard to make sense of what is going on. A psychologist can sometimes help us to understand these processes and make it a bit easier to manage.

Physiotherapist

You may meet a physiotherapist after surgery. They are concerned with helping to ensure that your body is functioning to the best of its ability. You will be familiar with sports physios helping athletes recover after they have been injured, and in a way, your body is injured by surgery. The physiotherapist will help by giving you exercises in order to ensure your full recovery. After breast surgery you will normally be given arm exercises, but only if you have had surgery under the arm. If you have not been given any exercises, then you should ask to see a physiotherapist. If you are still experiencing arm stiffness some weeks after surgery, you should also ask to see a physio.

Occupational therapist

The occupational therapist is a professional who is trained in the use of techniques and aids to help you adjust to changes in what you are able to do. They are associated with providing wheelchairs and special aids for the home, but they are also trained in stress management and may be able to teach you relaxation techniques to help you cope with your stay in hospital.

Dietician

Most people are familiar with the idea of a dietician being able to help with a weight-reducing diet, and you may find that you have trouble with your weight while taking certain medicines. They are also able to advise on a wide range of eating-related queries. You may want to talk about what would be a healthy diet after having had breast cancer, or to discuss the use of diets recommended by practitioners in complementary medicine.

Complementary therapist

Some hospitals provide complementary medicines to help you through the breast cancer experience. This is because they recognise that these therapies may have something to offer in addition to what you can gain from traditional medicine. Most doctors are happy for you to use complementary therapies as they recognise that this is your choice. They would be concerned if you were using a complementary therapy *instead* of conventional medicine, but they would recognise that that is also your choice. The hospital may have a masseur, reflexologist or aromatherapist and some hospitals provide access to acupuncture.

Support groups

There may be a support group in your hospital run by the breast care nurse or clinical psychologist. These can be helpful for sharing ideas with other women in the same situation as you. A group can help you feel less alone as you get to know other people going through the same traumas that you are facing. However, you may find that you have to face their distress at times when they need support and this kind of sharing is not helpful for everyone. There are a variety of types of support group: some are led by volunteers and some by professionals. If you want to go to one, I suggest that before you go you find out all you can about what they try to accomplish as a group and go with an open mind.

Voluntary organisations

There are a variety of organisations that offer help, advice and information. There is a comprehensive list at the back of this book. Some, like Cancerlink (see Useful Addresses), will put you in touch with support groups as discussed above, while others are there primarily to provide information. Breast Cancer Care is the main organisation that specially caters for women with breast cancer. They will put you in touch with other women who have had breast cancer, provide loads of information about breast cancer and will also fit and provide breast prostheses and bras. They even have a partner's network, for partners to chat over the telephone to get support from someone else who has been there.

Friends and family

While it goes without saying that your friends and your family will be your main source of help, it is not always easy to know how to tap into this. Val has talked about this in some of the previous chapters. You will need to decide who you want to know about your cancer, and when you have decided this you will need to think about how you want to approach those people. Sometimes, thinking of practical things that they can do to help is a great way of coping with their uncertainties. Everyone likes to know what they can do to help.

Written information

You should get lots of written information from all sorts of people involved in your care. If you need written information and don't get it, ask for it. The breast care nurse is a good source of information; she may have books and even videos that you can borrow.

Follow-up visits and investigations

After you have finished all your treatment for breast cancer, you will be asked to return to the hospital on a regular basis for check-ups. Usually the doctor will examine your breast and ask you how you have been. If you have noticed any changes in your health, or if there is anything you are worried about you should mention it at this time. You should also raise any queries that you might have about side-effects. Most people get very anxious about these visits and when they arrive at the hospital they find that they are in and out in a few moments. It all seems a lot of worry and you don't get a lot out of it. So how can you make the most of these visits? I think it is very helpful to make a list of queries before you go. Tell your doctor that you have a list as soon as you see him. He may want to save answering the questions until he has examined you, but at least this way he knows in advance.

The other thing to know is that it is very unusual for the doctor to find something of which you are not already aware. You should tell the doctor if you are concerned by any of the following: any unusual lumps; pain that will not go away; shortness of breath; lack of appetite and weight loss; and unexplained weakness or headache. If you get any of these in between your appointments and you are worried about them, then do not wait for your scheduled appointment. Ring up and ask to be seen sooner. I personally think it would be more helpful if women were not given any appointments other than for their yearly mammogram, but were advised to return to the hospital if they were worried about anything.

Mammograms

You should get a repeat mammogram at least every two years. This is the one test that might throw up something unexpected because it can pick up very early changes in your breast that you are not aware of. It can find a new cancer in the other breast, or can detect early recurrence. A mammogram is a good way to find cancer in the breast as it can be detected very early and the outcome of treatment is better when cancer is found early.

Private health care

Many people now have private health care and feel that this is a good time to use the benefits that it brings. The vast majority of what I have described will be the same whether you are having your care under the NHS or private care. You may be able to get to see a specialist more quickly, but on the whole most NHS clinics will see you very quickly if it is thought that you have cancer. There are a few other advantages. These are mostly about convenience rather than whether you get better care. You should always see the consultant personally rather than one of his team and you may be allocated a longer time to consult him. When you need to spend any time in hospital you will normally have a private room with private washroom facilities. This can be a great boon when you are feeling ill and vulnerable and makes it easier to sleep at night. However, some people prefer to be in the company of others and may feel isolated in a single room. If you choose to have all your treatment as a private patient it may be worth checking out whether your plan covers the whole course of treatment as some plans are rather limited.

Six questions to ask when you go to the hospital:

What tests will I have?

Why am I having these tests?

What do they mean?

Who can be with me?

When will I get the results?

What services does this hospital provide to help me through this experience?

8
Surgery and reconstruction

Most people with breast cancer will need some form of surgery at some time. There may be occasions when chemotherapy or tamoxifen is given before surgery, but there is nearly always a decision to be made about what sort of surgery is going to be performed. These days most surgeons are keen not to remove the whole breast as the evidence shows that women who have the lump removed and have radiotherapy do just as well as those who have the whole breast removed. Unfortunately, there are still circumstances when a mastectomy is required, such as when the lump is large, or it is positioned right behind the nipple. In this case some women may prefer to have a breast reconstruction. Not every surgeon is skilled in reconstruction, in which case you may need to have the mastectomy first and a reconstruction done later by a plastic surgeon. There will be lots of issues of this nature that you will need to discuss with your surgeon. If your surgeon cannot offer you what you want or need, always remember that you can ask to see someone else.

Going into hospital

You will usually be admitted to hospital the day before surgery so that final checks can be made about your general health. Some places will do this on an outpatient basis so that you can go in on the morning of the operation. It is usual not to have anything to eat or drink for some hours before you have a general anaesthetic as the drugs can make some people sick, which could be dangerous when you are under the influence of the anaesthetic. If you know your operation is late in the day you can have a light breakfast and it is a good idea to have a drink.

What to take
The disadvantages of hospitals are: hard beds, plastic covered pillows, food you are not accustomed to and a general lack of privacy and comfort.

There is not a lot of room to put many personal possessions, but those that increase your comfort are worth having with you.

Suggested list:
pillow
dressing gown and slippers
well-fitting bras (it can be more comfortable to wear a bra over your
   dressing as it supports the breast)
night wear (pyjamas may be best as then your top half can be
   examined without you having to get completely undressed)
squash and nibbles (such as biscuits)
tissues
light, easy-to-wear and comfortable clothes, such as a track suit
   (which you can wear over bulky dressings the day after surgery)
a cassette radio with ear plugs and cassettes
earplugs and eye shades if you are bothered by other people around
   you at night
books/magazines – you will be surprised how little you want to do
   and how poor your concentration is
toiletries and towel (they will supply a towel but you may prefer
   your own)

While most hospitals will cater for special diets the choice is often limited and you may want to bring in snack food that is more to your taste. There may also be simple meals that the hospital is prepared to provide to order, such as omelettes, soup, fruit and yogurt.

Choice of surgery

Lumpectomy

If the lump is small enough, the surgeon can just cut out the cancer, plus an area of tissue around the lump which looks as though it is clear of cancer. This is to make sure that no cancer is left behind which could not be seen at the time of surgery. This is usually called a lumpectomy, although some surgeons refer to it as a wide local excision. Sometimes it is called a quadrantectomy. The more tissue that is removed at surgery, the bigger the scar will be and the more likely it is that your breast will alter in shape as a result. The type and size of scar will also vary depending on where the lump is in your breast. It is worth checking with your surgeon exactly how much of the breast tissue he intends to remove and what the scar will look like. You may also need to know if the breast will have a dent in it, if it will be the same size as the other breast and if the position of the nipple will be affected at all. If you have any concerns about the expected result, ask him what your options are.

After the operation

After the operation, most women feel well enough to get up the next day (or even sometimes the same day). For many people it is not particularly painful and a few paracetamol seem to control the discomfort. If you have more pain than this, don't put up with it. Everyone has a different experience of pain and there are stronger painkillers that can easily be used. If you have pain, then it stops you from doing the things that you want to do.

As long as there is no leakage, it is best to leave the dressing over the wound undisturbed. Stitches are removed about 7–10 days afterwards. During this time you can reduce the chance of introducing infection by keeping the dressing or wound dry. If the dressing does get wet, or if there is any leakage, it can be changed and a clean light dressing used in its place. Infection is unusual but can occur. Signs to look out for are increased soreness, redness around the wound (or dressing), a rise in your general temperature or feeling generally unwell. While you are in hospital you will find that the nurses check your temperature regularly, to monitor possible signs of infection.

A nurse will usually remove stitches in the outpatient department. Most people find this a straightforward process. I have had occasions when I have prepared people, taken out the stitches, and then they have asked me when I am going to start! After the stitches have been removed, you can wash the area as normal.

After-effects of surgery

In the first few weeks after any surgery people generally feel tired. In the first few days after breast surgery I have noticed that some women have an immediate buzz and feel much better than they expected. I think there are lots of reasons for this: the operation and the awful waiting are over; something has finally been done towards the road to recovery; and, often, they don't feel as ill as they had thought they would. When they get home sometimes there is a real low patch. Tiredness catches up with them and there is no one around to ask for help if anything goes wrong. The body is giving a message and the answer is to rest when feeling tired.

Complications following surgery

Pain

You might expect an operation on the breast to be particularly painful. This is not normally the case. People are often surprised how little pain there is. Clearly the larger the operation, the more pain there is and surgery under the arm is often more painful than in the breast itself. Regular use of a mild painkiller for a few days may be all that you need. It is worth taking these as you are unlikely to do yourself any damage and you will get back to normal more quickly if you are not being held back by being in pain. Very rarely, people are left with pain that does not go away for months and months. This is not normal and you should tell your doctor if it happens. They may refer you to a pain specialist who should be able to help.

Numbness

If nerves have been cut during surgery, there may be areas that are numb. This happens with surgery in the armpit, when the back of the arm has a numb patch, which is strange at first. The feeling in this area may return, but often does not. It is a bit weird to get used to but is nothing to be alarmed about.

Infection

Any surgical wound can become infected, although this is not the norm. An infection can be easily cleared up with antibiotics. If not treated early it can make you feel quite unwell and delays healing. The scar that is left as a result may also be more unsightly as it may be larger. It is worth looking out for any signs, such as increasing soreness, redness or heat on the skin, or a general body temperature. Larger operations and reconstructions are more vulnerable to infection, in which case you may receive antibiotics to prevent the infection from occurring in the first place. These are referred to as prophylactic antibiotics.

Seroma – collection of fluid

Where body tissues have been damaged it is quite common for liquid to accumulate in the area. This is usually a clear, straw-coloured fluid called serum. If this does not drain away internally, but gathers into a lump, it is called a seroma. This is not dangerous but may be uncomfortable. If you get leakage of serous fluid, put a padding over the top of your dressing and see your doctor at the earliest opportunity.

Haematoma – collection of blood

A collection of blood under the surface is called a haematoma. This is like a large bruise and will discolour the skin in the same way as a bruise. It may also form into a clot and will then feel like a hard lump under the skin. This takes a long time to disperse and may lead to the formation of scar tissue. If there is a large amount of this it may cause the skin to pucker as it heals.

Scar tissue

It is common to feel scar tissue as a hard lump just under the skin. This can be a bit scary, as it can feel just like the cancer lump, or even bigger or harder than the original cancer. If you are worried about any lumps you should ask your surgeon, but at this stage it is almost certain to be scar tissue. As scars age they get shorter and fatter. This means that they can pucker the skin, although this does not usually happen. Scar tissue can be kept more soft and mobile by gently rubbing the area with a moisturising cream. Some experts believe that vitamin E can aid local healing. This massage should not be done in the first week or two when initial healing is still occurrng. The size and shape of the scar will depend on the size of the lump and the amount of tissue needing to be removed. You should ask your surgeon where, what shape and how big the scar will be, and if you have any options about this.

Cording – strings of fibrous tissue

In the weeks or months after surgery, the body sometimes reacts with an inflammatory response that causes long strings, or cords, of fibrous tissue down the arm or the side of the body. This may just be noticeable in the crook of the elbow or armpit, or you may be able to feel it all the way down your arm. These cords are not dangerous, but may be uncomfortable and it is important to keep them stretched as otherwise they may restrict the movement in your arm. You should ask to see a physiotherapist if they occur so that they can advise you and monitor your progress. These cords tend to disappear over time, but can take many months to resolve completely.

Surgery in the axilla, or armpit

It is normal for the lymph nodes under the armpit (or axilla in medical terms) to be removed at the same time as the breast lump. This is done to give further information about the disease and also to remove any disease that has spread to these nodes. At the time of surgery it is usually not possible to see if these nodes contain cancer cells; this can only be determined by examining them under the microscope afterwards. It is, therefore, difficult to know how many to remove. Some women do not need any nodes at all to be removed. This may be the case with very tiny cancers or those that are only DCIS (see previous chapter). It is hoped that in the future a very small cut could be made to remove only the first node. This is called a sentinel node biopsy. If this node is clear of cancer, then no further surgery will be needed. However, it is not yet certain whether this is appropriate as there is a possibility that other nodes will contain cancer cells even if the sentinel node does not. It is currently the norm to remove all the nodes that can be easily reached. Different people have different numbers of nodes in this area – usually about 10–15, but it can be anything up to 40.

Breast tissue has a good blood supply and so after surgery it is possible for internal bleeding to continue. To prevent bruising and the accumulation of blood it is common to have one or two drains into the breast, but there is not usually very much bleeding and after a day or two the drains are removed. The biggest problem with the drains is forgetting that they are there! It is easy to walk off and leave them behind, only to be brought up short. Sometimes they have a hook so you can hook them onto your bed. A useful tip is to put them into a bag and then you can carry them around discreetly. It can be easier to manage the drain tubes if you wear short tops, such as pyjamas, or sweat shirts, rather than a long night-gown. Once the drains are removed you can usually go home. Removing the drains is a simple procedure that takes place at your bedside and is done by the nurses. They will release the vacuum on the drain, take out the stitch holding it in place, and gently pull it out. For the majority of people this is a very simple procedure; they have a weird sensation as the drain comes out, but virtually no pain. For a small minority it can be quite painful, but it is over very quickly. If you are worried about it then you can take some painkillers beforehand and practise some deep breathing.

Surgery in the axilla is more likely to cause pain and reduced movement than breast surgery. The more lymph nodes that are taken, the more surgery that is required and the more severe the possible after-effects. Immediately after the operation, this area is quite sore and it is uncomfortable to raise the arm. Most surgeons advise that you practise certain exercises to help ensure a speedy return to normal. A nurse or physiotherapist should advise you about these. It is not a good idea to be too active very early on as this can cause increased swelling locally. It is not uncommon for a collection of fluid to gather under the armpit during the first week or so after surgery. This is a clear, straw-coloured fluid called serum. It is not normally painful, but can be a bit uncomfortable. It can be drained off if necessary.

It always takes a couple of weeks to get over any surgery. Regaining full use of your arm again may take 3–6 weeks. The sort of things that you will find difficult will be some domestic chores, such as hanging out washing or lifting heavy pans, so this is a good time to say 'yes' to all those people who offer help. On the whole it is beneficial to use your arm as normally as you can. If you need a mild painkiller to do this, then take it, as it will speed your recovery. You may worry that you will overuse your arm if you have dulled the pain, but you can do just as much damage by being overprotective. The trick is to get the right balance. Do gentle, everyday things, but nothing to excess. One young woman did feel that perhaps the 20 lengths she did in the swimming pool a couple of weeks after surgery might have contributed to the swelling that gathered in her arm and breast the next day!

You will usually be given some exercises to help get back to normal. If you are not told what to do then ask to see a physiotherapist or breast care nurse.

Mastectomy and breast reconstruction

A mastectomy is removal of all the breast tissue. This means all the milk-producing part of the breast, which are the ducts and the lobes, and usually also means the nipple, but not the skin. It should be possible to do this operation and leave a fairly neat scar across the chest wall. It used to be common to remove the muscle underneath the breast as well. This was called a radical mastectomy and left quite a dent in the chest wall, as well as some weakness due to the loss of muscle, but this is rarely necessary now.

For most people it should be possible to perform a breast reconstruction at the same time as the mastectomy. There was a school of thought that said it was safer to leave the reconstruction until at least a year after the original surgery in order to watch for possible recurrence in the site of the mastectomy, and to be sure that the reconstruction did not hide recurrence. This has been shown to be an unfounded fear. Problems that can occur are on the skin or just below the surface. There may be other reasons why immediate reconstruction is not recommended; if your surgeon suggests you avoid reconstruction, ask him for specific reasons. One of the reasons could be that the cancer surgeon is not trained or experienced enough to carry out reconstructive work. If your hospital has only a few women every year who want a reconstruction, then the surgeon will not be able to keep his skills up to date. In this case, you may be better off going to another surgeon who is more skilled in this area, such as a plastic surgeon, for your reconstruction.

However, a mastectomy with reconstruction is a bigger operation and some women will choose not to have this. They may feel quite happy to manage with a prosthesis (or without one). Some women say that they have never had much of a bust anyway so they won't miss it, others say that because they have always been small, they don't want to lose what they have got. It is easiest to get a good match for an average-sized bust. Someone with large breasts may find that the imbalance in weight causes difficulty with clothing and can be quite uncomfortable. In this case a reconstruction may not be perfect, but may be easier to manage than a large prosthesis.

A reconstructed breast is never quite like the original and in many cases it is quite different. Surgeons talk about forming a breast 'mound'. This is designed to be the same size and shape as the original breast, but as all breasts are different, this is not always an easy task. It is also common to lose the nipple, which makes quite a difference to the overall shape. Not only does it not look the same, but it does not feel the same either. There is often reduced sensation in the skin and sometimes significant numbness. Some women describe the reconstructed breast as being colder. When an implant is used it does not behave in the same way as normal breast tissue. It is very hard to achieve the normal 'droop' of breast tissue and implants are always a bit firmer and rounder. As one gets older this difference can become more marked. If a person loses or gains weight after surgery, an implant will stay the same, while the natural breast may alter size. It is possible to replace the implant if this happens.

One woman I cared for described how perfection was very important to her. She felt that with reconstruction she ran the risk of achieving a result that was not perfect in her eyes and that she would never be satisfied with it. However, having looked at the prostheses that we had to offer she felt she could achieve a good match when clothed. Then if she changed shape, she could change her prosthesis without any difficulty.

Others say that to have a breast missing is a constant reminder of having had cancer and that once they had their reconstruction they could put cancer behind them. Whatever you choose, it has to be right for you, rather than what your surgeon or anyone else thinks is the best thing for you.

Whether you are young or old is not necessarily a predictor of whether reconstruction is right for you. I have known young women who are very confident of themselves and their bodies, who say that they can't be bothered with the extra surgery. If their normal lifestyle is casual and their normal clothing jeans and baggy shirts, then a reconstruction may not be worth the effort. The older I get, the more I think I would choose a reconstruction if I were faced with the choice. As my body ages and I notice the wrinkles more, I begin to think that I would like to hang on to whatever I have got. Single women tend to express concerns about how to manage new relationships and a mastectomy can be a barrier to intimacy. How do you tell a new partner that you only have one breast? Is it easier just to avoid the situation? A reconstruction can make this a little easier.

Although things can go wrong with reconstruction, I feel that the biggest problems occur for those people who do not have a clear idea of what they are getting and why they want a reconstruction. I have known women who have a reconstruction that looks great, but they hate it because it was not what they expected. Conversely, I have known some women who have had reconstructions that were well below average in the way they look, but the women were perfectly happy because it gave them what they wanted.

How can you tell what your reconstruction will look like? This is difficult to answer, as everyone is different. An average 36B is probably the easiest size to match well. If you have very large or very small breasts it is much harder to match your own breast. A reconstructed breast tends to be quite round, so if your own breasts are pointed or droopy then this is less likely to be achieved. Most surgeons will have photographs of some of the work they have done. These are helpful to look at as they give you a much more realistic idea of what you might get. I always showed women a variety of photos so that they could see how different each person is. One thing to beware of is that most of these photos do not have the person's face in them (unless they have given special permission) and are not taken to be flattering. Seeing just a part of a person's body gives a stark effect that makes the overall appearance worse than it is in reality. Some women who have already had reconstruction may be happy to talk to you and show you what it really looks like. The best way to find someone is to get in touch with Breast Cancer Care, who have a list of volunteers who have had breast cancer and are happy to talk to others going through the same experience. One woman looked at the pictures I had and then met up with someone who showed her her own reconstruction. The woman preparing for surgery described the pictures as much worse than the real reconstruction. This woman then asked to see my pictures, as she had had her surgery elsewhere, and realised that what she had was not as good a result as those shown in the photos. These days many surgeons are skilled in performing reconstruction. You need to check with yours how often he does this kind of surgery so you can be sure that you will get the best result for you. In making a decision about reconstruction I believe that the most important thing is to be clear about the reasons for having it done, and then proper consideration can be made of the risks and benefits for each individual.

Different kinds of breast reconstruction

Reconstruction with implants

It is possible to remove most of the breast tissue under the skin while leaving the skin and nipple in place. At the same time an implant is used to replace the breast tissue. This operation usually looks very good because all the outside of the breast has not changed. However, this can only be used for a few women, such as those who need a mastectomy for *in situ* carcinoma.

Normally, much of the skin over the breast is removed, as this is a place where breast cancer cells can return. One option is to place an implant under the remaining skin and to stretch the skin by expanding the implant. The implant is stretched during a few months by injecting saline solution into a tube that feeds into the implant. The injection site is usually placed under the arm and can be felt as a hard object just under the skin. This can be a bit uncomfortable at first, especially if it happens to lie under the side panel of the bra strap. Plenty of padding generally helps to relieve the discomfort. The implant is stretched until it is a bit bigger than the opposite breast, which allows the skin to stretch sufficiently to gain a more normal 'droopy' effect. The excess saline is then withdrawn. At this point either the tube is removed or a permanent silicone implant used to replace the expander.

Reconstruction with body tissue

Skin can be taken from other parts of the body in order to create a new breast mound. The skin has to be of sufficient bulk and supported with a good blood supply, so it is taken with the underlying muscle. The most common sites are from the back or the abdomen (tummy). This is usually necessary if the woman has larger breasts as an implant alone may not be of sufficient size. Sometimes a tissue transfer is used as well as an implant.

Back flap (Latissimus dorsi)

An area of skin from the back, with its underlying fat and muscle, is raised from the body, but is still left attached to the blood supply. This flap is then swivelled around and inserted under the skin under the arm. It is brought through to the front of the body where it is sewn into place to form the new breast. Unless the original breast was small, it is necessary to use an implant as well. This operation gives a good shape and feel. The main disadvantage is having additional surgery on the back. This feels quite painful for a few weeks, and leaves a scar all the way to the spine on the back. This scar can be horizontal, in which case a bra strap usually hides it, or it can be nearly vertical, which would be hidden by a swimsuit. The body adjusts to the loss of the muscle by using other muscles to do the same job. Normal activities, such as swimming and golf, can be resumed afterwards. Very active people who use a lot of upper body strength, such as rock climbers or cross-country skiers, will notice the loss of strength.

Tummy flap (TRAM – Transverse Rectus Abdominus Musculo-cutaneous flap)

This flap takes tissue from the abdomen, or tummy. Because most women have a good layer of fat here, as well as excess skin, this means the reconstruction can be done without using an implant as well. It also means that women get a 'tummy tuck' at the same time. This leaves a scar all the way across the abdomen, which looks very unsightly at first, but soon fades into a crease and is usually covered by underclothes. The blood supply to this area is not as secure as in the breast and so this operation is not suitable for everyone. Women who have had previous abdominal surgery, those who smoke or are overweight and those with certain medical problems, such as hypertension, are advised not to have this surgery.

Nipples

A few breast restoration operations can retain enough skin to carry out a safe operation and also keep the nipple, but this is usually not possible as the nipple always has some breast tissue in it. As a consequence the woman has to decide if she wants to have a nipple reconstructed. Some people are happy to have a breast that fills their bra and allows them to go without a prosthesis. Others feel that the nipple is the final touch that makes them feel that their reconstruction is more like a real breast. It is usually better to wait until after the breast reconstruction before creating a nipple to ensure the proper position and size. This can be done by using skin on the breast and pinching it up to make a projecting nipple shape. This will need to have colour added by tattoo at a later date. It is also possible to take tissue from elsewhere on the body, such as the inner thigh. This has the advantage of being a darker colour to start with, but the thigh is usually quite sore for a couple of weeks.

It is also possible to use stick-on nipples or to have the whole nipple tattooed if one wants to avoid surgery. A tattoo can look very good, but does not stick out. Those women who want a nipple often do so in order that they will not look unequal when wearing a tee-shirt or swimming costume. One young woman I looked after went to see a seaside tattoo artist in order to have a nipple created. In talking to her he discovered that, although she had a good reconstruction, she still hated it, as the scars were very visible to her. He suggested that he could tattoo feathers on her breast, using the scars as the spines of the feathers. She was delighted with this suggestion and agreed. He helped her to turn her hated scars into a beautiful and positive part of herself.

Implants

Breast implants are silicone bags, which contain either silicone gel or saline fluid. Other fillings have been suggested but none have yet been shown to be safe. Implants with soybean oil have been withdrawn due to concerns over safety. Silicone implants have been around since the 1960s and over one million have been used, therefore there is a lot of information available about the safety of these implants. There are a variety of sizes and shapes, designed to give the closest match to your own breast in shape and feel. They will never be quite the same, but some are pretty convincing.

Some women I have known have said they do not like the idea of having something inside them that is not their own body. I think this feeling is becoming less common now that so many people have hip replacements, heart valve replacements and pacemakers, but you may want to consider how you feel about this.

There have been lots of concerns about breast implants and about silicone in particular. There are known to be some complications with implants, but there are also many alarming claims for complications that have not been shown to be true. The known ones are simple. There are occasions when any operation results in an infection and this can happen with breast reconstruction. If there is an implant in place, this can make it more difficult for the infection to clear and the implant may need to be removed, which can cause a problem as complete healing needs to take place before any further plastic surgery can be carried out. The breast may then heal with a lot of scar tissue and it can be difficult to regain a good breast shape subsequently. For this reason it is common practice to give antibiotics as a preventive measure to women having reconstructive surgery. Secondly, the body recognises the implant as foreign and so lays down fibrous scar tissue around it. Occasionally, especially with old-style implants, this can become firm, and for a very few women develops into what feels like a hard, round ball inside. This can be uncomfortable and does not have the appearance that you would want. Although these fibrous capsules can be cracked, this is not always successful and sometimes replacement implants have to be inserted.

If the skin is very thin the implant can become exposed, in which case it must be removed. The implant can also deflate, leak or move. However, it is relatively simple to replace an implant if necessary. Implants are pretty tough, but they are not indestructible. A sharp injury or strong pressure from a blunt injury, such as that which might be sustained in a car accident, could cause an implant to rupture. Mammograms are adjusted to ensure that they do not cause undue pressure. Implants generally last for many years, but are unlikely to last for a whole lifetime. The body will absorb any saline leakage. If silicone leaks, it will normally be contained within the fibrous capsule described above. Even when the implant is not broken, minute amounts of silicone may seep through the implant envelope and some of this may be found in other parts of the body.

Silicone is not only found in breast implants, it is also present in many other medical devices, such as pacemakers, artificial joints and drains. It lubricates syringes, so that every time you have an injection, you also take in a tiny amount of silicone. It is found in tablets, cling film, cosmetics, babies' dummies and also in foods. Every time you use lipstick you take in silicone.

It has been suggested that silicone implants interfere with the immune system, but there is no medical evidence to support this. It has even been suggested that they cause cancer, which has been shown not to be true. There was an old coating on early implants, that was linked with a cancer-forming substance, but it is highly unlikely that it ever caused cancer in anyone and has not been used for some years. There have also been claims that silicone leakage from implants could cause diseases such as arthritis. There have been a number of large studies comparing women who have implants with those who do not, and in each group, the incidence of these diseases is the same. Silicone implants are now believed to be perfectly safe. Even in the United States, where the controls on drugs and devices made to be used in the human body are very tight, silicone implants have been declared to be safe. I have been asked why, if they are so safe, the manufacturer Dow Corning stopped making implants and was declared bankrupt. This was not because they believed that the claims against them were valid, but rather because it was becoming so expensive to contest the hundreds of claims that the easiest way to deal with them was to wind down the firm.

Complications of reconstructive surgery

The complications of reconstructive surgery are much the same as for any other kind of surgery but there are three extra points to consider. One is that it is generally a larger operation, especially where there has been transfer of tissue from another part of the body. This does tend to lead to more pain – one woman said she felt as though she had been kicked in the back by a donkey! This rapidly improved, however, and although she described herself as a coward who hated pain, she was still glad she had undergone the surgery. A tummy flap also tends to be painful, as every time you move, or even breathe, you use your tummy muscles. Immediately after surgery, strong painkillers are given and it is often possible to have a pump containing painkiller so that you yourself can control the amount of painkiller that you get. This is called a PCA (patient controlled analgesia) pump.

The second point is that you may have an implant in place. Potential complications of implants have already been discussed and if it is necessary to inflate the implant this may increase the number of visits you make to the hospital. The third difference is where you need to take tissue from another part of the body, which leaves extra scars and may have an impact on the area in other ways. In the first instance there will be pain in two areas of your body, rather than just one. Where muscle has been removed it will make the muscle strength weaker in this area. With a back flap this is not normally noticeable, but with a tummy flap there is a possibility of a hernia occurring. It is not advisable to practise sit-ups after this operation.

Anyone who smokes may be more liable to poor healing after surgery. Smoking causes deposits to be laid down in the arteries, so that the blood supply is not as good. This is particularly of concern in those who have a tummy flap. Being overweight may also mean that the blood supply to an area is reduced and so may also lead to poorer healing.

All the pros and cons of reconstruction can be summed up as follows.

The benefits of reconstruction are:

- waking up from the operation with two breasts
- reduced feeling of loss
- reduced concern about loss of femaleness
- not needing to worry about how you look when undressed
- an improved self image
- a feeling of normality
- feeling more sexy than being without breasts at all
- not needing to wear an artificial breast form (or prosthesis)
- increased choice of clothing
- keeping a cleavage.

The disadvantages of reconstruction are:

- not being the same as your other breast
- concerns about implants
- a bigger operation and potentially more pain
- possibly more scars
- possibly requiring tissue transfer
- not matching up to what you had hoped for

Timing of surgery

There has been some research that suggests that women do better if surgery is carried out in the second half of their menstrual cycle, that is, in the week or two before a period. It is not yet clear whether this is a definite effect and many women may prefer to get on with treatment rather than wait a couple of weeks for surgery. However, if this is an area that concerns you, you should discuss it with your surgeon to find out the latest information on this issue and what it might mean for you.

Lymphoedema (arm swelling)

The lymph nodes in your axilla make up part of the channels of lymph fluid all round your body. In particular they help to drain the lymph fluid that bathes the tissues of your arm. There are other channels to drain this fluid, but occasionally these become overloaded for some reason and the fluid accumulates in the arm. This is called lymphoedema. This is not unusual in the first few months after surgery and generally disperses, but it can also occur any time after these nodes have been removed – even many years afterwards. If the arm swelling is left for long without any treatment, then it will become permanent. Advice that is available at the moment concentrates on trying to avoid this swelling in the first place and, if it occurs, to seek treatment early on.

The only way to avoid lymphoedema completely is not to have treatment in the axilla. However, if cancer grows here it can also cause a blockage, which would also result in lymphoedema. So a balance has to be made between having the least amount of surgery and ensuring that there is no cancer in these nodes. One option might be to remove only a few nodes and then if they contain cancer to give radiation treatment to the area. Unfortunately, a combination of surgery and radiotherapy seems to be worse than having more major surgery alone. It is most common, therefore, only to do the surgery.

Only a minority of women develops lymphoedema and it is not clear why some do and others do not. One of the most common precipitating factors seems to be infection in the arm. This causes local inflammation, which results in local swelling and can then lead to the whole arm becoming swollen. It seems wise, therefore, to take measures to prevent infection.

Measures recommended to prevent lymphoedema:
Try to avoid injury to the arm:
- wear gardening gloves
- wear oven gloves
- avoid having blood samples taken from that arm
- wash and treat any cuts with antiseptic ointment
- keep the skin in good condition to avoid cracked skin
- use mosquito repellent and treat mosquito bites with antiseptic
- avoid lifting heavy weights, eg suitcases
- avoid sunburn.

What to do if your arm swells?

If you notice any swelling you should speak to your doctor about it as it is important to rule out other causes before treating for lymphoedema. You can then be referred to a lymphoedema specialist, who may be your breast care nurse, or physiotherapist, or a nurse who specialises in lymphoedema.

Lymphoedema cannot be cured, but it can be controlled by keeping the arm in good condition and by using strategies that help the fluid to drain away from the arm. If the arm is at the same level as the heart it will drain naturally, so that you may find it is better in the morning. Using an elasticated sleeve will then prevent fluid from accumulating. The pressure from the sleeve can also encourage the fluid to flow back into the normal channels: the blood stream and lymphatic system.

Certain exercises can also help, but some activities may make it worse. It is worth getting specific advice about your own situation.

Receiving the results of surgery

The surgeon will usually tell you how the operation has gone and what he has seen at the time of surgery. He will do this as soon as he can after your operation, usually the same day, or the next morning. At the time of the operation he will send all the tissue that he removes to the pathology laboratory. The specialists here will use this material to make into slides that can be examined under the microscope. There can be a lot of slides and so this whole process takes a few days. The specialist makes a report on what he finds, which he then sends to your surgeon. Depending on the systems in your hospital, this can take a few days or up to a week. It is quite common to go home before these results are available, so you will need to come back for an outpatient visit to discuss these results. When they can, the doctors will usually tie this appointment in with the appointment to remove your stitches. You may want to bring someone with you to this appointment in case you do receive results of the surgery. Sometimes the treatment that you receive subsequently will depend on these results so you may like to have someone to help you to take it all in.

The first thing that you need to know is that the cancer has been completely removed. During the operation, the surgeon takes out all the cancer that he can see, plus some clear tissue around the edges. The pathologist will check under the microscope to see if there are any cells at the edge of the sample. If there are then there is a possibility that there is some cancer still in the breast, in which case the surgeon may suggest that you have more surgery. This is unusual, but can sometimes happen.

Further results will show whether there is any spread of the cancer to the lymph nodes in your armpit and will also be able to tell you the grading of the cancer. This gives an indication of the appearance of the cells and whether they look more or less like the original breast tissue (See Chapter 7). You should also be told whether the cancer cells have receptors on the cell surface for oestrogen. (See Chapter 7.) This will give some indication as to whether or not the cancer is likely to respond to tamoxifen.

Information about lymph nodes, grading and oestrogen receptors can give an indication of how likely it is that the cancer will return, and is used to help decide what further treatment to have.

Breast forms (prostheses)

If you have a mastectomy and do not have a reconstruction, you may choose to wear a prosthesis, or breast form. Losing a breast may cause a feeling of great loss, and can lead to a change in the way that you feel about yourself. For many women, the knowledge that they will be able to present a normal body image to the world is an important boost to their self-esteem and emotional recovery. The use of an external prosthesis is a good way of doing this. Other women feel that accepting the change in their bodies means that they do not need to hide it from the world, and so choose not to wear a prosthesis.

A breast prosthesis is a moulded form, usually made of a silicone gel, which imitates a breast in weight, shape and feel. It can be placed in a normal bra, where it feels very natural. When dressed, most people cannot tell the difference.

Immediately after surgery the scar will be too sore to wear a permanent prosthesis. However, at this stage many women prefer to have something temporary to restore their natural contour. A soft padding of artificial lambswool in a cotton cover will do this, and will be comfortable to wear. Because the pad is so light it does tend to sit very high in the bra, and so may not look very even. This can be minimised by loosening the bra strap on this side and tightening up the strap on the side of the remaining breast. The pad may also move, so it is advisable to pin or tape it into place. The breast care nurse can supply these pads. A permanent prosthesis can be fitted as soon as healing has taken place and the possibility of any swelling has gone. This is usually about six weeks after surgery. However, many women continue to wear the pads around the house as a lighter alternative to the permanent form.

Permanent prosthesis

The permanent prosthesis comes in many shapes and sizes. You should be able to try on a range to see which one suits you best. There are also a variety of types, so if you find you have any particular difficulties with one, discuss it with your fitter or breast care nurse, to see if there are any alternatives to suit you better. Most come in a pale shell-pink colour, although there are a few standard dark skin tones available. To get a good skin tone match is quite difficult. Some companies will dye the prosthesis to match the individual. There is also a semi-lucent dark prosthesis available, which takes up the colour of the underlying skin.

There are some prostheses available that can be stuck onto your chest wall using sticky strips. These are not recommended for at least a year after surgery or radiotherapy. The adhesive strips hold the prosthesis very firmly onto the chest wall and so can be worn without a bra. This can give a lot more freedom in the choice of what clothes can be worn. They can also be useful if you participate in active sports, such as tennis, which could cause an ordinary prosthesis to slip.

Partial prosthesis

Surgery and radiotherapy can affect the breast size and shape even when a mastectomy is not performed. Many women find that their breasts are quite dissimilar after treatment and it is difficult to get a bra that fits well. It may also be a source of embarrassment if it is obvious to other people that the breasts are different sizes. A partial prosthesis can effectively fill out the bra and restore symmetry. This is a shell of silicone exactly like a full prosthesis, which fits between the breast and the bra. Once in place it is generally very comfortable and does not move. Most women say they hardly know that it is there.

Nipples

There is usually a nipple shape on the breast form, but for women with prominent nipples this may not match their own very well. It is possible to obtain stick-on nipples of different sizes and colours, which can be stuck onto the prosthesis.

Bras

It should be possible to wear a normal bra to hold a prosthesis. This bra needs to be well fitting and of a medium to firm control, so that it provides good support. This does not mean that it has to be plain or 'matronly'. However, if you like to wear a bra that shows a bit of cleavage, you may find that this shows the edge of a prosthesis, so you may need to rethink what you prefer to wear. It is really worthwhile being properly fitted for a bra, either by a breast care nurse, or by a trained fitter in a specialist lingerie store or department. In the UK, Marks and Spencer carried out a survey that showed that seven out of ten women do not wear the right size bra. Don't forget that as you change size or get older, your breasts will change too. If your bra does not fit closely, you may feel that the prosthesis will slip, in which case you can sew in a pocket, or simply sew two ribbons across the inside of the bra cup.

Swimwear

The thought of swimming after mastectomy can be daunting, but with a bit of care it should be possible to find swimwear that can look very good. If you choose a swimsuit that has an inner lining, or fitted cups, a pocket can be sewn in and a prosthesis can be worn inside the pocket. You cannot keep a prosthesis in without a pocket as water will get between the skin and the prosthesis and cause it to float away from the body. There are foam prostheses made just for swimming, and some women just use one of the temporary pads. If you choose a costume that is slightly higher round the neck and armholes, it can help to hide the scars of surgery. There are also specialist companies that supply fashionable swimming costumes for women who have had a mastectomy (see Useful Addresses at the end of the book).

Charges

Prostheses are supplied free of charge for women who have had a mastectomy under the care of the NHS. They can be replaced when they wear out and they usually last for several years. You may want a replacement if you change weight in the mean time. If you have your surgery conducted privately, your insurance firm should pay for the prosthesis, and if you remain a private patient you will need to buy your own replacements. They cost around £70–£200. Breast Cancer Care is a charitable organisation that can help with information about stockists and will also help to fit prostheses (see Useful Addresses).

Six questions to ask your surgeon:

How much breast tissue will you remove and what will my breast look like afterwards?

How often do you conduct surgery of this kind?

What kind of complications might I expect after this kind of surgery?

How will I feel after this surgery?

What exercises should I do after surgery and for how long should I continue them?

What were the results of the surgery?

9
Other conventional treatments

While surgery is the main form of treatment for breast cancer, many women have other treatments as well. The purpose of this is to eliminate any cells that may have spread from the original cancer, but which cannot be detected. Unfortunately, because they cannot be detected it is never known for sure whether all the cells have been killed or not. Doctors tend to work on percentages and chances of cure which can all be difficult to make sense of. Most women I have come across say that this is all very well, but what does it mean for them as an individual? This is the question that the doctors cannot answer, and it is why it is important for women to think about what matters most to them so that their feelings can be taken into consideration when decisions are made about treatment. For example, as most women do not want to lose a breast, it would be easy for doctors to assume that all women would prefer to avoid a mastectomy if at all possible. However, for some women there is an equal choice between a lumpectomy with radiotherapy treatment or a mastectomy without radiotherapy. I remember one particular lady for whom the thought of a daily visit to the hospital for six weeks was torture as she suffered from agoraphobia. For her to have a mastectomy was infinitely preferable.

Other cases may be less clear. If a woman has a very good outlook because she has a very small cancer and lots of favourable indications, it may be that the chances of benefiting from chemotherapy are as little as 1 per cent. This means that 99 per cent of women with the same indicators will have chemotherapy and it will make no difference to their outcome at all. If that woman has a young family and feels fit enough to cope with the consequences of chemotherapy then that 1 per cent may seem very worthwhile. If, on the other hand, the thought of chemotherapy fills her with dread, then 1 per cent may not seem much at all.

The message is: think carefully about what matters most to you, and make sure you find out what all your options are.

Chemotherapy

The thought of chemotherapy fills many people with dread. Images of sick patients with no hair spring to mind. Chemotherapy for breast cancer is generally used in combination with other treatments, such as surgery and radiotherapy. There are many different types of chemotherapy, and a variety of combinations are useful in breast cancer. Many of these can be relatively easy to tolerate and you don't always lose your hair. One woman I knew said that she felt that she was a bit of a fraud, as she wasn't getting any side-effects at all. Some find the whole process very difficult and question whether it is really worth it for them. This is a question that is impossible for me to answer for you. One study asked people whether they would go through toxic treatment for a 1 per cent chance of a cure. The response was varied, depending on the background of the individual. Most doctors and nurses said they would have the treatment, but for those people who had actually had cancer the numbers were much higher. It is one of those situations when you don't know how you will react until you are faced with it. I think it is worth thinking very hard about what you are actually going to gain from the treatment and how much it is worth it for you. I also think that for many people it is worth trying the treatment to see what it is like, as many people will find it is not as bad as they fear.

Unlike surgery or radiotherapy, chemotherapy can kill cancer cells wherever they might be in the body. This means that it increases the chances of being cured from cancer. Using chemotherapy alone can cure some cancers. However, the best chance of a cure for breast cancer is to use a combination of surgery and chemotherapy, and sometimes radiotherapy and hormone therapy as well. It is known that younger women (under 50) are more likely to benefit from chemotherapy, but older women may also get some benefit. The older you are the less likely you are to gain any benefit from chemotherapy. You are also more likely to find it difficult to deal with the side-effects. This is one of those areas when age is more about how fit you are and what age you feel, rather than your actual age. Women whose tumours have worse prognostic signs, such as a large tumour, lymph nodes under the arm or high grade, are more likely to benefit from having chemotherapy.

Chemotherapy really just means treatment with drugs, which could mean anything. It should really be called cytotoxic chemotherapy. Cytotoxic means that it kills cells. It works by damaging the DNA of dividing cells, and so instead of producing two new cells, the cell dies. Unfortunately, it kills normal cells as well as cancer cells and this is why people get side-effects. However, normal cells are less likely to be dividing and they are also better at repairing any damage, therefore they will be less affected than cancer cells. Chemotherapy is usually given as a combination of different drugs, in order to get the maximum destruction of cancer cells, but to minimise the effects on normal cells. Most chemotherapy drugs are given by injection into the bloodstream. This is to ensure that the maximum amount of drug is given to the cancer cells anywhere in the body, without being digested by the stomach or the breakdown process started in the liver. There are a few chemotherapy drugs that can be given as a tablet or by other routes. Some of those given by injection are now being given as a constant drip, which is driven by a small, portable pump. The drip is given into a secure line that goes under the skin in your chest, rather than your arm, and may be referred to as a Hickman line. It is then attached to a little bag that you can wear around your waist. With this in place you can go home and carry on normal activities, including bathing and showering.

Chemotherapy is usually given after surgery, although it is becoming more common to give it before surgery. This may be in order to shrink the lump before surgery or as part of a study to see if it increases the overall cure rate. It is often given as one injection every three or four weeks. A total of six or eight injections will be given, which means that the whole course lasts for about six months. Any side-effects are often felt in the few days after the injection and these then wear off over the rest of the three weeks. Some side-effects, like tiredness, accumulate over the course of the six months and last for some months afterwards. For those who are quite affected by chemotherapy it can take up to a year finally to feel over it.

High dose chemotherapy

This kind of treatment for breast cancer is not common in the UK at the moment and is still undergoing trials. The idea is that the more chemotherapy given, the more cancer cells will be killed and so the cure rate will be higher. This can severely damage the bone marrow, which is where your blood cells are made, so some bone marrow is removed before the chemotherapy and restored afterwards. It is not clear yet whether this will improve the chances of cure.

Side-effects of chemotherapy

It is difficult to predict how you will feel with chemotherapy as everyone has different side-effects, even if they have the same drugs. Each drug tends to have a list of common side-effects and you should be warned about what to expect with your own programme. One of the things I have noticed over the years, is that whatever people normally get when they are run down, is what they will suffer from when they are on chemotherapy. If you know that you get mouth ulcers, then stock up on what you usually use to manage them. However, nausea doesn't seem to follow this pattern. I have known people who say that they are always sick, with every pregnancy, or on every journey, and then they are the ones who don't get sick at all! You will be given specific information on the side-effects of the drugs that you are to be given.

Nausea

Nausea is usually much more of a problem than actually being sick. There are a number of anti-sickness tablets (anti-emetics) that can be given and these should be taken before the chemotherapy is given in order to prevent the sickness before it occurs. It is much easier to prevent sickness than it is to control it once it starts. If your tablets are not helping you, do not assume that this is normal and accept it. Go back and ask for something different; there are lots of new and effective drugs around. Most people find that this nausea lasts for a few days and then starts to get better.

Fatigue

Tiredness is one of the commonest effects of chemotherapy and the hardest to deal with, as there are no tablets that can be taken to help. As you go through the treatment, you may become anaemic and this will increase your tiredness. You will have your blood checked frequently and this will detect if you are anaemic. This kind of anaemia is not a result of iron deficiency, so taking iron tablets is unlikely to help. There are some injections that can help to boost the production of blood cells, and these may be offered, or you may be given a blood transfusion. In general, the best way to deal with fatigue is to reduce your activity. Plan your day around rests and shorter periods of activity.

Infection

Because your bone marrow is very vulnerable to chemotherapy, fewer blood cells will be produced than normal. White blood cells, which fight infection, are the first to be affected. This does not mean that you will get more infections than normal, but rather that, if you get an infection, it is more likely to be severe. Don't try to avoid normal contact with people, but if you know someone is unwell with a nasty infection, it would be wise to avoid them. If you do get any kind of infection, make sure you get some antibiotics and don't just wait for it to get better on its own. If it is easier to get to see your GP, you can get these from him.

Hair loss

Losing their hair is one of those things that women dread, as it so notice-able to others. Until this happens there are times when you can forget you have cancer and you can get on with your life fairly normally. Now it seems that everyone will know because it will be so obvious and you will constantly have to deal with concerned acquaintances. Well, not everyone on chemotherapy loses their hair, and for those of you who do, Val has some advice on wigs and looking good in Chapter 13.

   Some kinds of chemotherapy are more likely to make you lose your hair than others. Some people just get thinning of their hair so that it is not noticeable to others. For some kinds of chemotherapy you can have an ice-pack on your head while the drug is being administered, so that it does not reach your hair roots. This is called scalp cooling. It does not stop hair loss altogether but may reduce it. It is worth looking after your hair and not using any harsh products while you are on chemotherapy as this may increase the amount that you lose. The main things to avoid are harsh dyes, bleaches and perms. Hair loss is also temporary – it will grow back after treatment has finished.

Skin and nails

With some programmes of chemotherapy you may find that your skin and nails are affected. It may help to take vitamin B as this is used in the repair of skin and nails, and it is also worth using a good moisturising cream. Don't forget that your toenails can be affected too. There are some chemotherapy agents which have a specific reaction on the palms of your hands and the soles of your feet. If you find these areas getting red and sore, make sure that you show them to your doctor.

Menopause

Having chemotherapy nearly always makes your periods stop. This may not happen for a couple of cycles, and they may become lighter before they actually stop. If you are 30 or under, the periods will generally return after chemotherapy has stopped. However, the nearer you are to 40, the less likely they are to return, and if you are over 40, they are unlikely to return. This means that you will be infertile and that you will suffer from the signs of menopause, such as hot flushes and night sweats. As this menopause is brought on suddenly it does seem that, for some people, it may be worse than a normal menopause (see the section on coping with the menopause on page 130).

While you are having the chemotherapy you cannot assume that you are not fertile and so you should continue using contraception. The pill is not recommended at this time because it is hormonal, so you should use a barrier method instead. If you have already completed your family when you get breast cancer, this may not be a problem for you, but if you were still hoping for children it can be a cause of great sadness. Although there have been cases in the press about women having their eggs preserved before they have chemotherapy, this would not generally be recommended, because of the delay in treatment and the necessity for high doses of hormones to be given in order to induce ovulation. If this is a very important issue for you, you may want to think about how much benefit you would get from chemotherapy, and whether it is something that you want to have.

Radiotherapy

Radiotherapy is often used as a back up (or adjuvant) treatment to surgery. It can also be given directly to a cancer and will cause it to shrink and die over a period of time. Radiotherapy kills cancer cells by disrupting their DNA, which means that they cannot carry out normal functions or divide into new cells. It can damage normal cells as well, but they are much better at repairing themselves and so are less susceptible. To allow normal cells time to repair and to cause maximum damage to cancer cells, radiotherapy is often given in small, repeated doses. This means that you may have your treatment on a daily, or every other day, basis, over several weeks. Depending on how the doses are spread this can be from 3–6 weeks.

The source of radioactive material is most commonly contained within a machine and X-rays are carefully directed to treat only a small portion of the body. It is possible to have radiation wires that can be inserted into the breast. This is common in France, but in the UK it is more usual to have radiation that comes from a distant source. Once you have had your radiotherapy treatment you are not radioactive unless you still have the source, for instance the wires mentioned above, inside your body. Radiation travels in straight lines. Breast tissue curves around the body and so you cannot treat the entire breast by using one beam of radiation, unless some of it goes through your lungs as well. It is usual to use two overlapping beams to cover the whole breast and not damage the lungs.

Planning the radiation is a precise exercise. In order to give the same dose every day in the same way, treating the whole breast and not treating the lungs, careful maps are made of the way that the machines should be lined up in relation to your body. This means that you have to lie on the treatment table for a long time while accurate plans are made. This time can be quite trying. It is often done within a couple of weeks of your surgery and you may still be sore, especially under the arm. However, you need to be able to hold your arms over your head, so that they do not get in the way of the radiation beam. You will need to be able to lie still, holding onto a bar behind your head, for at least half an hour. If you think that this will be difficult, make sure you practice your exercises to get movement back into your arm and take a couple of painkillers just before you go into hospital. It is also worth taking some distraction with you, for instance a small radio or tape player with earphones. If you have learnt a relaxation technique, then this is a good time to practise it.

In order to ensure that they can always line up the beams in the same way, the radiographers will put marks on your breast. Having people draw on you feels bizarre. Some of these marks may need to be left on to help guide the radiographers when they are setting up your treatment, so they must not be washed off during treatment. These days it is more common to make tiny little point tattoos to use as guides; these are permanent, so you don't have to worry about them washing off. You may be concerned about having permanent tattoos. They are not very noticeable, but you may want to discuss this with your radiotherapy doctor.

When you start treatment you will be given a specific time of day for your treatment. Usually the appointments start on time and the treatment only takes about ten minutes, so you can be in and out quickly, although sometimes a backlog can build up if there are any technical problems with the machinery. If your appointment time does not suit you, it is normally possible to reorganise this to a more convenient time.

Going into the treatment area can be daunting. It is a big open area and looks bleak and clinical. Once you are positioned on the table the radiographers all leave the area and you may feel rather isolated. They can see you on their monitors so that you are not really alone and there is also an intercom so you can talk to them at any time if you need to.

Side-effects of radiotherapy to the breast

The biggest problem with radiotherapy is the need to have it every day over such a long time, which can be really disruptive to your daily life. This is a good time to call in all those offers of help: picking up the children from school; the odd bit of shopping or cooking; or even lifts to the hospital. Some people I know have worked out a rota, with different people giving them a lift on different days of the week.

Many women find that they get very tired during radiotherapy. Some of this is due to an accumulation of disruption to your everyday life and having to go to the hospital so frequently. It is probable that there is a direct effect from the radiotherapy as well, although why this should be is not completely clear. This tiredness increases as you go through radiotherapy and can last for a couple of months after it has finished.

Radiotherapy only has side-effects in the area that is actually being treated. This means that you will not lose the hair on your head, although the hair under your arm may be affected. It will affect the skin and most people get some soreness which is similar to mild sunburn, so it is itchy and red. A few people get a bad reaction in the skin, leaving it raw and needing a dressing. Nurses attached to the radiotherapy unit can help to advise you about the care of your skin, and you may be told not to use scented products as this could increase the reaction. Some doctors suggest that you do not wash the area, but there is little evidence that washing increases skin soreness. It is more common now to allow washing, but it may be advisable just to pat the area dry rather than to rub it, which might increase the chance of soreness. Some people hardly notice any change in their breast or skin at all.

After treatment the skin in the area may get a bit thicker and darker in colour and the nipple may also get a bit crusty. These effects tend to resolve over about six months. It is generally recommended that you cover up the irradiated area when sunbathing for a year after treatment has finished.

The breast may also become more sensitive during treatment and this takes some months to resolve. There may be some changes in sensation that never completely go away, and from time to time there may be odd pains that were not there before.

If you have radiation treatment under your arm, this will cause internal scarring as well, which can result in increased stiffness and reduced movement. Very rarely, the nerves that pass in a bundle under the armpit can also be affected and can cause tingling, numbness or even reduce the use of the arm on that side. The lymph nodes under the arm can also be affected and this can cause arm swelling in the long term. This is most common when both surgery and radiotherapy have been used. Surgeons and radiotherapists are trying to find ways of ensuring that the armpit is properly treated and that the damage is minimised so that lymphoedema does not result.

Hormone (or endocrine) therapy

It is known that hormone levels in the body affect the breast. Each month during the menstrual cycle oestrogen causes stimulation of the ducts in the breast and progesterone causes the milk producing alveoli to mature. In order for cells in breast tissue to recognise the signals from hormones they must have hormone receptor sites on the surface of the cell. There are receptor sites for all the different hormones and different tissues in the body have more or fewer receptor sites for each hormone. Breast tissue normally has many oestrogen receptors and so does skin tissue. During a lifetime of oestrogen stimulation some ductal cells may lose the proper regulation of growth and develop into cancer cells. Some of these cancers resemble the cells from which they originated and still have oestrogen and progesterone receptor sites on their surface. These cancers may also still depend on oestrogen in order to grow and they tend to be affected by drugs that interfere with the hormones in some way. If oestrogen can be blocked, or less of it made, then the cancer will be starved and will shrink.

One of the puzzles for many of the women I have spoken to over the years is that hormone treatments are often more effective in those women who have finished their periods and are now postmenopausal. They find it hard to understand how the cancer can respond to a reduction in oestrogens when they have already stopped making oestrogen! There are two keys to understanding this puzzle. The first is that postmenopausal women are more likely to have cancers that contain oestrogen receptors – what the doctors refer to as oestrogen receptor positive (or ER+ve). Therefore, these cancers can be treated by hormone manipulation. The second key is that even though the ovaries are not working after menopause, women still produce small amounts of oestrogen, mostly in fatty tissue. The amount they produce is only about 10 per cent of that which was previously produced, but interfering with this can be very effective.

Tamoxifen

The best known antioestrogen is tamoxifen. It is now made by a number of companies and has a variety of trade names, such as Tamofen® and Nolvadex®. Tamoxifen does not stop oestrogen from being made, but cells take the tamoxifen up and use it in preference to oestrogen. It has some of the effects of oestrogen, but does not stimulate breast cancer cells to grow. It has been shown to be very effective in preventing breast cancer from returning and so is frequently given as well as surgery. This is known as an adjuvant treatment. Surgery is the mainline, or primary, treatment and tamoxifen is the back-up, or adjuvant treatment. Most postmenopausal women will be given tamoxifen and so will some pre-menopausal women, especially if they have a cancer that is ER+ve.

Tamoxifen is a very easy drug to take. Only one tablet per day is taken and for many people it has no side-effects at all. However, this is not the case for everyone and there are side-effects of which the main two are weight gain and hot flushes. For a long time I was not sure whether tamoxifen really caused women to put on weight. I knew plenty of women who were not taking tamoxifen and still said they put on weight, because it is very common for women to change their lifestyle when they have cancer. The perpetual diet goes out of the window, 'comfort eating' increases and exercise is severely curtailed. Those who have nausea with chemotherapy can find that eating small amounts frequently helps to reduce nausea, so it is very common to put on weight after having breast cancer. However, research has now shown that, although this is true, and on average women do gain weight after breast cancer, it is also the case that those who are taking tamoxifen put on more weight than those who are not. The average weight gain is 2–3kg but this can be helped by a reducing diet.

Some women can suffer from hot flushes, although this is not the rule and they are generally not as bad as during a normal menopause. (See the section on menopausal difficulties on page 130 for help with this.) Tamoxifen does not cause the menopause, but it can affect menstrual flow, making it heavier for some women and lighter for others. It also has the effect of stimulating the cells that line the womb, or endometrium. Very rarely this can cause cancer of the womb. This caused a lot of anxiety when it was first discovered, but the numbers are so small in relation to the numbers of lives saved from taking tamoxifen, that doctors still feel it is a safe drug to prescribe. It does mean that if you have any unusual bleeding it is important to get it checked out with your doctor. Endometrial cancer can be easily cured if it is caught early. Tamoxifen can increase the chance of suffering from blood clots, but it reduces the chances of heart disease and strokes and helps prevent the bones from thinning in old age (osteoporosis).

Clearly there are risks as well as benefits in taking tamoxifen, as with any drug. One of the questions that still raises uncertainty is the best length of time to take it, when using it as an adjuvant treatment. It is known that women who take it for five years do better on average than those who take it for two years, and that at five years the risks are out-weighed by the benefits. Most doctors think that this may be a sufficient length of time to get maximum benefit and minimum risk, so it is normal to stop at five years.

Tamoxifen is also used for women when breast cancer has returned. In this case it is usual to continue using it for as long as it works, which can be many years.

There is a lot of research taking place at the moment to see whether tamoxifen can prevent breast cancer from occurring, and there is evidence emerging that it can reduce the risk. But there are still a lot of questions to ask, such as who will benefit most, when should women start, how long should they take it, how can the side-effects be minimised and are there other similar drugs that would be better?

Ovarian ablation (preventing the ovaries from producing oestrogen)

Women who still have periods continue to produce large amounts of oestrogen, largely from their ovaries. This can be stopped in a number of ways. Chemotherapy often stops the ovaries from working, and the near-er a woman is to menopause the less likely the periods are to return. The ovaries can be removed by surgery (oophorectomy), or stopped from working by radiotherapy. It is also possible to stop them working by using a specific set of drugs. These drugs work by interfering with the chemical messengers produced by the brain, which tell the ovaries to make oestrogen. When these drugs are discontinued, the messages start getting through again and the ovaries start to work again. Examples of these drugs are goserilin (Zoladex®) and leuprorelin.

All these methods of stopping the ovaries working will result in a menopause, either temporary or permanent, which will make the periods stop and result in infertility. If you want to have children after breast can-cer you will need to discuss whether this is the right treatment for you. It might be possible to use drugs, such as goserilin, which can be reversed after treatment. In the short term the effects of menopause are hot flush-es, sweats, vaginal dryness and reduction in sex drive.

Coping with the menopause

When I started working with women with breast cancer menopausal difficulties were rarely talked about. It has now been acknowledged that

70 per cent of women will have some menopausal effects after treatment for breast cancer. This is partly because it has been caused by the treatment: chemotherapy, tamoxifen or ovarian ablation. It is also the case that breast cancer becomes more common at the age when women are entering, or have gone through, their natural menopause. As it is known that oestrogen can stimulate breast cancer it is therefore presumed that hormone replacement therapy (HRT) might stimulate breast cancer. Any woman diagnosed with breast cancer is recommended to discontinue HRT if they are currently taking it. This may also cause menopausal signs to return.

A great many women can pass through the menopause without suffering any problems at all, while others may have symptoms lasting for years. Hot flushes and night sweats are the most common effects. For those people who have entered menopause suddenly due to treatment, hot flushes and night sweats can be more frequent and more severe than might otherwise have been expected. I have come across women whose life has been made intolerable by being woken up in a cold bed, dripping with sweat, many times a night. They wake up exhausted and bedraggled, unable to function normally. Some choose to sleep apart from their partner in order that only one of them has a disturbed night. For others it is the hot flushes in the day that make life difficult. As soon as they enter a warm environment, or often for no perceptible reason, their face, neck and upper body start to heat up, flush and then drip with sweat. This can cause great embarrassment and some choose to curtail their social life so that they will not have to suffer in public.

Some people find that hot drinks, especially caffeine, alcohol or spicy foods, can trigger flushing. Women who smoke also seem to suffer more frequent and more severe hot flushes. It may be worth trying to work out if you have any triggers that make it worse for you, and it is certainly worth wearing layers of clothes so that you can adjust them according to how you are during the day. If you can wear absorbent materials, such as silk or cotton, that can help you feel more comfortable too. I think that many old fashioned devices, such as fans and eau de cologne, were made fashionable by women who did not talk about menopause, but suffered from it all the same. Today you can get hand-held electric fans and I have come across a spray canister that gives a fine spray of deliciously cooling moisture. Other women carry wet wipes or simple sprays containing lavender water. One piece of advice I heard was to think of it like the summer heat, just stop fighting it and let it wash over you until it passes. There is some evidence to suggest that regular practice of relaxation techniques can reduce both the incidence and intensity of hot flushes.

Although women diagnosed with breast cancer are advised to discontinue HRT if they are taking it, it is not known whether or not it is safe to use HRT. It is known that HRT gives protection against heart disease and osteoporosis (thinning of the bones), both of which can be major concerns for older women. It is possible that the risks of HRT are outweighed by the benefits, even for someone who has already had breast cancer. Trials are being conducted at the moment to try to find the answer to this question. My feeling is that, if the effects of the menopause are making your life a misery, taking a course of HRT may well help and that this weighs heavily in the balance against the uncertainty about its safety.

There are other drugs that can be tried. Some doctors will prescribe progesterone, which is helpful for some women. There are some non-hormonal drugs, which constrict the blood vessels going to the head; they may be effective, but often have side-effects, such as headaches. There is also a range of herbal remedies, which I have heard many women say is effective. Some of these may contain herbal hormones that mimic our hormones, and so are effective in this way, but I have a concern that we do not know enough about how these substances work. It is also the case that we have no idea what kind of doses will be given, as there is no regulation for herbal medicines, because they are classed as foods. Other complementary medicines may be of some benefit; I know of women who have been helped by acupuncture and homeopathy.

Pregnancy and breast cancer

Breast cancer can occur while a woman is pregnant. This can make the cancer difficult to detect as there are changes in the breast due to the pregnancy. However, cancer diagnosed during pregnancy has the same chance of cure as when it occurs at other times and it is not necessary to terminate the pregnancy because cancer has occurred. However, if chemotherapy or radiotherapy are to be used during the early months of the pregnancy this may put the unborn baby at risk of abnormalities, in which case termination may be suggested. The surgery for breast cancer in pregnancy is the same as when the woman is not pregnant, but if radiotherapy is required this should be delayed until after the baby is born. There may be some chemotherapy drugs that can be given in the late months of pregnancy, but it is not known what effect tamoxifen would have on an unborn baby.

When all treatment for breast cancer has finished, many women will no longer be fertile. However, if they are still fertile and wish to have children, this does not seem to increase the risk of cancer recurrence. Most doctors advise women to wait for at least two years, by which time they have passed the time when most recurrences happen. They have also had a chance to have two years' treatment with tamoxifen. One woman I knew had suffered many miscarriages and had longed for a baby before she discovered that she had breast cancer. After her treatment for breast cancer she was over 40 and was uncertain that her periods would return. She regularly kept me informed of any signs of a period and some time later was delighted to be able to tell me that she was pregnant. She is now the mother of twins!

New treatments

In the last ten years there have been massive strides in scientific understanding about how cancer develops. This means that completely new ways of treatment are being invented as we write, and many of the old ways of treatment are being improved. There are new, more effective and less toxic chemotherapies and a mass of new hormone therapies. There are also brand new agents, which act by altering the environment in which cancers grow. These should all take us a long way forward in breast cancer treatment. I think both complete cure and complete prevention are still many years away, but I also think that it is possible that we may see substantial reductions in the death rate over the next 20 years.

Complementary therapies

I believe that complementary therapies have a major role to play in all health care. One of the greatest benefits of the complementary approach is that it helps people to take control of their own health, rather than leaving it completely in the hands of health care professionals. I believe that health is more than the presence or absence of disease. Most of us live with some level of ill health at many times during our lives. Health can be said to be about people being able to live the lives that they choose to live in the way that they choose.

I also believe that we have to be discriminating with complementary therapies in the same way that we are with conventional medicine. Many complementary therapies, such as relaxation and massage, have immediate and proven benefits to people. Others, such as acupuncture and reflexology, have a long history of use and, while they have not been fully explained according to Western medicine, there may be beneficial effects that we do not understand.

When it comes to herbal remedies and other supplements I believe the ground is much more shaky. The problem is not necessarily that they do not work, rather that we do not know enough about how they work and how safe they are. Many modern medicines originated in herbal remedies. Where would we be today without aspirin? Other natural sources have given us powerful medicines, such as antibiotics, chemotherapy agents and painkillers. Often the natural form is too toxic for use and the synthetic form is much milder and has many of the toxins removed. However, many people express a belief that anything that is 'natural' is therefore safe. This is clearly not true and is potentially dangerous. A further complication is that many of these 'natural' remedies are sold in health food shops as foods, which means that they do not undergo any of the rigorous safety checks that all modern drugs must undergo. The checks to which foods are subject are quite different from those of drugs and are usually associated with hygiene. Not only do we not know what many of these products actually do in our bodies, but they are also variable. Each plant source will have a varying concentration of active ingredient and the methods of preparation also mean that the amount of active ingredient in the bottle or tablet that you buy is potentially wildly different. I believe that you need to consider the natural remedies that you take as seriously as you consider the conventional medicines.

Six questions to ask your doctor when considering treatment:

What are my options for treatment?

How much will they benefit me?

What will the short- and long-term effects be?

How long will these effects last?

What can I have or do to help minimise these side-effects?

What is the latest thing available?

10
Living with secondary disease (advanced cancer or metastatic disease)

Neither Val nor I have had advanced breast cancer, so we can't tell you how it feels, but I have met very many women who have had it and they have taught me a few things. I have found that many women carry on living normal lives for many years even with breast cancer throughout their bodies. I remember bumping into people in the garden centre or high street and thinking that no one would ever know that this ordinary, healthy looking woman had advanced breast cancer. Of course, this does not last forever and many women still die of breast cancer. It is also true that there will be illness before they die and sometimes it can be hard to go through this. But people adjust as their circumstances change and so their goals change. One woman of about 35, who had undergone a variety of treatments for metastatic disease told me:

> 'You know, if I were me a couple of years ago looking at me in this bed now, I'd probably be feeling very sorry for me and I couldn't imagine what it must be like to be so ill. And now that I'm here it doesn't feel so bad at all. I'm still me – I still feel the same, I still want to live my life to the full, I just have different challenges, that's all.'

I have also learned that there is always hope. What you hope for may change, but there is always something to hope for. When people think about cancer, in my opinion there are two major concerns in their mind. The first is that they might die and this would mean leaving their loved ones. The second is that they worry that they will suffer, and in particular, that they will suffer pain. It would be untrue to suggest that people do not suffer. If you have been through treatment for cancer then you already know about suffering. However, it should not be necessary to suffer great pain. Modern medicines are very advanced and it is extremely rare not to be able to control pain. I find that sometimes people are afraid to take strong painkillers, especially morphine, either because they are afraid of becoming addicted, or because of what it might mean about their illness. These fears are unfounded. People who take morphine for pain do not become addicts, as the morphine works on the pain first. I am a strong believer in taking painkillers if it means that you can do the things that you want to do. If we soldier on bravely, then we can physically do less, and the pain wears us down, until we are chronically tired and irritable. This makes us snappy with those we love and with whom we want to spend our time. Far better to take the painkillers and be cheerful. There can be hope, therefore, for some good quality life and a dignified death.

This is not to say that being diagnosed with recurrence is anything other than devastating. The first time around everyone is very buoyed up with hopes of a cure. This time it feels very different. All the feelings that occurred the first time are there, but there is the added feeling about whether all that treatment was worthwhile, and also the knowledge that the end of your life is something that you will have to contemplate, probably long before you had hoped. All the things that you had wanted to do with your life may no longer be possible.

It is an immediate and natural concern to think about death when diagnosed with cancer or when cancer returns. While we don't like to talk about it, we all face death as the ultimate truth of life. Everyone should prepare for the end of life. I'll never forget one young man, who knew that his life was limited, asking me to learn from him what he had had to learn in such a hard way. His message was to live life for today and live each day to the fullest. He had worked very hard to provide a beautiful house and home for his wife and family. But he commuted such long distances and worked such long hours, that he rarely got home before his daughter went to bed, and he was often too tired to enjoy the evenings with his wife. Once he had cancer (he actually had melanoma, not breast cancer), he sold the big house in the country and bought a town flat. He could still do his work, but he could be with his family much more. I often try and think of his story. I may be well today, but who knows what tomorrow might bring? When Diana, Princess of Wales, died, one woman told me that she used to envy her, thinking she had everything, but Diana's death showed her that nothing is certain. Even though this woman had breast cancer, she was better off than Diana.

People are often more afraid of the dying process than death itself. No one can tell you what this will be like, but there are many doctors and nurses who are experienced in helping people face difficult situations and they have much to offer, if you ever feel the need for their help. Many people with cancer later express gratitude for the opportunities that they have had to get their life in order, to sort out their affairs, to re-evaluate their life and to appreciate it in a different way. They often become less afraid of death.

My 35-year-old friend sorted out a lot in her life. She had two little girls, but was separated from their father. However, she married a man she was very much in love with and whom the girls adored. She settled her financial affairs so that they would not be in need. Together they worked out how they would manage when she had gone; they discussed the children's upbringing, what values they held and where they would go to school. She had more years than she had hoped for with her family, and together they grew into a strong and loving unit.

Local or regional recurrence

It is possible for cancer to come back in the breast that has been treated and this is known as local recurrence. It may just be where the original cancer has been inadequately treated and can be treated by surgery. If there are some lymph nodes left in the armpit at the original surgery, then one of these could contain cancer, which could grow at a later date. This is called regional recurrence. Again, this is treated by further surgery. Having a local or regional recurrence does not necessarily mean that you have cancer cells elsewhere in the body (metastatic disease).

It is also possible to develop a new cancer in either breast, which is not a recurrence of the original cancer. Usually, if cancer occurs in the untreated breast it is a completely new cancer and can be treated in the same way as the first one. If there is a new cancer in the treated breast, then it will be necessary to have a mastectomy, as the breast cannot be treated with radiation more than once.

What is metastatic disease?

Once breast cancer has spread from outside the breast, it is possible to keep it under control for many years. Although some people die within two or three years of diagnosis of metastatic disease, many people live a long time with good health despite having breast cancer. I have known people who have lived for over 20 years with metastatic disease. However, it can never be completely eliminated for sure. The cells that have spread to other parts of the body are still breast cancer cells, but they are growing in the wrong place and usually behave abnormally. These are known as metastases, or secondaries, and breast cancer that has spread is known as metastatic, or secondary, disease.

Where can it go? The most common places for breast cancer to come back to are the skin, the bones, the lungs and the liver. It is also possible to get secondaries in the bone marrow, brain or ovaries. Secondary breast cancer in the lung or brain is not the same as lung cancer or brain cancer, where the cells of that particular part of the body have started to grow without the normal checking mechanisms. It is important to know this because the treatment given for secondary breast cancer in the lungs is different from that given for lung cancer.

What to look out for

I have found that once someone has had cancer, they are worried about any little thing that crops up in their body that they haven't noticed before or can't explain. However, there are a few specific things to look out for, so you can limit your worrying to anything that fits these criteria. The most common problems to look out for are pains that are not usual for you and do not go away. If you have always had headaches and you continue to get them, they are unlikely to be anything to do with breast cancer. Also, if you have been doing some unaccustomed exercise, such as a clear out in the garden, then it will not be surprising if you get some aches for the next few days. However, if you get pains that you cannot explain and that do not improve over a week or two, then it is wise to seek advice from your specialist centre. Other signs might be shortness of breath, lack of appetite and weight loss, and unexplained weakness or headache.

Sometimes local recurrence just looks like little skin bumps and it is worth looking out for these in the area where you have been treated. If you are uncertain whether a bump is just a spot or pimple you can wait a while to see if it goes away. If it does not get better, see your doctor. You can ring up and make an appointment in between clinic visits if you are worried.

What investigations are done

If you have gone to the clinic with a concern, the doctor will first find out how you have been generally and will also examine you. He will probably examine both breast areas, under your armpits and also your abdomen or stomach area. Many doctors start their examination with the unaffected breast, so that they can feel what is normal for you. It is then easier to check the treated breast, which will have scarring in it and so feel different. In order to check out any new pains it is likely that you will have an X-ray of that area.

X-rays

X-rays will be taken of any area that is causing any pain. It is also routine to do a chest X-ray, as breast cancer can recur within the lungs. X-rays can also show up if cancer has caused any damage to the bones.

Bone scan

You may also be advised to have a bone scan. This is not painful, but may take 2–3 hours. A very tiny dose of a radioactive marker is injected into your veins. This is allowed to circulate round your body and will be taken up by the bones. In order to encourage the circulation, you may be asked to drink a lot of fluid. After a certain time, you will need to sit or stand in front of a scanning machine so that it can detect where the radiation has gone. The machine is usually in front of you and it is not large like a CT or MRI scanner. You will be required to keep still for several minutes while the picture develops. This scan picks up any areas of increased activity (or 'hot spots') in the bone. Other conditions, such as arthritis, can show up on this scan, so even if it is abnormal it is not necessarily due to cancer. Healing also shows up as hot spots, so if you have had an injury in the last few months this could be detected by this scan.

Ultrasound

Ultrasound is useful for looking at the soft organs in your body, such as your liver or ovaries. This ultrasound is done in the same way as for the breast (Chapter 7). A blunt ended probe, which emits sound waves, is run over the abdomen. The waves that are bounced back create a picture on a monitor, which is read by the doctor. These images are difficult to interpret and what the doctor sees here needs to be put into context with the rest of your medical history. This is why they rarely tell you what they see as, though they may see some abnormalities, they may not be able to tell what these are. It is usually necessary to put together the information from a variety of tests before it is clear what is happening in your body.

CT scan (computerised tomography)

A CT scan is a series of X-rays which are put together by the computer in order to create a 3-dimensional picture of what is happening inside your body. This is sometimes known as a body scan. People have asked me 'Why can't I just be put into a body scan to see if there is any cancer in my body?' Unfortunately, metastatic cancer cells are still just individual cells that cannot be distinguished from any other cells. A CT scan will only detect where a new lump has started to form. The other difficulty with this kind of scan is that multiple X-rays need to be taken in order to build up a complete picture. It would take hours and a lot of radiation to scan a complete body and probably wouldn't give any very useful information. This sort of scan is usually done where there are some indications of a problem and the doctors know which part of the body to scan.

In order to have a CT scan you need to lie flat on the scanning table. The X-ray machine is like an enormous polo mint, which is positioned around the part of your body that is to be scanned. You are not enclosed by it, and it is open at both ends. While you are having your scan the radiographers and doctors are not in the room with you. This is for their safety, because they are working with radiation all the time. However, you can talk to them and they can hear you and reply. In order to increase the quality of the images, you may need to have an injection with a special dye. Some people find this makes them feel a little nauseated and so you are usually asked not to have anything to eat or drink for two hours before your scan.

MRI (Magnetic resonance imaging)

An MRI also creates 3-dimensional images, as well as giving a lot of other information, such as the amount of blood flow to an area. This uses no radiation and so is safer than CT scanning; it uses a strong magnetic field. You are advised not to take anything into the area that might be affected by magnetism, such as credit cards and computers. If you have a pacemaker you should let the radiographer know. It is usual practice to be asked to complete a checklist before you go into the scanner, so you do not need to worry about forgetting any of this.

For this scan you need to lie flat on the scanning table, but your whole body has to be right inside the scanner. It is open at both ends and you can still talk to the radiographers; as it is like being in a tunnel, some people find it claustrophobic. If you need this kind of scan and you are worried by claustrophobia, you should talk to your doctor and discuss how to manage the experience. Many people take in a portable cassette player, so that they can listen to music.

Blood tests

There are a variety of blood tests, which can give valuable information about what is happening in your body. Again, it is not possible to say whether there are any cancer cells in your body by doing a blood test. If the sample of blood taken does not contain cancer cells, this does not mean that there are none elsewhere in your body.

What it can tell is if cancer is in some of your body organs. If there is any damage to your liver, then enzymes are released by the liver, which can be detected in the blood. Some of these enzymes are very sensitive and may be present after a few alcoholic drinks. Any damage to the bones causes the release of a slightly different set of enzymes. The bones may also release calcium if they are damaged.

How can advanced cancer be treated?

The main purpose of treating advanced cancer is to help relieve the distress or discomfort from symptoms of the cancer. This is called palliation. As it is not likely to eliminate the disease, the treatments used are generally much less aggressive. It is always worth thinking about how much benefit you are getting from a treatment and how much it is affecting you. If you find the side-effects worse than the disease, ask for something different. It is common to be given more than one treatment: chemotherapy or hormone therapies are given to treat the whole body; radiotherapy is given to treat specific areas. The treatment that is given for advanced cancer is different for each individual, depending on the way in which the disease presents. There is no automatic treatment at this stage and it is important that you discuss with your doctors why they have chosen to give you a particular treatment and what benefit they expect you to gain from it.

Radiotherapy

Radiotherapy is useful for killing off cancer cells that have set up in the bones. When cancer is in the bone it can make it weak, and it also causes pain. Once the cancer cells have died the bone can heal again, so the strength improves and pain is eliminated. Occasionally it feels a bit worse before it feels better, as radiotherapy can cause local swelling, which may aggravate the pain.

Radiotherapy is also good for treating any cells that crop up in the brain. The brain has a protective barrier, which means that toxic substances in the blood are less likely to affect it. This means that chemotherapy, which is carried by the blood, does not reach the brain, and so is not generally very effective here. However, radiotherapy is effective in this area. Unfortunately, when you use radiotherapy on the head you will lose the hair in the treated area and it does not always grow back again.

Hormone therapy

If you have a tumour which is responsive to hormone changes, there are many different sorts of hormone therapy that can be used. Most people will already have used tamoxifen when they were first treated for breast cancer, so this is unlikely to be used now. If you are still having your periods, removing your ovaries would work as a treatment by cutting out the oestrogens in the body. As discussed in Chapter 9, there are also drugs that can be used to stop your body from producing oestrogens and these could be given instead of having surgery to remove your ovaries.

Once the ovaries are no longer working there are more drugs that can be useful in treating breast cancer. This is because the body still produces a small amount of oestrogen elsewhere in the body, which is nothing to do with the ovaries. This oestrogen supply can be cut off by a group of drugs called aromatase inhibitors. The first of these was a drug called aminoglutethimide, which although effective, had a lot of side-effects and is not normally used now. It has been replaced by a series of new drugs, which are more effective and have fewer side-effects. Unfortunately, these drugs are expensive at the moment and some Health Authorities have been reluctant to allow them to be used. You may come across Arimidex®, Aromasin®, or Lentaron®. These have very few side-effects and many people do not have any side-effects at all. You might notice some hot flushes or some nausea, but these tend to fade with time.

There are various other hormone treatments that do not cut out oestrogen, but may inhibit it working in some other way. Drugs that are like the normal female hormone, progesterone, can do this. You may have heard of Megace® or Farlutal®. These are generally well tolerated, but do have some side-effects. The main one is increased appetite and weight gain, which can be significant and difficult to combat, but it is possible to maintain a steady weight with a careful reducing diet. It is helpful to seek the advice of a dietician if you need to take these drugs. They can also cause increased sweating and fatigue.

Once breast cancer has responded to treatment with one hormone therapy, it is likely that it will respond to another. In this way, you can go from one hormone treatment to another, getting a good response with each. I have also known women have all the different hormone treatments and then come back to tamoxifen and get another response. The biggest disadvantage with hormone therapy is that it can take weeks, or even months, before it is clear whether the cancer is going to respond to this kind of treatment. If you are suffering severe effects of disease, then it may not be appropriate to wait that long to see if it is going to work. In this case, it is better to use chemotherapy.

Chemotherapy

Chemotherapy can be very effective in treating disease that has spread to the lungs or the liver. There is clearly a balance to be made between having treatment that makes you feel ill and treating a disease that makes you feel ill. The doctors are very aware of this and try not to give chemotherapy that will make you feel very unwell. But as each person reacts differently, this can be difficult to predict. So it is important that this kind of treatment is given only after careful consultation with you, so that you know what you have to gain from having the treatment, and so that you can make the decisions about how much you want to have it.

Symptom control

Treatments that kill cancer cells are the best way of controlling symptoms, or signs, of the disease. However, there usually comes a time when there are no anti-cancer treatments that are working. This does not mean that there is nothing that can be done to relieve the distress caused by these symptoms. The major symptom of advanced cancer is pain, but it can also cause other problems such as breathlessness, nausea or fatigue. As mentioned above, radiotherapy can be highly effective in controlling pain due to secondaries in the bones. If pain is more generalised, there is a host of painkilling drugs (or analgesics) that can be given in a variety of ways. Using them in combination with co-analgesics can often enhance their effect. Co-analgesics are drugs that do not act directly as painkillers, but which can help to reduce pain. Some analgesics can cause nausea or constipation, so it is often necessary to give other preparations to prevent these complications.

Breathlessness is sometimes caused by an accumulation of fluid in the lungs, which can be drained away. Chemotherapy drugs can then be inserted back into this area to prevent re-accumulation of the fluid. If breathlessness is caused by blocked lymph drainage around the lungs, steroid drugs usually help.

Nausea can be caused by a variety of factors and again there are a variety of drugs that can help. If the one you get is not helping, ask for another. One of the causes of nausea is high levels of calcium in the blood. This may happen if there is damage to the bones. The signs of high calcium levels are nausea, thirst, constipation, confusion and eventually coma. A number of drugs and high levels of fluid, usually given by intravenous infusion, to flush out the excess calcium, can easily treat this. This problem can be fatal, but as it is easily treated it is worth being aware of it.

Fatigue can be one of the most difficult symptoms to treat and often requires a significant change to lifestyle. If it is caused by anaemia, then it can often be relieved by blood transfusions. Steroids may also help.

When to stop treatment

This is clearly an individual decision, but I hope it is clear that it is never necessary to stop all treatment, as something can always be given to help relieve discomfort or suffering. The question is rather to consider when to stop taking some treatments, which may be causing more side-effects than they are helping to relieve.

How long have you got?

I remember one woman who was very ill in hospital and who we all thought was going to die in a few days. There was one treatment we hadn't used, and although we didn't think there was much chance it would work, it was a simple tablet and so she gave it a try. Within a couple of weeks, she was back on her feet and off home with her family to enjoy a few more months of unexpected time with them.

There does come a time when all the treatments available have been used or don't seem to be working any more. I think that you have a right to know this, although you may need to ask, as some doctors find it very hard to say that they cannot find any treatment that might be effective against your disease. Even then, no one can tell you how long you will live. It may be a few days, weeks, or much longer. I feel that it is helpful for you to know, so that you can decide how you want to spend that time. It used to be the case that doctors wouldn't tell patients when they were dying as they thought that they wouldn't be able to cope with the knowledge. In fact, most people want to know, so that they can use the rest of their time with a different outlook, rather than constantly striving just to live. I am often surprised by how well people actually do cope. One woman I helped look after had found the whole cancer experience very difficult to cope with and always seemed to struggle with coming to terms with the diagnosis and any treatment she had. When I knew that she was dying I was concerned for her, as I knew that this was what she had always dreaded, and I did not know how she would face it. When I went to see her, she welcomed me warmly, saying how glad she was to see me, as she particularly wanted to thank me for all I had done for her and so that she could say goodbye. She seemed a different person. She not only knew and had accepted that she was dying, but she was clearly in control and knew exactly what she wanted for her last hours. She then died that night.

Hospice care

Hospices are usually connected with palliative care, or symptom control. Many people fear that this means that their doctors have 'given up on them'. But more and more cancer centres work in conjunction with hospices, realising that they have built up an expertise in symptom control, which can help cancer patients at all points of their disease. One woman I knew asked for referral to the local hospice as she felt she would like the benefit of their knowledge and experience. A couple of years later she proudly came to tell me how she had been discharged from the hospice, as she had not been using their services. They had told her to ask for a new referral if she ever needed it. Many people use hospices as a place to stay for a short while, or when needing extra help with symptom control. Some hospices provide specialist Macmillan nurses, who can come to your home to give help and advice. The point with hospices, as with all medical services, is to use what they have to offer in a way that helps you. With the expertise available in hospitals and with advice from specialist palliative care consultants, it should now be possible for women to spend their last days in comfort, and to die with dignity.

Benefits and other sources of help

At all stages of your illness there are many sources of professional help available for you. Your GP or health visitor can advise you about these. Through the hospital you will also have access to social services, who may be able to support you practically and financially, especially if you are self-employed or a single parent. This can include help with travel costs, nursery or playgroups, meals on wheels and the orange badge for car parking concessions.

Many people are not aware of what they are entitled to or are too embarrassed to ask for help. However, these services are in place to try to help you live life to the full and try to minimise the pressure on you and your family. If they are available for you they can make a big difference to you. I remember one woman saying that she did not need an allowance that she was entitled to, but at the same time she was very dispirited as she found it difficult to get out much, as she was dependent on friends to take her. We discussed how her allowance would enable her to afford taxis when she wanted to do the odd bit of shopping and she realised that this extra bit of independence was just what she needed. Filling in forms can also be daunting. Don't be afraid to ask for help from your GP practice, Macmillan or breast care nurse.

Breast Cancer Care produces a helpful leaflet called 'Breast cancer and benefits', which is available free. It explains about Statutory Sick Pay; Incapacity Benefit; Severe Disablement Allowance; Disability Living Allowance; Attendance Allowance and Invalid Care Allowance. You may also be entitled to Income Support; Housing Benefit or Council Tax Benefit. Cancerlink also produce some useful leaflets in this area.

The Benefits Agency (check the business numbers section in your phone book) produces 'Which Benefits?' a general guide, as well as leaflets on individual benefits. These are available from your local social security office, post office or library. If you need someone to talk to, your local Citizens Advice Bureau is an excellent place to visit.

If you have children don't forget that the school can be a valuable source of help, providing support and continuity for your children. You may not always want to speak to the teachers about what is happening to you. However, if they know, then they can be accommodating about flexible attendance at school, especially if children have to be taken out at short notice.

Travel insurance

Your travel insurance will not cover you for any claim relating to your breast cancer if you do not declare your diagnosis. There are a number of firms willing to consider travel insurance for women with breast cancer, and Breast Cancer Care produces a leaflet listing their names and telephone numbers. It is a good idea to ring around several companies as they can vary a great deal in what they offer. Your Post Office can supply the E111 form, which entitles you to benefit from reciprocal health arrangements that operate within countries of the European Union.

Independent Financial Advisors offer impartial advice, specific to a client's needs. For IFAs in your area call IFA Promotions on 0117 971 1177.

11
Mind therapies

In the last decade there has been an explosion of interest in complementary treatments for the mind and body. It's estimated that nearly five million people visit complementary practitioners every year. My interest in complementary treatment began on a trial and error basis when I was first diagnosed with breast cancer. I decided that orthodox, Western medicine had a lot to offer, but I was daunted at the battering my body and mind seemed likely to get as a result of surgery, chemotherapy and radiation. How could I help my body heal? And how could I hang on to peace of mind and still enjoy life at the same time?

Somewhere in my brain the word 'holistic' had lodged. I felt that I needed help as a whole person; what good would chemotherapy do me if it destroyed the cancerous cells in my body but left me permanently anxious and miserable?

I had practised meditation since my middle twenties, and already knew how much it was helping me to get through those frightening, early days. So I set out to try anything else available that could strengthen my mind and support my spirit. I have tried many of the complementary treatments outlined in this and the next chapter and will share my views on them. Some may appeal to you; others may not. The most important thing to remember, though, is to make sure you consult a qualified, registered practitioner in whichever treatment you choose.

Much of the resistance from hospital doctors to complementary treatments stems from the fact that there is little high quality research into the safety and effectiveness of such treatments, and that not enough practitioners are suitably registered and supervised. My advice here is to use common sense. As well as checking that a complementary practitioner is a member of a professional body, ask to see evidence of qualifications and find out in advance how much the treatment will cost. Personal recommendation is usually a help when you are looking for a practitioner, as the standard of their skills can vary. Most therapies can be taken alongside conventional medical treatment, but you should tell your physician what you are doing.

A state of relaxation is key to many of the complementary therapies.

Practitioners say that the body's own healing abilities are more effective-ly activated when we are in a calm, relaxed mood. This is why many, though not all, of the therapies take place with soothing music playing in the background and in a peaceful atmosphere. My feeling is that they are probably right. After all, your brain works better when it is focused and calm rather than when you are frenetic and panicky, so it seems likely that other bodily functions follow suit. Even if this is not the case, the empha-sis placed by complementary practitioners on relaxation usually provides a boost to your spirit and your emotions, which certainly accounts in part for their rapidly increasing popularity.

I have focused on *complementary* treatments, which can be used alongside conventional cancer treatments, rather than *alternative* thera-pies, which are intended for use *instead* of conventional treatment. This is partly because my own experience is with complementary therapies, and partly because the essence of this book is a guide to hospital medicine and what you can do to make the most of it for yourself with the aid of complementary treatments. If you want to turn your back on Western medicine, there are routes you can take, but they are better explained in books other than this by people who have pursued them.

For ease of reference, this and the next chapter are roughly divided into strategies which focus on your mind and those which focus on your body. Although, of course, holistic practitioners believe that techniques for helping your mind have a direct effect on your health, and that certain kinds of physical treatment or exercise, like yoga and acupuncture, bring mental as well as physical well-being.

In his book, *Cancer as a Turning Point*, the psychologist, Dr Laurence Le Shan, describes the work he has carried out with cancer patients over the past 45 years. Basically, he turns routine psychological thinking on its head. Instead of looking at a cancer patient and asking 'What is wrong with this patient?' 'How did they get that way?' 'What can be done about it?' He asks instead 'What is right with this person?'

His approach is to find out people's dreams – what would make them glad to get up in the morning; what would give them a spring in their step and a zest for life? And when he has extricated a patient's innermost hopes, he works with them to make those dreams come true – whatever they may be – from the seemingly mundane, like learning to play the piano, to making big changes in jobs and relationships.

He believes we all have a unique song to sing in life; that there is a special music in our heart that we have to hear and experience. As he says: 'When we are actively singing our own song, we realise that it is only philosophers and depressives who ask "What is the meaning of life?" When we are using ourselves in the way we are built for, we know.'

Trying some of the complementary therapies discussed in this and the next chapter will, I believe, help you get through treatment for breast cancer. You may find, as I have done, that they not only do that, but they also widen your horizon. They give you a sense of peace and fulfilment and boost your spirit as well as your body. If you are fortunate, they can help you find a way through illness, not just to better health, but to a richer life.

Transcendental meditation

My feeling is that meditation heals my body and my spirit. If you have a family and a job and you are trying to cope with treatment for cancer on top of it all, it is hard to imagine that you could find even five minutes for yourself when you can close the door on the rest of the world. Many are the times that I have put off meditating in order to attend to tasks (or people) that seem to be screaming for my attention. All I can say is that my experience has taught me that if I want my day to go as well as I could hope for, I do better if I have meditated first. Whether it's a scary hospital appointment or a battle round the supermarket, meditating beforehand means I am a hundred times better at coping with whatever life throws my way.

The benefits of meditation are now widely acknowledged. In some European countries, regular meditators are awarded lower premiums by life assurance companies, as meditation has proven health benefits. It raises your pain threshold and reduces your biological age. There are even some businesses that encourage employees to begin the day with meditation.

I grew up in a house where meditation was part of normal, daily routine. My father had practised a form of transcendental meditation (which I'll explain later) since the early 1960s, and as a little girl I can remember curling up on his lap, enjoying the peace of my parents' bedroom, while he sat with his eyes closed meditating. It was known in the family as 'Dad's half hour'. I didn't know any other adults who did this, but that didn't worry me. I found the idea of such a ritual comforting, and when I was in a stressful job in my mid-twenties, I decided it was the ideal time to learn to meditate for myself.

There are lots of ways of relaxing that are called 'meditation'. One of the best descriptions I have heard explains it like this: prayer is talking; meditation is listening. It focuses the mind in a state of relaxed awareness.

For me, meditation means repeating a 'mantra' – a word or a series of sounds – inside your head until the noise and bustle of the outside world disappear and you are left in an inner world of stillness, silence and calm.

This form of meditation is called Transcendental Meditation or TM, because the suggestion is that you rise above the everyday worries of the world into a quieter, more spiritual place. Millions of meditators over the years have described the experience as a feeling of 'coming home'. Scientists have proved that the pattern of your brainwaves alters and other calming, chemical responses take place in the body during such meditation.

Ideally, it should be practised for two half hours a day, first thing in the morning and in the early evening. It is always better to meditate before a meal, rather than after one when your body is trying to digest and you are far more likely to fall asleep. While night-time sleep gives you physical refreshment, I have found that meditation gives mental refreshment and energy for the myriad tasks you have to do each day. Also, when you are rocked by fears or uncertainties, it offers an hour a day when you can jettison your worries and take the mental equivalent of a country walk in warming sunshine to the real part of yourself. You feel much better at the end of it.

Experienced meditators can meditate anywhere, but to begin with it's good to have a specially chosen chair which supports your back, so you can sit comfortably with your head, neck and spine erect. If your feet don't reach the floor, find a lower chair, or put a cushion underneath them.

You need to close your eyes and place the palms of your hands just above your knees; some people like to turn their palms outwards. In some schools of meditation you need to attend a simple initiation ceremony when someone tells you in privacy the word you can use as your mantra. Other people choose to repeat a word like 'peace' or 'calm' silently in their heads. As other thoughts creep into your mind, you simply note them and let them go and return to the mantra, without getting cross for being distracted or feeling annoyed with yourself for failing to concentrate. After a while, the repetition of the mantra begins to slow, and then you can taste a rich, still silence which is full of love. It can last for moments or for longer. This is often the link to the 'coming home' feeling that meditators describe.

There are, of course, a lot of spiritual associations tied to meditation. It forms an important part of most world religions, and if you start to meditate you may find that you become more interested in the spiritual side of life. Some meditators would say that it is more helpful if you receive it from a strong, established tradition, so that you can be supported in the early stages of learning to meditate. But you don't have to subscribe to a religion to appreciate the physical benefits of meditation: lower blood pressure, a slower pulse rate and a reduction of stress chemicals in the body. In fact, one group of Americans learned to meditate reasonably well using the word 'Coca Cola' as a mantra. I don't know if that would work for me, but it proves that you don't necessarily have to focus on higher things for meditation to be effective.

Try and find a quiet corner of your home for regular meditation. I have painted our spare bedroom a calming shade of blue, and it doubles as my meditation room. I like to light a candle before I start, and I usually glance at my watch and decide what time I want to stop. I don't know quite how the body's internal clock works, but almost always I open my eyes at the time I have decided to stop. If you are not certain that this would work for you, you can set an alarm clock, preferably one that doesn't have a loud tick as this can be distracting. One friend discovered his mobile phone had an alarm function which he used when he began to meditate.

On a final note – don't worry if you try meditation and feel you are not 'good' at it. Our brains love to chew over worries and thoughts constantly. They are not used to being told to switch their focus. What you are going to cook that night, remembering a dress that needs to be dry cleaned, or at stressful times, fears about your health, will all inevitably surface while you are trying to meditate. *It doesn't matter*. Simply pick up your mantra again and again.

I firmly believe that if you have the intention to sit down and give your body and mind some peace, it will repay you, even if you don't feel the impact of it immediately. Just stick with it and give it a chance to work.

Other forms of meditation

Relaxation tapes

Many people with cancer find listening to relaxation tapes very helpful. They can either be restful music or a voice that can guide you to relax your body and then your mind. One friend of mine wakes early in the morning and listens to a relaxation tape before she gets up. She also listens to a tape before she falls asleep at night. The tapes for her provide a focus which make her feel that she is contributing something positive to her own well-being.

Visualisation

Visualisation is a technique for using your imagination to create what you want in your life and to make improvements in your health and happiness. It is the process of forming positive thoughts and images in your mind which will then be communicated to your body. It is important to do this when you are in a relaxed state; first thing in the morning or just before falling asleep are good times because the mind is usually more receptive at these times. It is also important to practise a little every day, especially when you first begin.

In her book, *Creative Visualization*, the American writer Shakti Gawain argues that it is such a powerful process that even five minutes of conscious, positive visualisation can counterbalance hours, days or even years of negative patterns. She believes there are three necessary elements to effective visualisation:

1. *Desire*. Do you truly desire the goal you are visualising?
2. *Belief*. Do you believe that your goal can exist? Do you believe that it is possible for you to attain it?
3. *Acceptance*. Are you willing to accept what you are seeking? Sometimes we pursue goals without actually wanting to achieve them.

You don't need to have a vivid imagination to be able to visualise, it is something that we all do when we daydream. Sometimes it helps to imagine you are watching a television screen or to remember a past experience when you begin visualising.

Studies have shown that it is possible to boost the immune system with positive healing images during visualisation. During my last bout of chemotherapy, I woke up one morning feeling as if I was about to get 'flu – one of the danger signs you are told to look out for during chemo. I phoned the hospital, as I had been told, and the nurse advised me to call in at the Marsden so they could analyse my white blood cell count and check that my immune system was not completely wiped out. I decided to try visualisation to give myself a boost before I left home. I lay in bed for half an hour, wrapped the duvet around me so I was warm and comfortable, and imagined my white blood cells working effectively in my body. I told myself that my body was fit and strong and that my blood count would be fine. Previous tests had shown it varying: 4.8, 5.2, and 3.9. (The white blood count of a healthy person is between 7 and 10). When the result came back that morning after I had practised visualisation, it was 7.1. I didn't bother with any visualisation when I returned for my final chemo session three days later and my blood count was down to 3.9.

Of course, there is absolutely no scientific basis to this one result. I can only say from my own experience that I feel visualisation has something to offer. As the day that I visualised wore on, I felt much better. Whether it was because my immune system was functioning well, or because of something that took place entirely in my head, I honestly have no idea.

Research into Psycho-neuro-immunology (PNI) has shown that visualisation and positive emotional support can increase production of the body's natural killer cells which wipe out cancer cells. Whether or not this proves to have any long-term significance in eradicating cancer remains to be seen. But it is a fact that over the years many people with cancer have used visualisation because it gives them a sense of control over their bodies, and that alone makes them feel better.

Alison, a friend of mine, learnt visualisation techniques shortly after she was first diagnosed with breast cancer when she found she was having trouble controlling her emotions.

'It was the one thing that really helped me through. When I was lying in my hospital bed and I couldn't sleep, I'd just take myself off somewhere else. And there were times when I was under various scanner machines, when I was left lying around for quite a long time, and I'd use visualisation to let my mind go somewhere nicer. It got me through the really nasty bits; it really helped.'

If you want to try to visualise cancer vanishing from your body, Dr Ian Gawler makes four very useful points in his book, *Peace of Mind*:

1. The image for the cancer needs to be of something that is weak and confused as well as disorganised and vulnerable. This is actually a realistic view. Cancer cells have no natural defence mechanisms. They have no useful function; they simply get in the way and cause problems. They lack the organisation or beauty of a normal cell.
2. Your body's defences need to be seen as being organised and purposeful, powerful and effective. Again – another realistic view. Your immune system has regularly eliminated cancer from your body before. It is a splendid defence system which has enormous potential.
3. Any treament being used should be visualised as being strong and effective against the cancer. And it should be seen as being gentle on the rest of the body, causing no side-effects at all or minimum side effects from which the body will quickly recover.
4. The images should be as vivid, clear and positive as possible.

There are people who choose to visualise violent images: their cancer being devoured by piranha fish, for example, or an axe shattering it into oblivion. I have never felt comfortable with this sort of imagery; I prefer to think of a wave of healing sweeping through my body, touching and restoring every cell to perfect balance and health.

Affirmations – positive statements about yourself – can also be used when you are feeling relaxed and open. Most people tend to have a fairly negative picture of themselves; affirmations reverse this to focus on the positive and upbeat. Try statements like:

> 'I deserve to be healthy and feel good.'
> 'I am energetic and full of vitality.'
> 'My body is balanced and in perfect harmony with the universe.'

Or anything else that feels as if it might work for you.

It does feel extremely strange to say these things at first. Try it out and see if it helps. There are a few rules to remember about affirmations.

1. Put your affirmation in the present and not the future, ie not *I will be healthy* but *I am healthy*.
2. Affirmations are not meant to contradict or change your feelings or emotions, so always choose to say something that feels completely right for you.
3. Affirm what you *do* want and not what you don't want.
4. Keep it short and simple.

Hypnotherapy

I first came across hypnotherapy when I was pregnant. I saw an article in a local magazine about a hypnotherapist who was looking for women to take part in an experiment to see if hypnotherapy could be used to help in labour. As one of life's natural cowards, who hopes to avoid pain at all costs, I phoned the hypnotherapist and agreed to take part in her programme.

It was pretty straightforward. I visited her about half a dozen times before I gave birth, and she taught me how to relax deeply. She explained that hypnosis is not about getting someone to submit to your will (something most people would sensibly resist), but about making people feel sufficiently relaxed to allow the hypnotherapist to plant helpful suggestions in their subconscious. We agreed that when I felt labour pains, I would place my hands on my stomach and feel a gentle warmth washing away any discomfort. On my final visit to see her, I took Colin, my husband, and he was given a script to read which would slowly relax me.

The test of all this came when I went into labour. As the pains began to increase from mild twinges, Colin suggested we try the hypnotherapy. I was sceptical; I didn't know if I could be bothered. But he gently persuaded me to give it a try.

So I imagined myself dropping down in a lift, becoming more and more relaxed as the lift descended, and then stepping out into a beautiful garden by the sea. As I walked barefoot across the grass, I could smell the scent of the pink and red flowers nearby; then I walked down a couple more stone steps to a wooden bench that had been warmed by the sun. As I sat on the seat, staring at the blue sky and feeling a light breeze brush against my cheek, I imagined the white, fluffy clouds above me forming into numbers, starting at 99 and then slowing changing shape, counting down backwards. At this point I felt deeply relaxed. As I felt the labour pain begin, I would put my hands on my stomach and feel a soft heat spread through my hands and ease the pain away.

This worked incredibly well until the doctor in charge decided that my contractions needed speeding up and I was put onto a drip which meant they were fiercer and faster. It was much harder to carry on with the hypnotherapy, but soon after that Oliver was born. By then I was convinced that hypnotherapy was more than worthwhile.

Two-and-a-half years later, knowing that I was facing chemotherapy, I decided to get in touch with the hypnotherapist again. She recorded a relaxation tape which gave me suggestions that I would feel calm and relaxed when I arrived at the hospital. She said the drugs would help me and I would feel no sickness or discomfort. I used to play this the night before chemotherapy and, if I had time, during the morning before my 2pm appointment. The fact that I felt only a slight feeling of nausea after my chemo, rather than the violent vomiting some people experience, I put down to the excellent anti-sickness drugs the hospital gave me and the fact that the hypnotherapy kept me calm.

Certainly, when people experience sickness *before* going for chemotherapy, something hospitals term 'anticipatory nausea', hypnotherapy is worth exploring. After all, it makes sense to try something that works on a subconcious level when it is something in your subconscious, rather than a physical reaction, which is making you sick. But as with all complementary treatments, make sure your hypnotherapist is registered. And if you see one and it doesn't work, don't give up, try someone else. Some personalities don't gel, and as with any skill, whether it's surgery, massage or playing a guitar, some people are better at it than others.

Counselling

Counsellors have come in for a lot of criticism. This is partly because counselling was perceived as a service that was lacking in regulation – virtually anyone could advertise their services as a counsellor – and partly because there is still a tendency in Britain to admire people who keep quiet and don't complain about their situation. Doctors, who receive little training in counselling people, can be sceptical about its benefits. You have only to look at the scant resources most cancer hospitals divert to psychological medicine to see that it is generally not regarded as a high priority.

However, for women with breast cancer, talking things through with a trained counsellor can be a great support. Counsellors can teach coping techniques; the one I saw when I was first diagnosed was excellent at giving me tips to minimise my anxiety. And I believe that it is helpful to talk to someone outside your friends and family who will listen to your thoughts and fears in an entirely non-judgemental way. Everything you say is kept confidential. There is no danger of what you say being repeated as gossip. This doesn't appeal to everyone, of course, and if it's not for you, don't be pressured into feeling that you 'ought' to see a counsellor. Personality type can come into whether or not counselling might help you (see the Myers Briggs Type Indicator discussed in Chapter 5). For every person who feels great spilling out their feelings, there will be someone else who prefers to work things through in their head and talk when they are ready, or not at all.

Anna, a friend of mine who had worked as a cancer nurse, said that as she spent much of her time telling her patients they should talk to a counsellor about their situation, booked to see one herself when she was diagnosed with a rare chest cancer. She walked into the consulting room, sat down and waited to start. The counsellor smiled sympathetically, tilted her head to one side and asked what it was that Anna wanted to discuss. It suddenly dawned on Anna that it wasn't the right time for her to do it. So she said 'Nothing, thanks' and got up and left the room. Never feel pressured to talk. Remember that you always have this choice and do what feels right for you.

Your breast care nurse will have received some basic training in counselling, but you can always ask your GP or hospital consultant to refer you for counselling if you want to talk to someone else. The charity Breast Cancer Care offers a helpline, personal support and telephone support groups too. (See the Useful Addresses section at the back of this book.)

The Bristol Cancer Help Centre

Many cancer patients who are interested in using complementary mental and physical techniques contact the Bristol Cancer Help Centre (BCHC), which was set up nearly 20 years ago. Its pioneering, holistic approach has gradually become increasingly accepted by mainstream practitioners, who no longer see it as a threat to the lives of their patients. What is most encouraging is that the practitioners at Bristol, who initially gained a reputation for being against orthodox medicine, and hospital doctors, who were cynical about the holistic approach, seem to be coming together to acknowledge that perhaps they can both benefit people with cancer.

The Centre teaches people to look after themselves on all levels; physical, emotional and spiritual, and thousands of visitors have benefited from staying in such a welcoming and hospitable sanctuary for the body and soul. Unfortunately, it costs more than £1 million a year to run the Centre and after a major sponsor recently withdrew, the staff were faced with no option but to virtually double the fees for patients. Although the Macmillan Cancer Relief Fund will sometimes subsidise up to 50 per cent of a patient's fees, and there are some bursaries available, it remains an expensive place to visit.

According to Dr Roger Lichy of the BCHC: 'It is one of our dearest wishes that at some time in the future our services will be free to everyone, but at the moment we have to charge what it actually costs us to run the courses.'

For further details about the Bristol Cancer Help Centre see the list of useful addresses at the back of this book.

Learning a relaxation technique

A simple breathing and relaxation self-help exercise is useful for all sorts of conditions, not just for people with cancer. If you practise the simple exercise outlined below, you will find that it can offer an immediate and sometimes quite dramatic reduction in the level of tension and anxiety in your body. Almost everyone can practise relaxation and feel the benefit from it.

Preparing to relax

Tell the people you share your home with that you will need at least 20 minutes to practise relaxation undisturbed. Allow enough time to finish slowly and gently; don't leap up and rush out of the front door immediately afterwards.

Try to ensure there are no distractions; switch on the answerphone if you have one. Make sure you feel comfortable and warm.

You can sit or lie down. If you choose to lie down, use something which is firm, rather than a bed or a sofa; find a comfortable position, either sitting or lying. It's best to sit on a chair with a supportive, straight back, or to lie on a warm floor. If you lie on a squashy sofa or a bed you will be more inclined to fall asleep. Loosen any tight clothing and remove your shoes.

You may want to record this exercise onto a tape and play it through headphones, rather than needing to read it while you are trying to relax at the same time. The exercise includes a beach scene, which appeals to most people, but if your ideal is a field or a mountain, it is fine to imagine that, as long as you supply plenty of details to make it as real as possible in your mind.

Relaxation exercise

To begin the relaxation, close your eyes and become aware of the rhythm of your breathing.

Gradually, begin to slow the rate of your breathing. As you breathe out, let go and push away any tension. Let the tension go as you breathe out. Concentrate on making your breathing slow, controlled and relaxed.

Start to feel yourself becoming heavier each time you breathe out, sinking deeper into the bed or chair. Feel yourself becoming heavier, warmer and more relaxed each time you breathe out.

Think of a word you associate with being relaxed. This could be a word like 'calm', 'relax' or 'peace'.

Breathe in through your nose, and as you let the air go, say your relaxing word to yourself.

Breathe in . . . and relax . . . and in . . . and relax . . . and in . . . and relax.

Now return to a steady pattern of breathing, letting the word go from your mind.

As you breathe in, slowly count to four . . . now exhale and release the air to a slow count of four . . .

So it is: in, two, three, four and out, two, three, four, and in, two, three, four and out, two, three, four . . .

Place your hand flat on your stomach. Inhale deeply through your nose and take in enough air to expand your chest and stomach. Feel your hand move up as your stomach rises.

Exhale slowly through your mouth, emptying your lungs to flatten your chest and stomach. Feel your hand move up as your stomach rises. Exhale slowly through your mouth, emptying your lungs to flatten your chest and stomach. Feel your hand move down as your stomach lowers.

As you sit or lie there feeling relaxed, imagine yourself walking along a beach. It is a beautiful, warm, sunny day and the sky is dotted with tiny white clouds. Try to imagine the sound of the waves lapping against the sand and hear the cries of the seagulls overhead.

The beach stretches out in front of you; notice the warm, soft, golden colour of the sand. As you walk along the beach, feeling perfectly relaxed and carefree, enjoy this feeling of freedom and calmness.

You wander further along the beach and notice a large sand dune in the distance. Walk towards it and slowly begin climbing to the top. The sand feels soft and inviting beneath your feet as you climb higher and higher. Find a spot at the top of the sand dune and lie down. The sand is warm under your body. You feel the sand caressing your skin; you feel heavy and relaxed.

Hear the sound of the waves in the distance and feel the warmth of the sun on your skin as you lie there, perfectly relaxed and supported in the sand.

This is a special place for you. You can visit this place whenever you choose. This is a place where you feel calm, relaxed and secure, free from tension and worries. Enjoy it for a while. When you feel ready to return, retrace your steps down from the dune and back along the sand.

After a relaxation session

- Leave the imagined surroundings slowly.
- Become aware of the real surroundings by listening to the sounds around you.
- Be aware of how relaxed you feel.
- Start to move very gently by stretching your fingers and toes and moving your head.
- Blink a few times and when you are ready, slowly stretch your arms, legs and back and sit up.

12
Body therapies

This chapter explores the more physical, 'hands-on' varieties of complementary treatments available which are suitable for women with breast cancer. But I should stress here that the thinking behind all complementary treatment is 'holistic'. Practitioners aim to treat the whole person, not just their illness. People who offer physical treatments like reflexology and aromatherapy will expect them to have some psychological benefits too. So the split between this chapter and the last one doesn't reflect a real-life divide.

Massage

Massage is one of the oldest therapies around. Until the nineteenth century, massage was commonly referred to in medical textbooks. Then drug therapy became more popular, and massage was ignored for a while. But in recent years, hospitals have begun to accept that massage has a valuable role to play in helping their patients.

For some reason, we are less inclined to touch people who are ill. Whether it's because we subconsciously worry that we might hurt them, we'll catch something, or our touch will be unwelcome, I have no idea. But there is a pyschological condition called 'skin-starvation' which more often applies to older people, who can go for months and even years without being lovingly touched by another human being. When you are ill, whatever your age, it's possible to experience skin-starvation. Your body is seen only as something that has gone wrong. Surgeons cut you, radiotherapists beam radiation into you and oncologists fill you with powerful drugs. It is not difficult to lose the feeling that your body is something that can bring you comfort and pleasure.

Massage is a reminder that gentle touch can be beneficial and healing. It is a wonderful instrument for offering solace, comfort and relief from pain. Some massage colleges offer a post-graduate course in cancer massage, so it's worth finding someone with that qualification if you feel you would like specialist help. If you have had a massage you'll already know its benefits. If you have never experienced one, give it a try. You are in for a treat.

Aromatherapy

Aromatherapy is a treatment now on offer in several cancer hospitals, although I suspect that demand for it outweighs its availability at present.

It can have a powerful effect, so always consult a trained, registered professional. There are mixed views as to whether it is suitable if you are undergoing chemotherapy, so talk to your doctor before you make a decision.

Aromatherapy uses aromatic, highly concentrated essential oils, diluted in a suitable carrier oil, mainly for massage, but also to inhale or occasionally to apply directly to the skin. There are about 150 essential oils which have been extracted from the leaves, flowers, fruit, stems, wood, bark and roots of plants and trees.

Smell is a much under-rated sense; I find it has the ability to trigger a change in mood, and combined with a relaxing or stimulating massage, the benefits are considerable. But aromatherapy oils do not only affect your sense of smell. The chemical constituents are carried in the bloodstream to all areas of the body, where they react in a similar way to the effect of manufactured drugs, which is why it is critical to make sure that your therapist is properly trained and knowledgeable. On average, it takes around 90 minutes for the oils to be absorbed through the pores of the skin into the body.

Professional aromatherapists usually prefer massage as the most effective way of getting the oils into the body. The value of a gentle touch and the scent of the oils make a potent, healing combination.

Reflexology

First practised by the ancient Egyptians and Chinese, reflexology is a therapeutic foot massage which benefits the whole body. By applying gentle pressure to particular areas of the feet (and sometimes the hands), the whole body can be treated via points known as 'reflex areas'. If you have never come across reflexology before, it sounds bizarre. The idea that someone rubbing your feet could improve health levels in the rest of your body verges on the weird and the theory behind reflexology is currently rejected by orthodox medicine. But there are thousands of people who visit reflexologists regularly and are convinced of its benefits. I am one of them.

I stumbled across reflexology when the beauty salon I used to visit for its sunbeds and legwaxing, started to offer reflexology as another treatment. I liked the idea of my feet being massaged – after all feet take quite a battering on a daily basis – and the therapist set to work.

Before a treatment begins, the reflexologist will take a full medical history from you so that they can focus on the kind of treatment that will suit you, if they decide that you are a suitable candidate for reflexology. (Most people are, by the way. It is only in comparatively rare circumstances that a reflexologist will decide that it is not appropriate to give any treatment at all.)

Usually you sit in a reclining chair and the reflexologist will place your feet in their lap. They will be wiped gently and powder is sprinkled over them to absorb moisture or make them smooth if they are very dry.

Then they will begin to work, usually starting with the right foot, although practitioners can differ over this. They apply very gentle pressure with their thumbs which provokes different feelings in the person receiving the treatment. These can be interpreted by the therapist to indicate which parts of the body are working well, and which are not. The treatment aims to have a balancing and relaxing effect. It usually takes around an hour.

Most courses of reflexology take at least three treatments, usually one a week. Four to six treatments is normal. Then some people choose to continue with it, say once every six weeks, to maintain improvements in their health and help prevent further imbalances.

I began reflexology shortly after my chemotherapy began. I would have a treatment every couple of weeks, coinciding with the week of the chemo. There is currently some debate about whether this is a good idea. I have heard of one doctor who felt it wasn't wise to stimulate the immune system soon after receiving chemotherapy. As there is no scientific research on this, it seems to be that the best thing you can do is to use your common sense. Discuss it with your oncologist, and find out their views. Then make a decision for yourself.

I felt that reflexology gave me a much needed boost after chemotherapy and I have no regrets about the decision I made at the time. I decided that if poisonous substances were speeding round my body to kill cancer cells, I was happy for my body's natural killer cells to be stimulated as well. As with so much in terms of complementary therapy, and even the choices now available in orthodox medicine, do what you think is right for you.

Acupuncture

Acupuncture is part of traditional Chinese medicine. It has gained a degree of credibility among orthodox Western medical practitioners after various studies have shown that during acupuncture the body releases endorphins, natural chemicals which can relieve pain, relax muscles and increase feelings of well-being.

The treatment consists of placing a number of very fine metal needles into any of the 800 specially designated energy points beneath the skin. This manipulates the body's energy flow, 'chi', which needs to flow harmoniously through the body. Where it becomes blocked or stagnant, it can trigger illness. Having had two lots of chemotherapy over recent years, I have to confess that I felt I had had my fill of needles, and therefore acupuncture never really appealed to me, but there are plenty of people around who will sing its praises. It is thought to be particularly effective in helping control nausea, reducing pain, and combating hot flushes triggered by the menopause.

Shiatsu

Shiatsu is a form of Japanese massage. Like acupuncture, it is based on the belief that good health relies on a harmonious flow of energy through the body. Pressure is placed on the appropriate points to maintain this. Unlike other forms of massage which are based on skin-to-skin contact, shiatsu is either carried out with a sheet between the client and masseur or with the client remaining fully clothed. On the odd occasion when I have had a shiatsu massage, I have bounced out of the treatment room feeling full of energy and generally on top of the world. I can recommend it but, as ever, check you are consulting someone properly qualified first.

Yoga

While yoga is not generally accepted as a complementary treatment for cancer, from my own experience I believe yoga has a useful role to play, both in helping you recover after surgery and in balancing your body and mind while you are coping with the stresses of treatment and its aftermath.

There are several different kinds of yoga; some are more energetic than others, but they are all based on similar principles.

The yoga 'asanas' or poses not only produce physical benefits, but are mental exercises in concentration and meditation. They work on the internal machinery of the body, especially on key pressure points which, by no coincidence, are also the Chinese acupuncture areas.

I took up Sivananda yoga four years ago, and it has been a great help to me ever since. I attend a class that lasts for around an hour and a quarter on a Sunday evening, and as well as helping to keep my body reasonably flexible – yoga stretches and elongates your muscles – it calms my mind. In fact, it is in the period of relaxation, when you lie flat on the floor at the end of a class, that your body begins to renew and rejuvenate.

My instructor, a former ballet dancer, has a gentle voice to match his fluid body, and on occasions when I have felt anxious and found it hard to sleep, I have heard Keith telling me to '*inhale*, two three, *exhale*, two, three' and almost immediately I have relaxed and slipped into a deep sleep.

After the first operation on the lymph nodes under my right arm in 1994, I experienced 'cording', which is when tight bands appear in your arm which make it difficult to stretch your arm fully without a degree of discomfort. This was before I had begun yoga, and it went on for several months. After the operation on the lymph nodes under my left arm four years later, the same thing happened again. But this time I was attending my weekly yoga class, and I had booked a one-week yoga holiday in Crete five weeks after the date of the operation. Before we set off, I was thoroughly fed up. I was determined to go on the holiday, which I was looking forward to, but I couldn't see how I could practise yoga when I couldn't raise my left arm higher than my shoulder.

When we arrived, I told the yoga instructor about my predicament. He suggested that I shouldn't try and force anything, but I should join in the daily class to the best of my ability. Perhaps the heat of Crete in August helped. Perhaps it was the yoga. But by the end of the week, movement was fully restored to my arm and the cording had disappeared, never to return.

If yoga works on a physical level, it's my belief that it works on a psychological level too. Concentrating on the breath, part of yoga practice, is a form of meditation, and I have used 'yoga breathing' to help calm myself and also to cope with pain or discomfort. Before the drains were removed from my body after operations, I did some yoga breathing: inhaling and exhaling slowly through the nose from the pit of my stomach three times. If you can do this, it means you aren't tense and so you are less likely to experience discomfort when the nurse takes the drains out. (Of course, you need to warn your nurse about what you'll be doing, but once they understand it's for your benefit, they are always willing to wait for a couple of seconds while you prepare yourself.)

Practising yoga gives my mind and body a focus. And if you have any doubts about its effectiveness in keeping you looking young, try and guess the age of a yoga teacher – they are always at least ten years older than you think.

Spiritual healing

There are about 20,000 healers in the UK, which is twice the number of Anglican priests and nearly two-thirds the number of GPs.

In recent years, the image of spiritual healing has changed. It has moved away from something that is edging towards the spooky to be generally accepted, even by some branches of orthodox medicine, who have begun to admit that it may have considerable merit. Hospitals prefer to talk about 'therapeutic touch' rather than healing, but the treatments and the end results are similar.

Healing involves no pills or potions. The healer is usually silent, though not always, and moves his or her hands at about four inches' distance around the patient's body. Sometimes, with the patient's consent, they will touch the clothed body, usually focusing on the head, shoulders and feet.

It is not necessary for the patient to have any religious faith. Most healers talk about a higher force, and being channels for healing energy from that force, rather than being responsible for healing themselves. They prefer patients to keep an open mind about the benefits of healing, but even that is not strictly necessary for it to work.

They say that spiritual healing is about unblocking the healing mechanism that flows around the body, mind and spirit to keep them in perfect order. When a healer lays his or her hands on you, they act as a conductor, or channel, for the healing energy which flows from the divine force to where it is needed.

How healing works is not understood scientifically, but there is increasing evidence to suggest that it is effective. In one study, 46 healthy volunteers had incisions made on their arms; half were then unknowingly given no-contact therapeutic treatment. Their wounds healed significantly quicker than those of patients who had not had the treatment. And in a trial at St Bartholomew's Hospital in London, nurses on the intensive and coronary care unit who were trained in therapeutic touch treated 53 seriously ill patients over a year. Those patients slept longer, became less anxious and needed less pain relief.

When you visit a healer for the first time, they will spend around 20 minutes talking to you in confidence about your life and the mental, emotional or physical problems you may be experiencing. You will be asked to remove your coat and your shoes and lie on a couch or sit on a chair in a warm and comfortable room. Soft music may be playing to make you feel relaxed. A healing session can last between 20 minutes and an hour. You may be aware of a sensation of warmth coming from the healer's hands or a feeling of tingling or pins and needles.

Most healers would expect your condition to improve within six sessions. About 70 per cent of people who visit a healer report an improvement in their condition or a cure. There are no side-effects.

It is worth remembering that healing is not the same as curing. Healing does not always work at the physical level, but often while the illness may remain, the patient finds that her ability to cope with it is greatly improved. It is why healers can talk about people being 'healed' before they die. In this instance, they are referring to the fact that spiritual healing can help people make peace with themselves and others, and die in a state of calmness and tranquility.

You can contact a healer through The National Federation of Spiritual Healers (NFSH) (see Useful Addresses at the back of this book). The NFSH insists that its members adhere to a strict Code of Conduct and complete two years' probation working alongside another healer before they can become full members. Healing is not a money-making exercise. It is usually offered for less than £20 a session; often a healer will ask for a small donation only. The most important thing to remember when choosing a healer is that someone who suggests that you give up your conventional medical treatment is likely to be a charlatan. No reputable healer would guarantee to cure your cancer. All they will promise is to do their best to help your body heal itself.

I have visited two healers in the last five years, and they have had very different styles. The first was recommended to me by a friend who was coming to terms with a life-threatening condition. Her hairdresser had propelled her towards a healer she had found extremely helpful and supportive. I liked the idea of getting referred to a healer by a hairdresser; it appealed to me as reassuringly down-to-earth, and so I contacted her myself.

Initially, I was drawn to her warm and friendly manner. We often chatted for at least an hour before we started the healing and I found it refreshing to talk to someone beyond my friends and family about the big issues surrounding my health. She talked as if she was also psychic, which made our conversations all the more fascinating. She sensed things about me that no one else knew, and while that is intriguing in itself, I feel I should issue a word of warning here about dealing with people who behave as though they have gifts of insight which are more profound than the rest of us.

It is very reassuring when such individuals say they think you have a rosy future, but if they seem hesitant or reluctant to endorse any plans you might tell them, it may shrink the edges of your confidence. No psychic will ever say bluntly that you are going to die, but the merest hint that there isn't a smooth path ahead can send your emotions plummeting.

When you first have an illness like cancer, some people (like me) develop an incredible sensitivity to the behaviour and attitude of others insofar as it corresponds to their future. For example, women who have been told they are not suitable candidates for chemotherapy (in fact because their cancer is unlikely to have spread) have told me that they wondered if it was because they were going to die anyway, and the hospital wanted to save money on costly chemo drugs.

Your thoughts in those early days are not always rational and your state of mind can be heavily influenced by your perceptions of other people's behaviour. So talking to someone who says they are psychic can be uncomfortable. Although most healers are more 'in tune' with other people than the average person in the street, choose someone who will stick to straightforward healing if your nerves aren't up to metaphysical discussions, or hints about your future that you may find unsettling.

Having said all this, meetings with my first healer stirred my interest in spirituality and set me on a road of discovery in terms of expanding my awareness of myself and other people. That is a valuable gift and one for which I shall always be grateful.

The second healer I have seen also works as an aromatherapist, and visiting her is much more like visiting any health professional. She is polite and friendly, but restricts her conversation to my immediate concerns about my body. She may well be psychic, but she gives no clues as to where she sees my future. I have no idea of her effect on my body, but I feel she has a kind heart and she offers me a sense of reassurance and peace.

Reiki

Reiki is a form of healing that is thought to have originated in Tibet thousands of years ago. It was rediscovered by a Japanese monk born in the middle of the nineteenth century. Primarily it is a hands-on system of healing, where the healer touches various points of the patient's body during a session that can last for more than an hour. In common with spiritual healing, the practitioner becomes a channel for healing energy; he or she does not make any claims to be the source of the energy themselves. Some more advanced practitioners incorporate symbols and signs into their treatments. This sounds like hocus-pocus, but there are plenty of people who testify to Reiki's effectiveness.

My personal feeling is that the gentle touch of another human being is soothing and reassuring and it is possible that it alone triggers the release of chemicals in the body which relieve pain and promote well-being. And as for the sceptics who refuse to believe in anything that cannot be quantified scientifically, I have always wondered how they handle the concept of love. I don't think any scientist has been able to measure love, but there's no denying that it exists, and that either lack or a surplus of it affects us all.

Nutrition

Numerous books have been written about cancer and diet. Some of them are full of common sense; others seem quirky and restrictive. There are several well-established connections between diet and the causes of cancer, in fact Western scientists believe that diet plays a part in the development of up to a third of all cancers. What science has not proved, however, is that changing your diet once you have cancer means that you can eradicate the cancer from your body.

There are plenty of complementary practitioners who would disagree with this. There are people around who believe that getting rid of toxins in your body by various means, including what you eat, is a sure way of getting rid of cancer; but these methods have not been proved scientifically. My feeling is that it is a good idea to eat as healthily as you are able *and to keep the process of eating as joyous and guilt-free as possible.*

People with cancer can be made to feel guilty about getting the disease. Someone once asked me, 'Did they say what you did to get it?' No woman is personally responsible for getting breast cancer. Where we do perhaps have a responsibility is to look after ourselves to the best of our ability and to make the most of the quality of our lives. Eating a reasonably healthy diet is part of that, but I don't see it as a reason to give up chocolate or drinking wine if doing so will make you miserable.

The basic ingredients of a healthy diet are:

- plenty of fresh fruit and vegetables (at least five servings a day)
- foods that are high in fibre, like wholewheat bread and grains
- less fat
- less sugar and salt
- moderate amounts of tea and coffee (the less the better, especially if you can replace them with herbal teas or water)
- more fish and chicken and less red meat
- moderate amounts of alcohol
- time to enjoy your food.

The Bristol Cancer Help Centre publishes an excellent cookbook. The principles of its nutritional programme are that food should be:

- vegan
- low in fat
- whole and unprocessed (with less sugar and salt than most people are accustomed to)
- as far as possible, organically grown
- eaten raw when practicable

I have eaten at the Centre and the food is absolutely delicious. The cake available at teatime beat the best of Marks and Spencer, and as far as I am concerned, that's the ultimate accolade. But I haven't adopted a vegan diet at home. I am not a keen cook, and I decided that I would simply increase the amount of fruit that I eat – which is something I enjoy – and substitute herbal teas for my normal tea and coffee, several times a day. Spaghetti bolognese and chilli are now made with soya mince in our house and that's about the limit of my change in diet.

Having said that, there are women who find drastically altering their diet very helpful. It gives them the feeling that they are exerting control over their bodies and they thrive on the extra energy that eating a vegan diet can give. Some hospital dieticians, however, are reluctant to endorse the Bristol approach. They tend to be worried by the exclusion of red meat and dairy produce, sources of calories and protein, from the diet.

Where both sides of the fence are united, though, is that eating should be a pleasure. The Arapaho Indians used to say 'Before eating, always take a little time to thank the food'. If your food feels like nasty medicine, then somewhere along the line you have got it wrong.

Homeopathy

Homeopathy is based on the theory that like is cured by like, which means that a substance which can cause similar symptoms to those of the illness being treated can be used in tiny amounts to treat those symptoms. The idea is that this helps stimulate the body's defences to help the body heal itself.

These minute substances used in treatment are called homeopathic remedies. When you consult a homeopath, they will ask you questions about every aspect of your life, not just your health. They will be interested in whether you feel the cold; if you have any phobias and even your level of libido. The remedies they may prescribe come in tablet form, liquid or creams. Medical opinion is divided over the value of homeopathy. It is on offer in some NHS hospitals, but it has never been endorsed as contributing towards a cure for cancer. Where some doctors feel it is of help, is in dealing with symptoms caused by cancer or by conventional treatments, like chemotherapy and radiotherapy.

There are plenty of women who have experienced a menopause triggered by their cancer treatment who feel homeopathy has been an invaluable source of help in limiting the side-effects of the menopause, in particular in reducing hot flushes and night sweats. As always, make sure that your homeopath is fully trained and registered, and discuss with your doctor any plans you have to use homeopathy while you are receiving conventional cancer treatment.

Chinese herbalism/Western herbalism

You may be hard pressed to find a hospital consultant who will support you using either of these forms of treatment while you are receiving conventional cancer therapy. Both systems are thousands of years old and based on active ingredients, as are many conventional medical drugs. The dilemma for a Western doctor is that he or she may not know enough about their possible interaction with the drugs they are prescribing for you to assess their safety.

As the focus of Chinese herbalism is mainly to improve your immunity and balance the healing system rather than kill disease, you may prefer to turn to it when your conventional medical treatment has finished, as a way of building up your strength. Western herbal remedies are prescribed not only to alleviate disease but to prevent it recurring, as well as to detoxify the body of poisons that may have been responsible for the disease in the first place.

There are thousands of herbs available in both systems of herbalism which can be toxic if they are administered in large quantities, so it is vital that you give your practitioner a full picture of any drugs you have taken or are still taking. Also check that they are fully qualified.

Bach flower remedies

Some women swear by these. They are based on the essences of flowers, diluted many times, and can be swallowed in a glass of water or dropped directly onto the tongue. They are taken to reduce psychological and emotional symptoms. The only one I have tried is the Rescue Remedy which tastes like brandy and is rather pleasant. Labelling on the packaging claims, among other things, that it provides support at times of emotional demand and assists the return to a more positive outlook when you need comfort and reassurance. I can almost hear the guffaws of the cynics as I write this, but it is possible that the very act of taking something to make you feel better contributes to an improvement in your mental well-being. After all, the placebo effect, which is when people in medical trials are given a sugar pill instead of the drug to be tested, has around a 30 per cent success rate, which is greater than some of the drugs that are in use. So perhaps there is something to be said for the benefits of taking something into your body that you *think* will help you.

The 38 Bach Flower Remedies can be bought at major chemists and in most health food shops.

Exercise

Hardly a complementary therapy, I know, but a much under-rated way of making yourself feel better. It has been proved scientifically that physical exercise both works off the effects of stress and helps to limit it. One study showed that regular physical exercise was more effective than psychotherapy in helping some people cope with depression.

Having been the sort of person who hated sport at school and always drove everywhere rather than walked, four years ago I joined a gym for a month's trial membership. I decided that if I only went once during that four weeks, it would turn out to be a hideous waste of money and I would abandon my plans to get fit. To my total surprise, I actually enjoyed it. Boredom is the biggest turnoff as far as exercise is concerned, and the advantage of visiting a gym is that there are plenty of different forms of exercise you can try, from Step to yoga. I have always disliked exercise bikes and there's no change there, I still don't use one, but now I quite like running stress out of my system on a treadmill.

As for the potential nightmare of being surrounded by hundreds of gorgeous skinny women in lycra – forget it. The female changing room at my gym offers plenty of reassurance that women come in all shapes and sizes. There's always someone fatter than you. Honest.

Of course, you don't have to splash out on gym membership to improve your fitness level. A brisk, half-hour walk four times a week can have the same effect on improving your mental and physical health.

If there is any secret to sticking to an exercise plan, it has to be that whatever you choose to do, whether it is swimming, walking or chasing your partner, you should do it because you enjoy it. You are guaranteed to give up if it feels like penance, so find out what you *like* and have fun.

13
Looking good and feeling better

The impact that cancer has on your appearance may affect you greatly or hardly at all. I'm the kind of woman who would take her makeup bag to a desert island, and I found losing my hair during my first round of chemotherapy one of the hardest aspects of dealing with my cancer. Other women are happy to ignore such side-effects of treatment as long as they are convinced that the drugs will restore their health. And I know of one woman who actually welcomed losing her hair, because it advertised to the world that she was experiencing a serious illness and she wanted other people to notice and treat her accordingly.

Different things make us feel good about ourselves. You may dismiss the contents of this chapter as a trivial waste of time. Who cares about mascara when you've been diagnosed with cancer?

Or you may feel that you don't want cancer to take over your whole life, and that there is something to be said for keeping up habits like wearing makeup if they make you feel good and in touch with who you are. If you have never bothered about your appearance before, it may even be fun to take the time to make yourself look as good as you can. Not necessarily to impress anyone else, but simply because, as the title of this chapter implies, when you look good, you inevitably feel better.

I first came across the Look Good . . . Feel Better campaign at the Royal Marsden Hospital, where women with cancer are invited to spend a couple of hours hearing about skincare and beauty techniques and are given a free box of makeup goodies, courtesy of the Cosmetic, Toiletry and Perfumery Foundation.

Treatment for cancer can create physical changes to your skin and hair; chemotherapy can mean losing your hair entirely. If you have a beauty routine and you normally wear makeup, you may need to alter it when you receive treatment for breast cancer, and there are tips on this you might find helpful in this chapter.

If you lose your hair, you need to make a decision whether to wear a wig, a scarf or a hat. Even if you hair doesn't fall out, it may thin and it will certainly need gentle treatment for a while.

I am inclined to react against the idea that if you find yourself temporarily stranded in the world of the sick, you have to give up the rituals and comforts you take for granted when you are well. OK, I can't wear my usual nail polish on my toes when I have an operation, because the anaesthetist needs to check that my toenails don't turn blue under anaesthetic (though why they can't look at my fingernails I have no idea). But I am damned if I am going to wander barefoot around hospital with unvarnished toenails. That's just not me. So I take in the polish and paint them myself or get a friend to do it as soon as I can after the operation.

I don't know anyone who *likes* the smell of hospitals; I find a squirt of perfume creates a pleasant cloud of normality. My favourite anti-hospital smell is Clarins Eau Dynamisante – light, fresh and not remotely antiseptic.

Even though I am an ardent believer in the power of a truly luscious lipstick to lift my spirits, I still felt a slight quiver of shock when I recently came across an American book, *Beauty and Cancer*. For some reason those three words look uneasy together.

Why? I think we react like this only because we allow all the negative associations with cancer to overwhelm us. (Americans seem to find it easier to be more positive and upfront about most things.) Women's magazines are full of advice on changing your hair and beauty routines when you go on holiday, as you get older; even when the weather changes. So why shouldn't we talk about beauty and cancer?

If looking your best gives you a lift, it makes sense to look your best when you are in greatest need of a boost – when you are diagnosed with cancer.

Looking after your hair

There are a number of steps you can take to look after your hair during treatment for cancer. Alas, none of them guarantee that you won't lose your hair. That often depends on the type of chemotherapy that is used and your individual reaction to it. But it is advisable to follow these suggestions, anyway.

- Have your hair cut short before treatment. This can help, as it stops the weight of long hair pulling on the scalp.
- If you have long hair, you may prefer to have it cut in stages to get used to the transition from long to short. Some people shave it as short as possible once they start to lose it. There isn't a right or wrong approach

to this, but the step-by-step approach might pay off if you are one of the lucky few who don't lose their hair. Some women find it upsetting if they have had their precious long hair cut incredibly short, only to find that they *don't* lose it through chemotherapy.

- Don't plait your hair or wear it up as this can damage and break it.
- Don't blast it with a hairdryer. If you can't give up the idea of a blow-dry, at least make sure you adjust the hairdryer to a cooler setting and use the softest brush you can find. Avoid curling tongs and hot curlers too.
- Don't sleep in rollers.
- Switch from nylon to a cotton pillowcase – nylon can irritate the scalp.
- Avoid the harsh chemicals used in perms and colouring for six months after finishing your treatment. (In America the advice is to wait for six to eight *weeks*, but consult your doctor first.)
- If your scalp becomes itchy or flaky, try gently rubbing in a small amount of unperfumed moisturiser.
- Use a gentle shampoo suitable for chemically treated hair (one that is suitable for perms or tinted hair).
- Always use a conditioner. The scalp produces natural oils which seal moisture into the hair shaft – moisture helps maintain strength. Conditioner benefits dry hair by supplementing the moisture it needs and replaces the moisture taken away by shampoos for oily hair.

Talk to your hairdresser. One friend wrote a note to the hairdresser and beautician she had visited regularly to tell them about her diagnosis before her next visit. Rather than give them the news in a salon full of people (where sometimes you have to shout above the noise of the hairdryers to make yourself heard) she opted to tell them in her own way to give them the chance to think about her news before they saw her. I think this is a brilliant idea, especially if you know your hairdresser well and they are likely to feel a sense of shock when you tell them.

I asked to talk to my then hairdresser somewhere quiet, so I told him about my diagnosis in his office at the back of the salon. He was supportive and sympathetic, but stunned. Looking back, I think a note would have been better.

Can you prevent hair loss?

In recent years, 'scalp-cooling' has become more common in hospitals treating breast cancer. This works on the principle that by cooling the scalp, you cut back on the amount of chemotherapy drugs that reach the hair follicles. This reduces and, in some cases prevents, hair loss.

Hospitals differ in their application of scalp-cooling techniques. The most basic approach is to use a 'cold cap' by wrapping an ice pack in towels. Fifteen minutes before the chemo is given, a cold, wet bandage is wrapped around the head, pads cover your ears to protect them from the cold, and the cap is put on and held in place with a bandage. You keep it on during the treatment and for up to an hour afterwards. There are now some more sophisticated versions of this, including a hood that works on the principle of an old-fashioned hair dryer which circulates cold air, and a gel version which remains cold for a long while and is kept in place with velcro.

Scalp-cooling works incredibly well for some women; others find that their hair loss is patchy, and for a few it makes no difference at all.

The experience is usually described by doctors – who have never had it – as 'not pleasant'. Most of the women who have experienced it would say that that is an understatement, but it is bearable if you are well wrapped up and given plenty of hot drinks while it takes effect.

Coping with hair loss

Chemotherapy works by attacking rapidly dividing cancer cells and disrupting their growth. Unfortunately, this also affects other normal cells in the body which grow quickly, including the hair follicles. As a result, it is possible that within a few weeks of beginning chemotherapy your hair may begin to fall out. For some women this is so slight, it is hardly noticeable. Others lose increasingly big clumps of hair over a period of weeks and months.

It took two-and-a-half months for most of my hair to fall out; after each wash the bath plug became increasingly congested with hair and every morning there would be more hairs on my pillow. Losing my hair made me feel unfeminine and ugly. I tried a number of scarves and hats as the problem grew more severe. Eventually I bought a wig and, I have to say, it changed my life.

I made an appointment with Trendco, a wig specialist, in London one December morning and took my Mum with me for moral support. We were ushered into a private room and the stylist brought out a selection of wigs which were similar to the shortish, blonde highlighted crop I favoured at the time. Most of them looked OK, but they all looked like dull imitations of my own hair.

Generally, you are advised to buy a wig which is as similar to your own hair as possible. That's great if it makes you happy. But none of these wigs made me at all happy. Then the stylist had a moment of inspiration. She brought out a red, shoulder length creation that was not dissimilar from the kind of wig that Cher might wear on one of her more flamboyant days. I put it on and fell in love. We walked over to a window and yes, it was *really*, *really* red. I bought it. My Mum says that seeing me laugh at my red-haired reflection in the driver's mirror on the car journey home was a such a tonic for us both that she has never forgotten it.

My wig – nicknamed 'Wilma' – got me through from early December to the following April when my hair began to grow again. I bought new clothes and makeup to match – I decided to go for autumn shades – and when my hair grew back, I dyed it a similar shade of red. (No one told me that you are supposed to wait for six months before colouring or perming your hair when it regrows. I was so thrilled to have strong, healthy hair again that I probably would have ignored that advice anyway.)

While some people find it reassuring to buy a wig which is similar to their usual hair style, my experience demonstrates that sometimes cancer gives you a chance to try out something new. One dark-haired friend fancied a dramatic change and promised herself a long, straight blonde wig if she needed chemotherapy. When it turned out that she didn't, and her hair stayed on her head, she settled for a pair of bright green contact lenses instead.

Choosing a wig

The regulations concerning wigs on the NHS differ according to the area of Britain in which you live. Usually, you are entitled to a free wig if you are an in-patient when the wig is supplied. If you aren't eligible for a free wig you can still get one through the NHS at a subsidised rate, currently around £49. An NHS wig is free is you are over 60, or if you or your partner receive certain types of DSS support. Your breast care nurse will be able to advise you on this.

The problem with wigs supplied by the NHS is that they come in a limited number of styles and tend to be old-fashioned. In fact, for some women, one of their most depressing moments in hospital is being given a badly fitting wig via the Surgical Appliances Officer.

The good news, though, is that there are now plenty of attractive, relatively inexpensive wigs which can look as good, if not better, than your own hair.

Trendco, with branches in London and Hove (see Useful Addresses list at the back of this book) sells the excellent Noriko range of wigs which cost between £80 and £120. They are fashionable and fun, and if you work out how much you would spend on having your hair cut (and possibly coloured) over the five months or so that you may wear a wig instead, they are not exorbitantly expensive. Trendco also produces 'You Again', a free booklet with details of wigs and accessories for people with chemotherapy-induced hair loss.

The present rule is that VAT (Value Added Tax) doesn't have to be paid on wigs when hair loss is the result of treatment for cancer. You will need to complete a VAT form, however, which most stores will provide when you buy your wig, as the tax can't be claimed back at a later date.

Keeping your wig on

Fear that your wig will fall off in public haunts practically everyone, but there are steps you can take to make sure this doesn't happen. I remember meeting some commissioning editors, from a magazine I used to work for, who didn't know about my cancer. I arrived at their office for lunch one day and slipped into a major panic when they casually suggested braving the force nine gale outside to get to a restaurant they had chosen. I braced myself, ignored the rain and used my umbrella to buffer me from the howling wind as best as I could, praying that a sudden gust wouldn't lift my fabulous red hair into the air. I can hardly describe the sweet relief I felt when we arrived at the restaurant with my hair still intact . . .

A well-fitting wig shouldn't fall off, but people often feel happier with a 'belt and braces' approach. You can used hypo-allergic double-sided tape, on sale from wig suppliers, to ensure that it stays securely in place. If you are still worried, simply bend over and shake your head to test it.

Wig linings can occasionally irritate the scalp, which is why some people prefer to wear a fine cotton scarf or skull cap under their wig – both of which can also be bought from wig suppliers.

Synthetic wigs can be washed and left to drip-dry as they are usually pre-styled. Wig experts usually warn you that real-hair wigs should be professionally cleaned, but I used to wash mine occasionally in a gentle shampoo and comb it out to dry. I borrowed some curlers from my Mum and at night, when I could be bothered, I would stick a few curlers in it for extra body. I bought a polystyrene wig stand for it, but if I went away I would drape it across a lamp stand, over a vase, or on a two-litre bottle of water.

In a good wig shop, the assistants will also be trained hair stylists who will trim your wig to suit you. This may mean shortening a fringe or cutting a few soft layers around your face. It will also be completely normal for them to see women without any hair, so don't be embarrassed when you visit. One of the senior stylists at Trendco tells his clients about his sister who has lived with total hair loss since she was a child, and he finds that this makes them feel more at ease.

How soon will your hair grow back?

Sometimes your hair will start to grow back before you have finished your treatment. Usually, there's not much sign of re-growth until a few weeks afterwards. At first, the hair is baby-fine, but within three to six months you will have a full head of hair again. When my hair grew back it was much curlier than before – people kept asking if I had had a perm – and five years later it is still more wavy than before my chemotherapy, although I no longer have the luxuriant, pre-Raphaelite curls I enjoyed at the beginning.

As soon as my hair was long enough to cut into a reasonable shape, I abandoned my wig (about three months after the end of my treatment) and although I was occasionally mistaken for a man (if you are 1.73m (5ft 9in) with very short hair people are easily confused) I was still relieved to have hair again.

Hats and scarves

Some people never take to the idea of a wig, or they try one and find it is too hot. I loved hearing the story about the former Northern Ireland Secretary, Mo Mowlam, who wore a wig after treatment for a brain tumour. Apparently, when political negotiations got tough, she was known to whip off her wig, give her head a good scratch and then carry on as before. Sadly, how the politicians sitting around the table reacted to that has never been recorded.

Hats are a popular alternative to wigs, and come in all shapes and sizes; baseball caps are especially popular with younger cancer patients. In the US they can be bought with false hair attached to them, although I am unaware of any firm that provides that service in the UK.

I never managed to get to grips with scarves – I couldn't get the hang of tying them so they stayed on – but at that stage I hadn't come across *Beauty and Cancer* by Diane Doan Noyes and Peggy Mellody. The chapter on hair alternatives contains easy-to-follow diagrams on various ways of tying scarves attractively. There are a few guidelines to bear in mind if you are going to wear a scarf instead of a wig:

- Choose cotton, lightweight wool or cotton-blends – satin-type material tends to slip off the head easily.
- For a basic headwrap, choose a 65cm (26in) or 72cm (28in) square scarf. For something more fancy, you can use a larger square, up to 82cm (32in), and oblongs can be used as a trim.
- Track down more unusual designs at the remnant counter of department stores. John Lewis usually has an interesting collection of remnants.

As with any practical skill, you get better at tying scarves with practice. It is worth persevering until you get it right.

Basic headwrap

Figure 1A

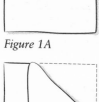

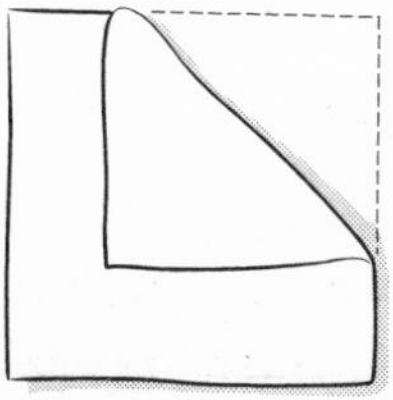

Figure 1B

Step 1: Lay scarf flat; wrong side facing you. Fold scarf into a triangle, leaving one point slightly longer than the other (figures 1A and 1 B).

Step 2: Drape scarf over your head with the shorter side on top and points at the back. Pull scarf down until about 5–7.5cm (2–3in) above your eyebrows (figure 1C).

Step 3: Tie scarf ends in a half-knot behind your head. The flap should be anchored beneath the knot (figure 1D).

Step 4: Tie scarf ends into a square knot (figure IE).

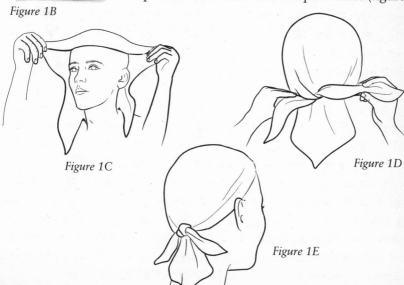

Figure 1C

Figure 1D

Figure 1E

Skincare

Your skin reacts to internal changes in your body as well as external influences like the sun, cold weather and pollution. Cancer therapies can alter the condition and texture of your skin, leaving it drier, more sensitive, and more likely to burn in the sun.

Every woman's magazine from *Cosmopolitan* to *Woman's Weekly* tells you how important it is to cleanse, tone and moisturise your skin, and that advice is not just there to fill the spaces between the adverts. Caring for your skin pays dividends by keeping it healthy. When you are having treatment for breast cancer it still matters.

Cleansing

You don't have to spend a fortune on expensive lotions (unless you do already and it's a habit that you enjoy). The best advice is to use inexpensive, fragrance-free, hypo-allergenic (which means there is little chance of an allergic reaction) and alcohol-free products.

It is advisable not to use any form of harsh cleanser which is likely to irritate the skin. Apply your chosen product gently to avoid pulling the delicate surface of the skin. If your platelet count is low, take extra care not to pull your skin too much or you might create bruising.

Moisturising

Even if your skin is oily and not dried out by chemotherapy, you still need a moisturiser. This is because moisturisers don't add oil to the skin, but keep you from losing moisture from the outer dead layers, and they add some grease which holds in natural oils. This keeps the skin soft and supple, helps your makeup to go on easily and provides a barrier against the wind, pollution and, if it contains a Sun Protection Factor (SPF), damage from the sun.

Facials

Although some French women would rather go without food than their weekly facial at the beauty salon, I have to confess that although I have tried professional facials a couple of times I have never enjoyed them. I think it's the agonising bit when they start squeezing open pores that puts me off. I'm happier at home, scaring my family with a bright green Tea Tree face pack from Boots. If you are a facial fan, however, keep it up because there's little doubt that they are good for your skin. It also gives you a brief oasis in the day when you can relax and just lie there while someone else works, which is a good experience for everyone now and then.

Sunburn

Certain chemotherapy drugs can make you burn more easily in the sun. Your doctor should warn you if this is likely. Use a higher SPF than you would normally (ideally, Factor 15 or greater) and reduce the amount of time you spend in the sun.

Contrary to popular opinion, sunbeds are not safer than exposure to the sun. Ultraviolet rays are harmful to the skin: it doesn't make any difference whether they come from the sun or an artificial source. In fact, current research suggests that sunbeds may cause more skin damage than natural sunlight and speed up the ageing process. You should avoid sunbeds if you have received radiotherapy as this can change the texture and suppleness of the skin and sunbeds can aggravate an adverse reaction.

Faking it

None of this means that you must spend the rest of your days being pale. As public knowledge about the risks of a suntan has increased, so too has the demand for fake tans, which have become increasingly sophisticated in recent years. Gone are the days of streaky orange knees and elbows. Ideally, you should exfoliate the areas of your body you intend to tan, then moisturise the skin, and finally rub in small amounts of the fake tan. As I am not one of life's great exfoliators, I just moisturise my skin with Aloe Lotion from The Body Shop (which kept my skin soft and supple while I had radiotherapy on my breast), and then apply Clarins Self Tanning milk. It's best to wait for 15 minutes before you get dressed and in about an hour you have an even, natural looking tan. There are lots of excellent fake tanning products around. If you want to look brown, try out a few and settle on the one that gives you the colour you like best. It's cheaper than a course of sunbeds or a week in the scorching sun – and a lot safer.

If you can't be bothered to apply fake tan but wouldn't be adverse to people commenting on how well you look, use a tinted moisturiser on your face. Most of the major cosmetics companies produce them and they give you a healthy glow. In hospital I found a touch of tinted moisturiser and a hint of lipstick worked wonders for my morale. They are easy to apply and give your face an instant lift.

Makeup

If you have never worn makeup before, there are plenty of women's magazines and books around that offer tips and guidance. If you would like someone to give you personal advice, wander around the cosmetics counters of your local department store and ask who offers a makeover and how much they charge.

Some of the counters have separate, private rooms available for makeovers, so you are spared the potential embarrassment of meeting your friends while you are perched high on a stool in the middle of the shop with a tissue tucked into your neck and half an eye made-up. Often the makeover is free, providing you spend a certain amount of money on the products they recommend, but always check first. Tell the beauty company representative if your treatment is affecting your skin in any way, and check that they use clean or disposable brushes and sponges – point out to them that your resistance to infection is lowered. They should have been fully trained in standards of hygiene, but there's no harm in double checking for yourself. Wash your own makeup brushes regularly too. Once a week is probably ideal, but once a month is better than not at all.

Eyebrows

Even if you lose the hair from your head as a result of chemotherapy, you won't necessarily lose your eyebrows and eyelashes too. You may find that they are scanter than before, however. The rule with an eyebrow pencil is to remember that eyebrows are not one solid line of colour. They are feathery and full. If your eyebrows have thinned, brush them first using an eyebrow brush (I use an old toothbrush) and then fill in the gaps with light, feathery strokes from an eyebrow pencil. As a general rule, the colour of the pencil should never be darker than your natural hair colour.

If you have no eyebrows at all, use two eyebrow pencils in contrasting shades, which match the tones of your natural hair. With one pencil create an eyebrow line of dots where your eyebrow should be, use the other to add feathery strokes coming from each of the dots, and set with a light dusting of translucent powder. There are excellent diagrams and full instructions on re-creating eyebrows in *Beauty and Cancer*. (See Further Reading.)

Eyelashes

If your eyelashes thin a little, they can be built up with mascara. Water soluble is best because it is the easiest to remove. Don't use mascara which is several months old though; most types of mascara contain animal fat which collects bacteria with age and you don't want to pick up an eye infection.

If you lose your eyelashes altogether, you may want to try false eyelashes which are available from most department stores. Alternatively, if you still have some eyelashes, you can add to them with individual clusters. Monica Lewinsky, the US cover girl (amongst other things) is a big fan of clusters of false eyelashes as they make your eyes look bigger and bolder.

Facial hair

Steroids and other drugs can produce facial hair which can be removed by various forms of waxing or electrolysis. However, if your resistance to infections is low, your best bet is to cover it up. First, brush it downwards with an eyebrow brush to make sure it is lying flat. Then cover it with a concealer. Don't apply powder over the concealer, though, as the powder will cling to the hair and make it more obvious.

Nails

Chemotherapy can cause damage to fingernails and toenails which affects their appearance and growth. Ridges can appear in your nails, and they may become dry and split easily. My normally long nails suddenly started to break after my first cycle of chemotherapy, so I kept them short but manicured until my treatment had finished. Some women are tempted by acrylic replacements, but the problem with these is that they can damage your natural nails, so you should steer clear of them while you are having chemotherapy.

I did paint my nails from time to time and they don't seem to have suffered any long-term effects. If you are tempted to use nail polish, avoid alcohol-based removers, which are drying, and use a lanolin-based remover instead.

Mastectomy and breast reconstruction

Debbie has discussed the medical approaches to mastectomy and breast reconstruction in her chapters. What follows here is an overview in the context of both operations and self-image.

For some women the idea of losing a breast – or both breasts – is their worst nightmare. For others it is no more than a minor inconvenience. Wherever you are in this spectrum of feelings, it is worth exploring what mastectomy means to you in terms of the way you look and feel.

Mastectomy

Debbie has talked about the mastectomy operation and the options available in terms of prostheses and clothing. The impact of a mastectomy on you as an individual will depend on how you feel about your breasts. This may not necessarily be connected to their size. Losing a small breast can be as devasting as losing a large breast. I once heard of a surgeon who told a 38-year-old patient: 'We'll do a mastectomy and it won't matter because you only have small breasts, anyway.' This is an outrageously insensitive remark. I can't imagine a fellow surgeon remarking to him, 'We'll do an operation on your penis, and it won't matter because it's only small, anyway.'

Some people opt for a mastectomy and no reconstruction because it is a more straightforward operation which is widely available in most hospitals. Others have friends who have had reconstruction and been unhappy with it, and this has put them off. Whatever your reason, choose a mastectomy because you have been through all the options and decided that *it will suit you best*. Don't be persuaded into it because it is the easiest option for everyone else.

Prostheses

Some women choose not to wear a prosthesis. Either they have small breasts and feel it is not necessary, or they don't feel they should have to conform to society's picture of what a woman should look like; they are proud of who they are. In her book *A Visible Wound*, Julie Friedeberger, a yoga teacher, urges women not to wear prostheses, but to come to terms with themselves as whole people who have no need of anything that 'covers up' the reality of what has happened to them.

It is an interesting point of view, but I feel that no one should be pressured into doing what is right for someone else. Clearly, she has found a sense of release and freedom in being open about her scar; for other women it is a private matter. They don't hide it because they are ashamed of it; they wear a prosthesis because it suits them physically and emotionally.

Cancer is an experience that can help you grow as a person. But it's tough having to cope with a life-threatening illness and not everyone feels they want to challenge society's preconceptions about physical norms at the same time. Some women with mastectomies are happy to go topless on the beach. I couldn't manage that myself, but I admire women who can. My feeling is that you should do what makes you feel better. If you feel more comfortable wearing a prosthesis – wear one. If you find it a chore and it feels awkward – don't bother.

What most people find surprising about mastectomy scars is that they aren't ugly. None of the men I interviewed said they found them off-putting, or that they desired their wives less after their mastectomy. What they were concerned about was that their partners would change *in other ways*. They were most worried that their partner's personality would be affected by cancer and that their relationship would suffer as a result.

Reconstruction

I chose to have a bilateral mastectomy with immediate reconstruction when I was diagnosed with a second primary tumour in my left breast, four years after I had been treated with a lumpectomy, chemotherapy and radiotherapy for a tumour in my right breast. When the second lump was diagnosed, I lost confidence in the ability of my breasts to stay healthy, and decided that I wanted the breast tissue taken out and replaced with breast implants.

At the time, I considered this as being comparable to the kind of cosmetic surgery that is advertised in countless newspapers and magazines. Virtually every Hollywood actress seems to have had a boob job these days, led by the majority of the female cast of *Baywatch* (the most watched TV show on the planet). In a strange way, it felt like a socially acceptable operation, especially when my surgeon offered me the option of bigger breasts that wouldn't droop. I was comfortable talking about the operation with my friends – especially when they boosted my ego by complaining about their small or droopy bosoms and wishing they could change them (though, not presumably, by getting breast cancer). In some ways it is like having cosmetic surgery, but in other significant ways, it is quite different.

As far as I am concerned, the advantages of immediate breast reconstruction are considerable. Because my surgeon considered it was safe to leave my nipples in place, my operation involved removing most of the breast tissue and inserting two implants behind my chest wall, against the envelope of skin that was left. This means I now have two breasts which are the same size (34D – a cup size bigger than I was before) which sit fairly high up on my chest, so I don't have to wear a bra if I don't feel like it.

In clothes they look great. Apart from the fact that the silicon implants point skywards when you lie down – they don't go flat like normal breasts – they give me a better figure than I had before.

Now to the disadvantages. I don't have any feeling in them. Surgeons usually warn you that you will lose 'erotic sensation' in the nipple. I have no sensation in either breast (apparently, this can occasionally happen when implants are inserted purely for cosmetic reasons, too). When I am undressed and I bend over, they don't droop. And because they are so firm, you can't wear a Wonderbra, or its equivalent, and get a deep cleavage.

I do know, despite these disadvantages, that I am very grateful to have them. I can get changed at the gym, lie on a beach or go into communal changing rooms and not have to worry about prostheses or being stared at because I have no breasts. That matters a great deal to me. To other women it might not be important at all.

Overall, in terms of looking good and feeling better, they are a success. Occasionally I might see a woman with a soft, squashy-looking bosom and feel sad that I don't have my old breasts any more. But I imagine that feeling is no stronger than seeing a younger woman look good in clothes you might have worn 20 years ago and now wouldn't consider. Time moves on and you have to move on with it. Regret over something you can't change is a waste of time.

A surgeon's advice

Breast reconstruction has been around for more than 30 years. The late Gertrude Shilling, who became famous for the outrageous hats she wore to Royal Ascot, was one of the first women in Britain to have a breast implant after she had breast cancer in the mid-1960s. She died in 1999, aged 89.

Nigel Sacks, the surgeon who carried out my operation at the Marsden, points out that success in immediate breast reconstruction relies on two things. First, make sure your surgeon has the technical expertise for the job, and secondly, check that he adjusts each operation for his individual patients. You don't want a surgeon who does the same operation for each of his patients, regardless of their breast size or what they want.

There is still a feeling among some surgeons in Britain that they won't offer immediate reconstruction to mastectomy patients – some suggest a wait of two years. According to Nigel Sacks:

'From the breast cancer point of view, that's rubbish. It's just an old wives' tale. There is no evidence that doing an immediate reconstruction hides the recurrence of breast cancer or delays other treatment like chemotherapy or radiotherapy.'

Some surgeons don't offer immediate reconstruction because they are not trained to do it. Others believe, and I was shocked at the arrogance of this, that women who have lived with a mastectomy for two years are *more grateful* for any kind of reconstruction and are, therefore, less critical of the surgeon's skills. Says Nigel Sacks:

> 'Women who go into surgery with two breasts and come out with a reconstruction have higher expectations of the surgery, and no matter how good a surgeon you are, you can't make a completely normal breast.'

I would suggest to surgeons that being honest about the limits of reconstruction and then allowing the woman to decide on the right course of action for herself is preferable to denying her reconstruction for two years to increase her gratitude. Sadly, we are still some way off achieving that in many hospitals.

Nigel Sacks reminds his patients that the main priority is to treat their breast cancer and then to get as good a cosmetic result as possible. He shows them pictures of previous reconstructions and tries not to raise their expectations too high.

As with all operations, your outcome rests mainly on the skill of your surgeon and the aftercare you receive, so make sure you are completely happy with the surgeon who is going to carry out your operation. It is always possible to get a letter of referral to another surgeon from your GP, if the first one you see fails to meet your requirements. If you have cover for private health care, you can see virtually anyone you choose, although I would recommend that you select an NHS breast expert who keeps his skills up-to-date and does private work as well, and not a surgeon who carries out private operations only.

Tattoos

If your nipple is removed during your mastectomy operation, for a while you will have to live with a breast with no nipple. Skin from your thigh can be grafted on to the breast and a tattoo in the shape of a nipple added to create a replacement. Some hospitals offer this service, but not all of them have trained tattooists available. Some women with an adventurous spirit have tattoos like ivy leaves or feathers on their reconstructed breast which distract attention from the fact that there's no nipple. One friend of mine visited a tattooist in south west London. He opened his shop specially for her and her husband one Sunday afternoon and charged her just £10 for the disposable needles. When she offered him more (to have tattooing done privately in hospital could have cost up to £500), he replied: 'I make my money out of guys who have eagles tattooed on their backs, not from women who have been through an experience like yours.' So next time you see a man covered in tattoos, remember he might be a sensitive soul underneath.

What to wear in hospital

Debbie has given plenty of sensible advice about things to take into hospital. (see Chapter 8). But while we are talking about looking good and feeling better, I'd like to make a personal plea that you treat yourself to a smart pair of pyjamas or a new dressing gown before you go in.

Sally

'I was such a diligent little housewife, I was busy filling the deep freezer for my husband to survive on while I was in hospital, when I really should have been more selfish and got myself a decent night-dress and dressing gown, instead of wearing my old bedraggled one.'

Loose fitting, front-opening pyjamas are the best bet, and wearing a smart pair when you receive visitors after your operation will make you feel better. As soon I can, I start to wear normal clothes in hospital. Not business suits, obviously, but lightweight trousers and tops which are comfortable to sit in. I have a theory that you are treated differently by medical staff when you are wearing normal clothes. Obviously, if you are feeling dreadful and just want to lie in bed, the most sensible thing to wear is night attire. But once you are up and about, get friends or relatives to bring in clothes that are easy to wear and which make you feel like *you* again.

Twenty things to do if you are feeling fed up

Debbie and I have put together a lighthearted list of 20 things you might try on days when you feel low. None are guaranteed to work. Some might not appeal at all, but it is worth giving one or two a go, and if they lift your spirits you can keep them up your sleeve until the next time you fancy a treat.

Remember the saying: 'Don't put off until tomorrow what you can do today. If you like it a lot today, you can do it again tomorrow . . .'

1. Eat a piece of dark chocolate. It contains theobromine, a chemical which boosts endorphins, the body's natural relaxant.
2. Talk to a friend and have a giggle. Do things you enjoy together at least twice as often as discussing problems.
3. Recall happy memories. This has a chemical effect on your body. Reseachers have shown that volunteers who recalled happy memories doubled their level of a protective substance called immunoglobulin A (igA) within 20 minutes; three hours later they were still up by 60 per cent. Guilty memories had the opposite effect.
4. Go for a brisk walk. Exercise is one of the best morale-boosters around.
5. Tune into the sounds around you when you are outside. Listen for birdsong.
6. Put a bunch of flowers on your desk or kitchen table.
7. Go to the garden centre and buy a sweet-smelling plant.
8. Have sex. An orgasm relaxes you and releases lots of 'feel-good' hormones. Even a cuddle cheers you up.
9. Plan a weekend away. It doesn't matter if you don't do it, the planning alone makes you feel better.
10. Choose a treat for someone you love.
11. Make something. A cake or a coat; it doesn't matter.
12. Visit somewhere quiet and peaceful, like a church or a garden.
13. Go on a guided tour of your home town.
14. Buy something you've never dared to buy before.
15. Clear out a corner that's always been a mess.
16. Polish something: your shoes, the piano, or your nails.
17. Put on a rock-and-roll record.
18. Learn tap dancing, ballroom or salsa.
19. Make the most of any sunshine. It releases serotonin which boosts your mood.
20. Go somewhere to watch the sun set.

14
The way ahead

Someone once said that hope is to humans what water is to fish. A fish has no idea what water really is, but if you take its water away, it flounders and dies. Equally, we might find it hard to describe exactly what hope means, but removing hope from our lives is like a blow to the heart.

In this chapter I talk about the concept of hope for women with breast cancer, whether their cancer is in its early stages or is advanced. And I touch on the spiritual side of our lives, which to cynics may sound like a lot of hot air. I think it is important to think about spirituality. After all, there's only air in your car tyres but without it you'd have an awfully bumpy ride.

I also include quotes from some women and their partners who have lived with breast cancer for years. They have talked about the long-term impact of the disease on their lives and how it has changed them as individuals and changed their relationships. I add my thoughts, too, on the emotional experience of breast cancer and the effect it has had on my life and my sense of the spiritual.

If you are flicking through this and feeling low, you might like some of the prayers, quotations and poems. I have chosen them simply because I like them, and they have helped me. I don't think you have to be a churchgoer or even a particularly religious person to find comfort in prayers. Sometimes, reading another person's prayer helps clarify your own thoughts and hopes, especially if you are feeling overwhelmed by fear and worry.

Why we need hope

Everyone who is diagnosed with breast cancer hopes for a cure and a long life ahead of them. For many women, that is what they will get, but to achieve it, they will probably need treatment that they may not find easy to handle. And for some women a cure will not be possible. I believe that keeping hope alive in difficult circumstances is crucial for everyone. Hope sustains you emotionally and physically. It keeps a balance in your brain and your heart. Hope is what spurs us on when life is tough, but it can waver and falter, and sometimes it can disappear altogether. Feeling hopeless from time to time is a natural reaction to a life-threatening illness. So how do you find a sense of hope amidst the panic and fear that can engulf you when you live with breast cancer?

My first tip is to remember that a sense of hope does not need to be restricted to regaining your health. Naturally, this is something we all hope for, but I believe that hope has a bigger role to play in a fuller picture of our lives.

Hope is about setting goals for yourself, which you may or may not be able to realise, but your achievement lies in taking practical steps towards them. If you are feeling low, you may think that there is no point in creating goals that you may not manage to carry out, but it is the process of moving towards the goal that is important. It is that process that makes you feel better. Hope is about planning a weekend away after your radiotherapy is over, or booking tickets for a favourite show to raise your spirits in the middle of your chemotherapy. If you don't feel well enough to go on the day, give the tickets to someone else, but the chances are that you'll make it. Hope can offer a small island of strength in a sea of worry and fear. For most of us cancer is about living with uncertainty. In the face of such uncertainty, what's wrong with hope?

False hope

Medical practitioners, in particular, tend to be wary when it comes to offering hope. They are concerned about giving patients so-called 'false hope' which they usually equate to a misleading diagnosis. I don't believe there is such a thing as 'false hope'. There is lying to a patient, which used to happen when families believed relatives needed to be protected from the news that they had cancer, and I certainly don't advocate that. Blithe reassurance that all will be well when someone is confronting an unpredictable illness like breast cancer is not helpful either. But an honest optimism that helps patients keep an eye on the joys and goals that are possible as long as life goes on is important. This is not the same as pretending to be upbeat, no matter what the situation. That attitude springs from fear of disability and illness, and patients can sense that at every level.

I don't believe doctors will be sued if they emphasise the positive. No one can guarantee the future and patients know this. If a doctor gives them a sense of hope, they will cope better with their lives. If a doctor takes away hope, and I'm not talking about whether or not a disease is curable here, a patient's morale plummets.

Hope is not the same as wishing

Hope is not the same as wishing. Hope is active, it is about seeing that the outcome you want is possible and then working towards it, no matter how small the steps you take. Wishing is the opposite. To me, wishing sounds as if it's accompanied by a sigh and a helpless shrug of the shoulders while you wait for a miracle to happen.

As Norman Cousins says in his book, *Anatomy of an Illness*:

> 'Not every illness can be overcome. But many people allow illness
> to disfigure their lives more than it should . . . There is always a
> margin within which life can be lived with meaning and even with
> a certain measure of joy, despite illness.'

I'd go one step further than this, and say that life can be lived with a *lot* of joy, despite illness. This is one of the important things to remember in keeping hope alive.

You are always so much more than your illness

It also helps to remember that you are always so much more than your illness. It was while I was buying a gardening book as a present for my cousin, the first Christmas after my diagnosis, that I came across *Love, Medicine and Miracles*, by Bernie Siegel. The self-help section of my local Waterstone's was next to the gardening shelves and the title leapt out at me. I bought both books and started to flick through what Bernie Siegel had to say later that afternoon. Within 24 hours I had read it from cover to cover. It certainly changed my attitude to my illness, and it was probably instrumental in changing my life.

Bernie Siegel is an American cancer specialist who realised that his emotional detachment from his patients and his purely surgical interventions were curing some of them, but many of them were left unhealed. Exhausted and frustrated by his lack of impact on his patients' lives, he decided to change his attitude and behaviour. He began to become more empathetic and emotionally involved with his patients, and started to encourage them to find an inner reason for living, to resolve conflicts and to mobilise their faith in everything they could possibly believe in. He developed a philosophy which said that patients who just want to get well through doctors alone or God alone were minimising their chances.

He asked patients to make choices based on what would feel right if they knew they were going to die in a day, a week or a year, whether or not that was the prognosis for their illness. He used that model to give people an immediate awareness of how they felt, and what they wanted to change. Then he would encourage them to make every change that they wanted.

It would be easy to sneer at this and say that what people really wanted was to have their cancer taken away, and he couldn't guarantee that, so he was wasting his time and that of his patients by asking about other aspects of their lives. But if you take that view, you are assuming that we all lead perfect, untramelled lives prior to being diagnosed with cancer. I have yet to meet someone who would say that. Equally, I would never suggest that our lives before cancer caused the illness. As I have said before, I have no truck with people who believe that cancer patients are somehow 'to blame' for creating their illness. Or that in some deep-seated way we choose to be ill. Choice affects *how* we are ill, not *whether* we are ill. Just because you have cancer, it doesn't mean that you have no choices left. You do have choices, which go far beyond your treatment options, and it is as important as before you had cancer that you make them carefully.

Looking at *Love, Medicine and Miracles*, I was encouraged to read on by Bernie Siegel's dismissal of the word 'terminal'. Once you have cancer, it is a word no longer connected solely to airports and buses; it acquires a terrifying significance. He points out that people aren't either 'living' or 'dying'. They are either alive or dead, and as long as they are alive, that is how they should be treated. To label someone 'terminal' means people have begun to treat them as though they were already dead. As Richard Bach, who wrote the story *Jonathan Livingstone Seagull*, puts it: 'Here's a test to find whether your mission on earth is finished. If you are alive, it isn't.' We need more medical staff to recognise this.

Getting well is not the only goal

Bernie Siegel says that getting well is not the only goal. Even more important is learning to live without fear, to be at peace with life and, ultimately, death. Then healing (which is not necessarily the same as cure) can occur and one is no longer set up for failure, by believing that one can cure all physical problems and never die.

His definition of spirituality is that it means the ability to find peace and happiness in an imperfect world, and to feel that one's own personality is imperfect, but acceptable. The only ingredient missing from that for me is that he doesn't mention the awareness of unconditional love and the true connection that we have with other people. It is still one of the best definitions of spirituality that I have come across. And he does go on to explain that the first step towards inner peace is to decide to give love, (to oneself and others) rather than to wait to receive it.

Loving other people is an ongoing process, and I think healing works the same way. I have always felt uncomfortable with the idea that you are either 'well' or 'ill' and must belong to one group or the other. 'Health' to me doesn't mean just the absence of illness or pain. It is about living a life which has balance, contentment, joy and peace, which means you can live a healthy life with breast cancer.

Stephen Levine, in his book *Healing into Life and Death*, suggests that rather than trying to beat an illness, you should meet it. That's a phrase I find very appealing. An illness you decide to 'meet' is much less terrifying than one you must 'beat'. It is even possible, then, to accept that things which we immediately judge as 'bad' may not turn out to be as negative as we first thought.

In Helen Thomas' book, *World Without End*, written soon after the death of her husband, the poet, Edward Thomas, she talks, in effect, about trusting bad luck as much as good:

'I came to realise that everything that is part of life is inevitable to it and must therefore be good. I could not be bounced high upon the crest of ecstasy and joy unless I also knew the dreadful depths of the trough of the great waves of life. We are born to die. If death were not, life would not be either. Pain and weakness and evil as well as strength and passion and health are part of a beautiful pattern of life. And as I grew up, I learned that life is richer and fuller and finer the more you can understand not only in your brain and intellect, but in your very being, that you must accept it all without bitterness, the agony without complacency, the joy. Dimly I perceived that it was because I was I that life came to me like this.'

The serenity prayer sheds some light on living in a state of acceptance rather than bitterness, too. It has long been used by groups that help people with addictions and problems of all kinds. Again, whether or not you believe in God, I feel the words offer a way of making peace with yourself:

> God grant me the serenity to accept
> the things I cannot change,
> courage to change the things I can,
> and wisdom to know the difference.

A few sentences written by a very dear friend have offered me comfort over the years:

> The past is never exactly the same again. Stop worrying about it; keep cheerful, for cheerfulness is your real shape. The clothes you are wearing must wear out; the smoothness of your skin must go; wrinkles must appear on your face; your body must lapse into the coils of time. Take all that in your stride, and play the part assigned to you.

Pain and suffering

I think it is important to distinguish between pain and suffering. I think it is possible for people to be in pain, but not to suffer greatly, and equally for people to suffer terribly with hardly any physical pain. Someone once remarked that pain is physical; but it can be worsened by sorrow which is internal – mental and emotional suffering.

If internal sorrow can increase physical pain, perhaps it is possible that internal happiness can reduce pain. Of course, no one can switch from being sorrowful to being happy in an instant, but there are some short-cuts which can help.

Music can play a powerful role in transforming sorrow. If I listen to the opening chords of the Canon in D by Johann Pachelbel, they act like a glue that can stick my wounded spirit back together. Certain classical music hits the spot fastest for me, but I am sure there are people who find the opening bars of Barry Manilow's *Mandy* just as effective.

Flowers are for our souls to enjoy

The Native American Indian tribe, the Sioux, had a saying 'flowers are for our souls to enjoy', and as a woman who dives into her local florist at least once a week, I can testify to the truth of that. Flowers are one of the nicest gifts to receive. Even the humblest bunch of red tulips is capable of brightening a room and its inhabitants. If people don't buy you flowers, buy them for yourself; they can work a mini-transformation in your heart. Sitting in a garden in the sun can work magic even quicker. If you don't have a garden, visit a park. I like the following poem, 'God's Garden', by D.R. Gurney, which is understandably popular with gardeners:

> The warmth of the sun for pardon,
> The sounds of the birds for mirth,
> One is nearer God's Heart in a garden
> Than anywhere else on Earth.

Moving beyond breast cancer

While most women's lives will move way beyond the immediate experience of breast cancer, I think there are few who would say that their lives afterwards have been untouched by it. Whether you perceive it as a crash course in facing up to your own mortality, or an insight into loss and gain, its impact stays with you. I've spoken to a number of men and women about the lasting experience of breast cancer on their lives. Here are a few of their remarks:

Mavis

'Your mortality is brought to the fore. I can remember the first September after my op, planting the bulbs and thinking "will I be here in the Spring?" Then I decided "am I going to fold up and let life pass me by, or am I going to get what I can out of life?" Now I often say that cancer has given me permission to do what I really want. I had to get a new passport to go to New Zealand last summer and I remembered that ten years ago, just after I was diagnosed, I'd got a ten-year passport, and I thought at the time, "that's a waste". I've just bought another ten-year passport. My life changed and it is better now, for having had cancer. I don't know if that's a sad thing to say, but it's true.'

Linda

'Having cancer made me look at my life, at what I thought was important and what was actually important. It made me realise that normal, everyday things are very precious. Material things don't matter. Perhaps I would have liked to have come to these conclusions through a different door, but I would have wanted to experience this change. I have found a sense of well-being. I don't think I would have wanted to go through life living only on the material level. I am glad I appreciate other things.'

Paul

'I think I've become a lot better at seeing the world from another person's point of view since my wife had breast cancer. And I have realised that it's OK to say "I don't know what to say". I've learnt that women don't necessarily want instant solutions, but they want to know that you have noticed them. I think the quality of our marriage is infinitely greater. We have a heightened sense of what is and what isn't important. We aren't going to wait until the mortgage is paid off or we retire until we do things. We get on and do them today. We have got used to the idea of marriage being like rock-climbing. One leads with the rope and then the other takes over. It seems natural for us to operate like that now.'

Sally

'Having breast cancer has meant that I don't think you should try to suppress your anguish or your anger, whatever you want to call it. I put on a bright, cheerful face at the beginning and everyone said "Oh, you're being so marvellous". Then six months later, my daughter gave me her cat because she couldn't keep it in her flat any longer. She was an adorable little black thing. One night she got out and was run over. I felt it was my fault and I just sat and cried. I cried for about a fortnight. And, eventually, I realised I wasn't crying for the cat any more, I was crying for myself. I had pushed down the grief and it just bubbled up. People are expecting you to be upset at the time and in a way, that's easier. You don't have to squash it down, because it will come back later and it might be much harder to cope with then.'

The Chinese hieroglyphics for 'crisis' are a combination of 'danger' and 'opportunity'. That is a good summary of my experience of breast cancer. When I was first diagnosed, I felt my life was in danger; I was frightened and panicky. To say I felt under threat is an understatement. Cancer felt like a menacing presence in my life; a sniper who had me as a target. I still feel like that from time to time, but over the years, that fear has lessened and the opportunities that cancer has presented have come to the fore.

My interest in complementary medicine, joining a gym and a drama group, taking up yoga, making new friends, even learning to tap dance, all these have stemmed from a desire to focus less on fears and worries for the future and to make the most of the here and now. In *Healing into Life and Death*, Stephen Levine quotes one woman who struggled against cancer for two years. As she prepared to die, she realised she had put so much on hold and that realisation pulled her back into life. She told him: 'If I ever get ill again, I don't think it will be as terrible as that last time. My life was so narrow and now it is so broad. Thank God I didn't die so small.'

I am not advocating that you should suddenly rush out and sign up at every evening class going, or drag yourself along to a gym if it really doesn't appeal to you. What I would suggest, though, is that you give yourself space to do what you know in your heart you would like. The crisis of cancer isn't a question of transforming yourself into someone else; *it is about being who you really are.*

In Nelson Mandela's inaugural address as President of South Africa he said:

> 'We are all meant to shine, as children do. We were born to make manifest the glory of God that is within us. It's not just in some of us, it's in everyone. And as we let our own light shine, we unconsciously give other people permission to do the same. As we are liberated from our own fear, our presence automatically liberates others.'

There is a story I like about the great Hassidic Rabbi, Zusya, which also illustrates this point. One day his congregation asked him to take a particular political action. He refused. They said: 'If Moses were our Rabbi, he would do it.' Zusya replied: 'When I die and stand before God, He will not ask me why I was not Moses. He will ask me why I was not Zusya.'

Stephen Levine says that healing is the optimum preparation for death. It can take place whether or not you are physically ill; healing is a whole-hearted opening to life, even in its subtlest turnings and changes.

It is not only the saints and the philosophers who can teach us about handling life and illness. The other day I was having my hair cut and I overheard a conversation between the owner of the salon and one of his clients, who said:

> 'I don't keep clothes for best, any more. What I do is make the most of every single day. So I wear nice clothes if I want to, no matter what I'm doing. I take each day at a time and think "how can I make the best of the next 24 hours?" And then I get on with it.'

What he was talking about is the experience that mystics describe as 'living in the present moment'. When your attention is focused solely in the past ('my life was OK before I had cancer') or in the future ('what bad things are going to happen to me now?') your mind is a breeding ground for anxiety, worry and regret. Naturally, you can't spend all your time living in the present – how would you plan holidays or make a shopping list? On the other hand, most of us spend hardly any time at all making the most of the moment. And, let's face it, the moment is all we actually have.

The following poem, 'Afterword: If I Could Live It Over . . .' by Nadine Stair is a good illustration of this:

> If I had to live my life over again, I'd dare to make more mistakes next time
> I'd relax.
> I would limber up.
> I would be sillier than I have been this trip
> I would take fewer things seriously.
> I would take more chances.
> I would take more trips. I would climb more mountains, swim more rivers.
> I would eat more ice cream and less beans.
> I would perhaps have more actual troubles, but I'd have fewer imaginary ones.
> You see, I'm one of those people who live seriously and sanely hour after hour, day after day.
> Oh, I've had my moments. And if I had it to do over again, I'd have more of them.
> In fact, I'd try to have nothing else, just moments, one after another, instead of living so many years ahead of each day.
> I've been one of those persons who never goes anywhere without a thermometer, a hot water bottle, a raincoat and a parachute.
> If I had it to do again, I would travel lighter than I have.
> If I had to live my life over, I would start barefoot earlier in the spring and stay that way later in fall.
> I would go to more dances.
> I would ride more merry-go-rounds.
> I would pick more daisies.

I would like to think that this book will help, but you don't need all the answers to solve the crisis of your breast cancer. Though you may feel hopeless from time to time, you are never helpless. You will find your own way through.

Glossary

Adjuvant therapy. This is treatment that is given in addition to a primary therapy. Surgery is usually the primary treatment for breast cancer and chemotherapy, hormone treatment or radiotherapy may be given in addition.

Advanced (metastatic) breast cancer. This is when breast cancer has spread from the breast to other areas in the body, through the blood or lymph system.

Aspiration. When a needle and syringe is used to remove fluid from a cyst or cells from a lump.

Atypical hyperplasia. Cells that are growing abnormally and have increased in number.

Axilla. The area underneath the armpit that contains lymph nodes.

Axillary dissection. This is when lymph nodes are removed from the axilla during surgery.

Benign. A lump or body tissue that is not cancerous. This means that it cannot invade neighbouring tissues or spread to other parts of the body.

Biopsy. Where a sample of tissue or cells is taken for examination under a microscope in order to make a diagnosis. This may be done with a large needle or by making a small cut in the skin.

Bone scan. A test to find out if there is any cancer in the bones.

Calcification. Small amounts of calcium in tissue, which appear as flecks on a mammogram. This is often associated with benign changes, but can sometimes indicate cancer.

Carcinoma. A specific type of cancer. These cancers arise from tissues that line the surfaces (epithelial tissues) of organs, glands or other body structures. The majority of cancers are carcinomas.

Carcinoma in situ. This is where cancer cells are present, but they are confined to the area where they began, and have not spread into surrounding tissues. This also means that they cannot have spread to other parts of the body.

Chemotherapy. The use of specific drugs in order to kill cancer cells. This is most commonly given by intravenous therapy, but can be given as tablets or in other forms.

Computerised tomography (CT) scanning. A technique used to make an image of the body by using a computer to organise the information, from multiple X-ray views, and construct a cross-sectional image.

Cyst. A sac that is filled with fluid. Breast cysts are benign.

Cytology. The examination of individual or groups of cells under a microscope.

Cytotoxic. Drugs which are poisonous to cells. A term usually used to describe cancer chemotherapy.

Ducts. Channels that carry body fluids. The ducts in the breast transport milk from where it is made in the lobules to the nipple. These ducts are made of epithelial, or lining, tissue.

Ductal carcinoma in situ (DCIS). Cancer cells that are confined to the ducts of the breast tissue.

Endocrine (or hormone) therapy. Treatment which controls disease by affecting the hormones in the body.

Excisional biopsy. This is where the whole of a lump is removed, usually with a surrounding area of healthy tissue, in order to make a diagnosis by microscopic examination.

Fat necrosis. This is where a lump of fatty material has formed after there has been a bruise or injury to the breast.

Fibroadenoma. This is a benign (non-cancerous) lump in the breast, which is made up of both structural (fibro) and glandular (adenoma) tissues.

Frozen section. Sometimes during surgery a sliver of tissue is taken and immediately frozen. This can be used to make a quick diagnosis but it is not 100 per cent reliable.

Histology. The study of body tissues. Histologic analysis is done to name and describe the extent and type of disease.

Hormones. These are chemicals that are produced by various glands in the body. They are designed to have specific effects on specific organs and tissues. They regulate many body functions such as growth and sexual functions.

Hyperplasia. Overgrowth of cells. Several types of benign breast conditions involve hyperplasia.

Incisional biopsy. This is where only a portion of a lump is removed in order to make diagnosis by microscopic examination.

Intraductal papilloma. A small wartlike growth that grows within a breast duct and can cause bleeding from the nipple.

Invasive cancer. Cancer that is no longer confined to the duct or tissue from which it arose, but has spread into nearby tissue. A diagnosis of cancer usually refers to invasive cancer.

Lobes or **lobules.** The tissues within the breast which produce milk. There are 15 to 20 lobes in the breast. These then branch into smaller lobules, and each lobule ends in scores of tiny bulbs. Milk is made in the bulbs and is carried by ducts to the nipple.

Local recurrence. Cancer which returns in the site of the original tumour.

Localisation biopsy. This is when a mammogram is used to locate the specific area that contains an abnormality that can be detected only on mammograms. The area is usually then marked by a thin wire so it can be removed for microscopic examination.

Lumpectomy. This is when only the breast lump and an area of normal surrounding tissue is removed at surgery.

Lymph fluid. Colourless fluid which bathes body tissues.

Lymph gland or **node.** Small mass of tissue where lymph fluid is purified and some white blood cells are formed.

Lymphoedema. Swelling of the arm caused by lymph fluid that cannot drain away. This is usually as a result of damage to the lymph drainage system by surgery or radiotherapy.

Malignant. A lump or body tissue that is cancerous. Malignant tumours can invade neighbouring tissues or spread to other parts of the body.

Mammogram. An X-ray of the breast.

Mastectomy. This is when all the breast tissue is removed.

Mastitis. This is when the breast has an infection. Mastitis usually occurs in women who are breast-feeding.

Menopause. The time when a woman's monthly menstrual periods cease.

Metastasis. The process by which cancerous cells spread throughout the body. New tumours set up in distant parts of the body are called metastases or secondaries.

Neo-adjuvant therapy. This is a treatment, which is given in addition to the primary therapy, but is given before the primary therapy. Surgery is usually the primary therapy for breast cancer and chemotherapy is given as an adjuvant. Chemotherapy can be given before surgery and then it would be called neo-adjuvant.

Oncologist. A doctor who specialises in cancer treatment.

Oncology. The study of cancer.

Oophorectomy. A procedure to remove the ovaries. Can be called ovarian ablation.

Prophylactic. Medical treatment given to prevent a problem from occurring.

Prosthesis. An artificial body part. In relation to breast cancer, this usually refers to an artificial breast form.

Radiation. This is energy, which is carried by waves or by streams of particles. Various forms of radiation, usually X-rays, can be used in low doses to diagnose disease and in high doses to treat disease.

Radiographer. This is a technician who is trained to administer radiation for the purposes of diagnosis or treatment.

Radiologist. This is a doctor who uses X-rays to make images of the body for diagnostic purposes.

Radiotherapist. This is a doctor who uses radiation in high doses in order to treat cancer.

Tumour. A tumour is a swelling or abnormal growth of tissue. It can be either benign or cancerous.

Useful Addresses

Breast Cancer Care
Kiln House, 210 New Kings Rd, London SW6 4NZ
Tel: 0808 800 6000
bcc@breastcancercare.org.uk

Bristol Cancer Help Centre
Grove House, Cornwallis Grove, Bristol BS8 4PG
Helpline: 0117 980 9505

British Association of Counselling
1 Regent Place, Rugby, Warwickshire CV21 2PJ
Information line: 01788 578328

For more information about the **Myers-Briggs Type Indicator (MBTT)**:
British Association of Psychological Type (BAPT)
PO Box 48, Honiton, Devon EX14 0XY
Tel: 01404 850267

British Complementary Medical Association
249 Fosse Road South, Leicester LE3 1AE
Tel: 0116 282 5511

British Herbal Medicine Association
Sun House, Church St, Stroud, Gloucestershire GL5 1JL
Tel: 01453 751389

British Homeopathic Association
27a Devonshire St, London W1N 1RJ
Tel: 020 7935 2163

Cancer BACUP
3 Bath Place, Rivington St, London EC2A 3JR
Tel: 020 7613 2121
Freephone (outside London): 090 800 1234
www.cancerbacup.org.uk

Cancerlink
11-21 Northdown St, London N1 9BN
Freephone: 0800 132905

Eloise Lingerie
PO Box 70, Bury St Edmunds, Suffolk IP30 0JT
Tel: 01284 828787

The Haven Trust
Effie Rd, London SW6
Reception: 020 7384 0000
Appointments: 020 7384 0098

Lymphoedema Support Network
St Luke's Crypt, Sydney St, London SW3 6NH
Tel: 020 7351 4480

Macmillan Cancer Relief
15–19 Britten St, London SW3 3TZ
Tel: 020 7351 7811

For more information about **Neuro Linguistic Programming**:
McKenna-Breen, Aberdeen Studios, 22–24 Highbury Grove, London N5 2EA
Tel: 020 7704 6604

The National Federation of Spiritual Healers
Old Manor Farm Studio, Church St, Sunbury on Thames, Middlesex TW16 6RG
Tel: 01932 783164

Nicola Jane
Unit 2, Dukes Court, Bognor Rd, Chichester PO19 2FX
Tel: 01243 790900 and 0800 018 2121

Stress Management Training Institute
Foxhills, 30 Victoria Avenue, Shanklin, Isle of Wight PO37 6LS
Tel: 01983 868166

Trendco (Wig Suppliers)
Head Office and Mail Order: Sheridan House, Western Rd, Hove, East Sussex
Tel: 01273 774977
Personal Callers: 229 Kensington Church St, London W8 7LX Tel: 020 7221 2646

For further, more up-to-date contacts, visit our website at
www.thebreastcancerbook.com

COMMONWEALTH ADDRESSES

NHMRC National Breast Cancer Centre
www.nbcc.org.au   email: directorate@nbcc.org.au
PO Box 572, Kings Cross
NSW 1340, Australia. Phone: (02) 9334 1700

Breast Cancer Network Australia
PO Box 4082, Auburn South Vic 3122
Phone: (03) 9660 6865

Cancer Society of New Zealand
www.cancernz.org.nz

Other NZ cancer related agencies:
Breast Cancer Aotearoa NZ   Tel: (09) 846-0578
Breast Cancer Foundation   Tel: (09) 575-5118
Breast Cancer Support Service   Tel: (04) 389-8421

The Cancer Association of South Africa
www.cansa.org.za   cansainfo@cansa.org.za
P.O. Box 13330, Mowbray 7705
Tel: (021) 689-5347

Further Reading

Alexander, Jane (1998) *Spirit of the Home*, Thorsons

Allen, Judy and Brock, Susan A. (2000) *Healthcare Communication Using Personality Type – Patients are Different!*, Routledge

Bach, Richard (1973) *Jonathan Livingstone Seagull*, Pan Books Ltd

Berger, Karen and Bostwick, John (1998) *A Woman's Decision: Breast Care, Treatment and Reconstruction*, St Martin's Griffin, New York

Carlson, Richard (1999) *You Can Be Happy, No Matter What*, Hodder and Stoughton

Chisholm, Kate (1998) *Fanny Burney*, Chatto and Windus

Cousins, Norman (1996) *Anatomy of an Illness*, John Wiley

DeGregorio, M. and Wiebe, V. (1994) *Tamoxifen and Breast Cancer*, Yale University Press, USA

Friedeberger, Julie (1996) *A Visible Wound*, Element Books Limited

Gawain, Shakti (1995) *Creative Visualization*, New World Library

Gawler, Ian (1989) *Peace of Mind*, Prism Press

Gray, John (1993) *Men are from Mars, Women are from Venus* Thorsons

Hay, Louise L. (1980) *You Can Heal Your Life*, Eden Grove Editions

Jeffers, Susan (1991) *Feel the Fear and Do It Anyway* Arrow Books

Kent, Ann (1996) *Life After Cancer*, Ward Lock, London

Kubler-Ross, Elizabeth (1997) *The Wheel of Life*, Bantam Press

LeShan, Lawrence (1996) *Cancer as a Turning Point*, Gateway Books, Bath

Levine, Stephen (1998) *Healing into Life and Death*, Gateway Books, Bath

Love, Susan (1995) *Dr Susan Love's Breast Book*, Perseus Books, Massachussetts

Moore, Thomas (1997) *Care of the Soul*, Judy Piatkus (Publishers) Ltd

Moran, Diana (1990) *A More Difficult Exercise*, Bloomsbury, London

Noyes, Diane Doan and Mellody, Peggy R.N. (1992) *Beauty and Cancer*, Taylor Publishing Company, Dallas, Texas

St Catherine's Hospice, *A Child's Questions*, St Catherine's Hospice, Malthouse Road, Crawley, West Sussex RH10 6BH (Tel: 01293 447333)

Sen, Jane (1996) *Healing Foods Cookbook*, Thorsons

Siegel, Bernie S. (1988) *Love, Medicine and Miracles*, Arrow Books

Speechley, V. and Rosenfield, M. (1996) *Cancer Information at Your Fingertips*, Class Publishing, London

Spiegel, David (1993) *Living Beyond Limits: New Hope and Help for those Facing Life-threatening Illness*, Vermilion, London

Thomas, Helen, *World Without End*

Index